THE CHARLTON
STANDARD CATALOGUE OF

WADE WHIMSICAL
COLLECTABLES

FOURTH EDITION

BY
PAT MURRAY

PUBLISHER
W. K. CROSS

The Charlton Press

TORONTO, ONTARIO • BIRMINGHAM, MICHIGAN

Canadian Cataloguing in Publication Data
The Charlton price guide to Wade
whimsical collectables

Biennial.
1995-
ISSN 1205-8025
ISBN 0-88968-200-3 (4th ed.)

1. George Wade and Son—England—Catalogs.
2. Miniature pottery—England—Catalogs. 3. Figurines
—England—Catalogs.   I. Charlton Press

NK8473.5.G46A4   738.8'2   C96-900410-6

Editor	Nicola Leedham
Graphic Technician	Davina Rowan

ACKNOWLEDGEMENTS

The Charlton Press wishes to thank those who have assisted with the fourth edition of the *Charlton Standard Catalogue of Wade Whimsical Collectables*.

Special Thanks

Many thanks to the George Wade Pottery and staff for providing information on the manufacture of Wade porcelain and the sales staff in the Wade shop, particularly Cynthia, for providing new information on Wade products and sending their sales leaflets. Many thanks to The Official International Wade Collectors Club. And special thanks to Gordon for his time, patience and photography.

Contributors to the Fourth Edition

The author would like to thank the following companies, institutions and individuals who graciously supplied photographs, pricing and technical information for this edition:

B.B.C. Television, England, **Brooke Bond Oxo Ltd.**, England, **C & S Collectables**, England, **Camtrak**, England, **David Trower Enterprises**, England, **G & G Collectables**, England, **Granada Television**, England, **Harrods** of Knightsbridge, **K & P Collectables**, England, **K.P. Crisps**, England, **Lever Rexona**, New Zealand, **P & R Collectables**, England, **Pat & Terry Collectables**, England, **Phillips Auctioneers**, England, **The Potteries Antique Centre**, England, **Redco Foods Inc,** U.S.A., **Red Rose Tea Canada**, **T & A Collectables**, England, **Robell Research U.K. Ltd.,** England, **James Robertson & Sons Preserve Manufacturers Ltd.,** England, **Tom Smith and Company Ltd.**, England, **U.K.I. Ceramics,** England, **Village Antiques & Gifts**, U.S.A., **William Cross Antiques & Collectibles**, Canada.

Barrie Reference Library, British Newspaper Library, Metro Toronto Reference Library, Stroud Public Library.

Averill Abbot, Gill Adams, Mary Andrews, Lawrence Ashby, John and Lisa Bonsey, Catherine and Stuart Barlow, Jane Broomfield, Jenny Chinnery, Peter and Lesley Chisholm, David Chown, Elizabeth & John Clark, Mrs. E. Clayton, Angel Clohessy, Adrian and Elaine Crumpton, Ben Dawson, Peter DeGraaf, Terry & Susan Dove, David Elvin, Janet & Mike Evans, Jean & Ralph Fure, Peggy Fyffe, Mrs. M.E Gamble, Betty and Dennis Hannigan, Charlie Harlan, P. Hatton, Mr. & Mrs. V. Harvey, Pauline Hilling, Marion and Gareth Hunt, Kathleen Johns, Dave Lee, Jane & Tina Lister, Gladys and Tom Lucas, Vera and Ian MacKay , Joanne & Don Mandryk, Pam and John Marshall, Michael A Matthew, Barbara Morgan, Margaret Neate, Lindsey Otter, Pam and Brian Powell, June & Geoff Rance, Russell Schooley, Joyce & Leonard Steers, Mr & Mrs T. Swinhoe, Alan Taylor, Glen and Karen Thorsen, Val Turner, Anita Wade, Kim and Derek Watson, Mr. & Mrs. Williams, Carol and John Woolner, Mary and Steve Yager and JoAnn Yadro. And all those who wish to remain anonymous.

A SPECIAL NOTE TO COLLECTORS

We welcome and appreciate any comments or suggestions in regard to the *Charlton Standard Catalogue of Wade Whimsical Collectables*.

If you would like to participate in pricing, please contact Jean Dale at the Charlton Press.

To provide new information or corrections, please write to Pat Murray, Box 746, RR #2, Stroud, Ontario L0L 2MO, Canada.

Printed in Canada
in the Province of Manitoba

The Charlton Press

Editorial Office
2040 Yonge Street, Suite 208, Toronto, Ontario M4S 1Z9
Telephone: (416) 488-1418 Fax: (416) 488-4656
Telephone: (800) 442-6042 Fax: (800) 442-1542
www.charltonpress.com e-mail: chpress@charltonpress.com

Set Six
farmyard friends
join WADE Whimsies

CONTENTS

WADE COLLECTOR'S FAIR AND EVENT FIGURES

THE OFFICIAL INTERNATIONAL WADE COLLECTORS CLUB MODELS
MEMBERSHIP FIGURES AND LIMITED EDITIONS

PRIVATELY COMMISSIONED MODELS

HOW TO USE THIS PRICE GUIDE

THE PURPOSE

This publication has been designed to serve two specific purposes. Its first purpose is to furnish the collector with accurate and detailed listings that provide the essential information needed to build a rewarding collection. Its second function is to provide collectors and dealers with current market prices for the complete line of Wade whimsical collectables.

This guide is divided into two sections: the models produced by and for the Wade product line and then those produced by Wade under commission for other corporations.

In the first section, the models are listed in order of their issue dates; in the second section they are listed in alphabetical order according to the issuing company.

STYLES AND VERSIONS

STYLES: A change in style occurs when a major element of the design is altered or modified as a result of a deliberate mould change. An example of this is *Snow White and the Seven Dwarfs*, 1938, (style one) and *Snow White and the Seven Dwarfs*, 1982-1984 (style two).

VERSIONS: Versions are modifications in a minor style element of the figures, such as the open- and closed-eared rabbits in the Red Rose Tea series. A version could also indicate a change in colourways; for example, the variety of hat colours of the *Lucky Leprechauns*.

THE LISTINGS

A Word On Pricing

The purpose of this catalogue is to give readers the most accurate, up-to-date retail prices for whimsical Wades in the markets of the United States, Canada and the United Kingdom. However, one must remember that these prices are indications only and that the actual selling price may be higher or lower by the time the final transaction agreement is reached.

To accomplish this, The Charlton Press continues to access an international pricing panel of experts who submit prices based on both dealer and collector retail-price activity, as well as on current auction results in the U. S., Canada and the U. K. These market prices are carefully averaged to reflect accurate valuations for models in each of these markets.

This catalogue lists prices for figures in the currency of a particular market (U.S. dollars for the American market and sterling for the U.K. market). The bulk of the prices given are not determined by currency-exchange calculations, but by actual activity in the market concerned.

Additionally, collectors must remember that all relevant information must be known to make a proper valuation. When comparing auction prices to catalogue prices, collectors and dealers must remember two important points. First, compare "apples and apples." Be sure that auction prices realized for figures include a buyer's premium if one is due. Buyer's premiums can range from 10 to 15 percent, and on an expensive piece, this amount can be substantial. Secondly, know whether a figure is restored, repaired or in mint condition. This fact may not be noted or explained in the listings, and as a result, its price will not match that of the same piece in mint condition. Please be aware of repairs and restorations and the effect they have on values.

A last word of caution. No pricing catalogue can, or should, be a fixed price list. This book must be considered as a price guide only, showing the most current retail prices based on market demand within a particular region for the various models.

A Word on Condition

The prices published herein are for models in **mint condition**. Figures with minor imperfections resulting from processing at the pottery will be discounted in the range of 10 to 20 percent from these prices. The early models with a cellulose glaze are almost impossible to obtain in mint condition, so their prices are for figures in reasonable condition, meaning that a minimum number of flakes of glaze are missing. The early figures in "strictly" mint condition will command a price much higher than the listed price. Models with minor chips, due to packaging by the commissioning company, are just "fillers" in collections and will command only a fraction of the mint price, in the area of 10 percent. Cracked or chipped figures are not really collectable. Models that are broken, repaired or have major chips are worthless and should not be collected.

Technical Information

The whimsical Wades in this book were produced in the George Wade Pottery, the Wade Heath Pottery and in the Wade Ireland Pottery between the 1930s and 1995. For each model, the name of its series, the year of production, the model's name, its size (the height first, then the width in millimetres), the colours and its present value are presented. All known backstamps of the models are listed above the tables. If the figures can be found with a variety of backstamps, then each backstamp is followed, in parenthesis, by the model numbers applicable to it. For a few listings, only approximate dates of issue are given, as they could not be confirmed by Wade. When known, the year the model was discontinued and its original issue price are also given.

INTRODUCTION

WHIMSICAL WADES

By the early 1950s, the Wade Potteries had filled the demand to replace industrial ceramics damaged in the war, and there was not sufficient work to keep the employees busy. This was when Sir George Wade decided to produce his now world-famous miniature animals—the *First Whimsies* — which he referred to as his "pocket money toys." They first appeared in spring 1954 at the British Industries Fair. The miniatures were intended for school children, but they soon attracted the attention of adults and became very collectable.

George Wade's policy was to limit the number of whimsical models produced, so they would not flood the market and lose their appeal. Models of the early 1950s were produced in sets, usually of five, and most sets were in production for only a year or two, some for as little as a few months. Whenever a large industrial order was received, the whole pottery would revert to the production of industrial wares, leaving some sets or series unfinished. Perhaps the pottery intended to go back to unfinished series, but because of slow sales, high production costs, copyright laws, or a new interest by the public, they were never completed.

In some of these cases there were only a few thousand models made, usually as a test run, and therefore they were not issued for nation-wide sale. To recoup production costs, some models may have been sold only in one area of the United Kingdom.

In 1958 the three English Wade Potteries were restructured under the name Wade Potteries Ltd., later renamed Wade PLC. Wade (Ulster) Ltd. was renamed Wade Ireland Ltd. in 1966.

Sir George Wade died in 1986 at age 95, to be followed a year later by the untimely death of his son Tony. With their passing, 120 years of Wade family involvement in ceramics came to an end.

In 1989 Wade PLC was taken over by Beauford PLC and renamed Wade Ceramics Ltd., which is still in production today. Wade Ireland was renamed Seagoe Ceramics and continued to manufacture domestic tablewares until 1993, when it reverted back to the production of industrial ceramics.

THE PRODUCTION PROCESS

The Wade Pottery manufactures a particularly hard porcelain body which has been used in many different products. It consists of a mixture of ball clays, china clay, flint, felspar, talc, etc., some ingredients imported from Sweden, Norway and Egypt. These materials are mixed in large vats of water, producing a thick sludge or "slip." The slip is passed into a filter to extract most of the water, leaving large flat "bats" of porcelain clay, approximately two feet square and three inches thick. The clay bats are dried and then ground into dust ready for the forming process. Paraffin is added to the dust to assist in bonding and as a lubricant to remove the formed pieces from the steel moulds.

Once pressed into the required shape, the clay articles are dried, then all the press marks are removed by sponging and "fettling," which is scraping off the surplus clay by hand, using a sharp blade. From the early 1960s, a new method of fettling was used, whereby the base of the model was rubbed back and forth on a material similar to emery paper. This resulted in a lined or ribbed base, which is the best method of identifying the majority of post-1960 Wade figures.

One or more ceramic colours is applied to the clay model, which is then sprayed with a clear glaze that, when fired, allows the colours underneath to show through. This process is known as underglaze decoration. On-glaze decoration is also used by Wade, which includes enamelling, gilding and transfer printing, and is done after the article has been glazed and fired.

Some whimsical Wades are hollow, usually because they were prototype models that were discarded or removed from the pottery by workers. Other models may be found in different colour glazes than the originals, due to one or more of the following reasons:

1. The first colour glaze was laid down for a test run, but when the models came out of the kiln at the end of the firing period (sometimes as long as three days), it was either too light or too dark. This occurred in the case of the black *English Whimsies* "Zebra," which was so dark when it emerged after its run through the kiln that the striped pattern could not be clearly seen. The colour glaze was then changed to beige.

2. When the model was shown to the client he did not like the initial colour, so another was chosen.

3. Some models were reissued in different colour glazes for use in promotions for Red Rose Tea and for Tom Smith Christmas crackers.

WADE MODELLERS, 1954-1994

Listed below are the modellers who helped to create whimsical Wade figures. The year that each modeller started working at Wade is given and, if known, the year he or she left.

After leaving Wade, many modellers went on to work for Royal Doulton, Szeiler, Sylvac, Dilsford Studio and other well-known British potteries. This accounts for the great number of other collectable models that bear a distinctive and characteristic likeness to Wade models.

Jessica Van Hallen, 1930
  Snow White set, 1938

Robert Barlow, Late 1930s
  Tinker, Tailor, Soldier, Sailor
  Comic Duck Family

Nancy Great-Rex, Late 1930s-Early 1940s
  Butcher, Baker and Candlestick Maker

William K. Harper, 1954-1963
  First Whimsies
  Bernie and Pooh
  Hat Box models
  Drum Box series
  Minikins series
  Noddy set
  Tortoise Family
  TV Pets
  Shamrock Cottage
  Irish Comical Pig
  Pink Elephant
  Flying Birds
  Disney Blow Ups

Leslie McKinnon, 1959-1961
  The British Character set
  Happy Families series

Paul Zalman, 1961
   Mabel Lucie Attwell models

Ken Holmes, 1975 to the present
   Dinosaur Collection
   Burglar and Policeman series
   Children and Pets

Alan Maslankowski, 1975
   Snow White set, 1982

MODEL BOXES, 1954-1995

Most collectors have seen or purchased Wade models in their original boxes. In order to catch the eye of a collector, early Wade boxes were made to be just as colourful, appealing and decorative as their contents.

When Wade models were issued in the 1950s, their appeal to collectors was not as avid as it is today; as a result, few boxes from the 1950s were kept by the original purchasers. Models in their boxes can command a higher price than a model alone, and depending on the age and condition of the box, the price of the model may increase by 30 to 50 percent.

In the 1970s the rising cost of paper and the fact that Wade produced an established collectors' product caused the company to produce less appealing containers. But by the 1980s, the boxes again became colourful and eye-catching, although they had lost the old-world charm of the boxes of the 1950s.

Box designs and colours can vary depending on the year of issue and the length of the production run. Some popular models that were reissued two or more times can be found in two, and at times three, different box sizes and colours (as in the *Happy Families* series, which was issued and reissued in three different box designs).

WADE MARKS, 1930s-1998

Wade Heath Ltd. and George Wade and Son Ltd. not only shared their pottery moulds, they also shared the Wade trademark during the late 1940s and into the 1950s. This makes it difficult to distinguish which pottery a particular model came from. As a general guide for those models produced in both potteries, the Wade Heath postwar novelty models have a green or greenish brown "Wade England" mark on their bases, and the postwar George Wade figures have a black or blue "Wade England" transfer on their bases.

Later, with the addition of Wade Ireland, it became even more difficult to determine the origin of a model. The potteries had a habit of helping each other out in order to speed up production. These figures all had the mark of the originating pottery on their bases and were packed in boxes from that pottery, even though they may have been made in another location.

A good example of this practice is the 1977 *Bisto Kids* set. During one of our conversations, Tony Wade told me that, although they were marked "Wade Staffordshire" on their bases, these models were in fact produced in the Wade Ireland Pottery. The George Wade Pottery had had another large order to complete, so Wade Ireland took over.

Similarly, some of the 1950s *First Whimsies* are believed to have been produced by Wade Ireland, although none of the models have a Wade Ireland mark, and the entire series of ten sets was packed in Wade England boxes.

Many small open-caste models (models with no bases and standing on thin legs) did not have enough space on them for a Wade label or an ink stamp. They were originally issued in boxes with "Wade England" clearly marked on the box or packet front. Once removed from their container, however, these models are hard to identify without the aid of Wade collector books (the *First Whimsies* is a good example of this).

Larger, more solid-based models were marked with a Wade ink stamp or with a black and gold label on their bases. But over the years the label or the ink stamp can wear off or be washed off by previous owners, leaving them unmarked.

Wade Heath

Ink Stamps

1. Black ink stamp "Flaxman Ware Hand Made Pottery by Wadeheath England," 1935-1937.
2. Black ink stamp "Flaxman Wade Heath England," 1937-1938.

3. Black ink stamp "Flaxman Wade Heath," 1937-1938.
4. Black ink stamp "Wadeheath Ware England," 1935-1937.
5. Green-brown ink stamp "Wade England," late 1940s-early 1950s.
6. Green ink stamp "Wade England [name of model]," late 1940s-early 1950s.

7. Black ink stamp "Wadeheath by permission Walt Disney England," 1937-1938.
8. Black ink stamp "Wade" and red ink stamp "Made in England," 1938.
9. Black ink stamp "Wade England," late 1940s-early 1950s.

Wade

Hand-painted Marks

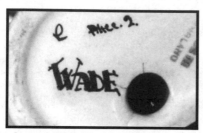

1. Black hand painted "Wade Alice 2," with black ink stamp "Made in England," 1930s.
2. Black hand painted "Wade Alice 7" and red ink stamp of leaping deer, 1930s.
3. Black hand painted "Hiawatha Wade England," 1937.

Ink Stamps

4. Black ink stamp "Wade England," late 1940s.
5. Black ink stamp "Wade Made in England," 1955.
6. Brown ink stamp "Wade England," with brown cricket in large C. Only seen on some of the *Happy Families* models.

Transfer Prints

7. Small black transfer "Wade England [name of model]," 1950s.
8. Large black transfer "Wade England [name of model]," 1950s.
9a. Black transfer "Wade Snippet No. 1 Mayflower Carried 102 Pilgrims to North America 1620-Real Porcelain-Made In England," 1956.
9b. Black transfer "Wade Snippet No. 2 Santa Maria Flag ship of Columbus 1492-Real Porcelain-Made In England," 1956.
9c. Black transfer "Wade Snippet No. 3 Revenge Flag ship of Sir Richard Grenville 1591-Real Porcelain-Made In England," 1956.
9d. Black transfer "Wade Snippet No. 4 Hansel-Real Porcelain-Made in England," 1957.
9e. Black transfer "Wade Snippet No. 5 Gretel-Real Porcelain-Made in England," 1957
9f. Black transfer "Wade Snippet No. 6 Gingy-Real Porcelain-Made in England," 1957.

10. Blue transfer "Wade England," 1956-1957.
11. Black transfer "Wade Porcelain England," 1961.

12. Black transfer "Wade Porcelain Copyright Walt Disney Productions Made in England," 1961.
13. Brown transfer "Wade Made in England," 1962.
14. Brown transfer "Copyright RHM Foods Ltd. & Applied Creativity, Wade Staffordshire," 1977.
15. Black transfer "Wade Made in England," 1978-1987.

16. Black transfer "Walt Disney Productions" in an oval shape, with "Wade England" in centre, 1981-1987.
17. Black transfer "Wade Porcelain England S/F [1-6]," 1984-1986.
18. Red transfer "Wade Made in England," 1985, 1994.
19. Black transfer "Harrods Knightsbridge," 1991-1994.
20. Black transfer "Wade Limited Editions Modelled by Ken Holmes [includes model name, series number and limited edition number]," 1993-1994.

21. Black transfer "Arthur Hare [Holly Hedgehog] © C&S Collectables Wade England," 1993-1995.
22. Black transfer "Wade," enclosed in an outline of the Isle of Wight and numbered, 1994.
23. Black transfer "[Limited edition number] © H/B Inc, Scooby-Doo, Limited edition of 2,000, Wade England, G&G Collectables," 1994.

24. Black transfer "1994 [1995] Mirror Group Newspapers Ltd © C&S Collectables Wade England," 1994-1995.

Impressed Marks

25. Impressed "Wade Porcelain Made in England," 1958.

Embossed Marks

26. Small embossed "Wade," 1954-1983.

27. Embossed "'Whimtrays' Wade Porcelain Made in England," 1958-1965.

28. Embossed "Wade Porcelain Made in England," 1958-1984.
29. Embossed "Wade Porcelain - Mabel Lucie Attwell © Made in England," 1959-1961.
30. Embossed "Angel Dish Wade Porcelain Made in England," 1963.
31. Embossed "Robertson," 1963-1965.
32. Embossed "Wade England," 1965-1994.

33. Large embossed "Wade Made in England," 1975-1984.
34. Embossed "Mianco [year of issue] Wade England" on rim of base, 1989-1995.
35. Embossed "Wade England 1990 [1991]," 1990-1991.

36. Embossed "Wade England 1991" on rim of base and ink stamp "GSG," 1991.
37. Large embossed "Wade," 1993-1994.

Labels

38. Small black and gold label "Wade England," 1954-1959.
39. Black and gold label "Genuine Wade Porcelain Made in England," 1959-1965.
40. Large black and gold label "Wade England," early 1970s-1981.
41. Black and gold label "Walt Disney Productions Wade England," 1981-1985.

Wade Ireland

Ink Stamps

1. Black ink stamp "'Pogo' Copyright, Walt Kelly, Made in Ireland 1959," 1959.
2. Black ink stamp "Made in Ireland," 1974-1985.
3. Purple ink stamp "Made in Ireland," 1974-1985.

Transfer Prints

4. Green transfer "Shamrock Pottery Made in Ireland," 1953-1956.

Impressed Marks

5. Impressed "Shamrock Pottery Made in Ireland," 1953-1956.

6. Impressed "Irish Porcelain Made in Ireland by Wade Co. Armagh," with shamrock, early 1950s.
7. Impressed "Made in Ireland," early 1970s.

Embossed Marks

8. Embossed "Irish Porcelain, Made in Ireland," with a shamrock leaf, 1953-1956.
9. Embossed "Shamrock Pottery Made in Ireland," 1959.
10. Embossed "Wade Porcelain Made in Ireland," 1970s-1980s.
11. Embossed "Made in Ireland, Porcelain Wade, Eire Tir-Adheanta," 1980-1988.
12. Embossed "Wade Ireland," 1984-1987.

7. Elephant Happy Family

8. Owl Happy Family

WADE MODELS

STORYBOOK FIGURES, NOVELTY ANIMALS AND BIRDS

Wade produced over 83 figures from the 1920s to the 1930s, mostly models of ladies; only "Alice and the Dodo," "Hiawatha" and the 1938 set, *Snow White and the Seven Dwarfs*, are classed as storybook figures. All these models were produced with an experimental cellulose glaze, which cracked and flaked when exposed to heat, damp and sunlight. It is rare to find storybook models from this period in mint condition.

A small number of comic animal models and some Walt Disney character models were produced by Wade Heath Ltd. for approximately three years before giftware production ceased at the onset of World War II. Some models are marked with a 1935-1937 mark ("Flaxman Ware Hand Made Pottery By Wadeheath England") or either of the 1937-1939 marks ("Flaxman Wade Heath England" or "Wadeheath Ware England"). Most have an all-over, one-colour matt glaze. All the following storybook and comic animal models are slip cast, and therefore hollow.

ALICE AND THE DODO

Circa 1935 -1938

"Alice and the Dodo" was produced in the cellulose glaze described above. It is rare to find these models in perfect condition.

Size: 130 x 80 mm.
Backstamp: **A.** Black hand-painted "Wade Alice 2" with black ink stamp "Made in England" (1)
B. Black hand-painted "Wade Alice" with red ink stamp of leaping deer (2a, 2b, 2c)

No.	Description	U.S. $	Can. $	U.K. £
1	Orange-yellow dress; black band; light brown bird; black beret	250.00	350.00	175.00
2a	Green dress; red band; dark brown bird; blue beret	250.00	350.00	175.00
2b	Pink dress; red band; dark brown bird; blue beret	250.00	350.00	175.00
2c	Blue dress; red band; dark brown bird; blue beret	250.00	350.00	175.00

DISMAL DESMOND

Circa 1935

This model of "Dismal Desmond," a weeping Dalmatian, is based on a British childrens comic character who featured in *Deans Rag Books* during the mid 1930s.

Size: 165 mm.
Backstamp: Ink stamp "Wadeheath England" with lion (1934-1935)

No.	Description	U.S. $	Can. $	U.K. £
1	White; black markings; brownish red tears, collar	620.00	825.00	360.00

NOVELTY ANIMALS AND BIRDS

Circa 1935

Baby Bird

Baby Bird, small   Baby Bird, large

Backstamp: **A.** Black ink stamp "Flaxman Ware Hand Made Pottery By Wadeheath England" (1)
B. Black ink stamp "Wadeheath Ware England" (2)

No.	Name	Description	Size	U.S. $	Can. $	U.K. £
1a	Baby Bird, Large	Mottled green	200 x 165	160.00	190.00	95.00
1b	Baby Bird, Large	Pale orange	200 x 165	160.00	190.00	95.00
1c	Baby Bird, Large	Yellow	200 x 165	160.00	190.00	95.00
2a	Baby Bird, Small	Orange	90 x 65	65.00	90.00	45.00
2b	Baby Bird, Small	Yellow	90 x 65	65.00	90.00	45.00

Cheeky Duckling

Backstamp: Black ink stamp "Flaxman Ware Hand Made Pottery By Wadeheath England"

No.	Name	Description	Size	U.S. $	Can. $	U.K. £
1	Cheeky Duckling, Large	Blue	180 x 115	145.00	190.00	95.00
2a	Cheeky Duckling, Small	Blue	150 x 85	110.00	145.00	70.00
2b	Cheeky Duckling, Small	Orange	150 x 85	110.00	145.00	70.00

Duckling

This duckling was in production from c.1937 to 1939.

Backstamp: **A.** Ink stamp "Flaxman Wade Heath England" (1937-1939) (1a)
                B. None (1b)

No.	Name	Description	Size	U.S. $	Can. $	U.K. £
1a	Duckling	Beige brown	95	120.00	150.00	75.00
1b	Duckling	Green	95	150.00	200.00	100.00

The shape number for Jumbo Jim is 331.

Backstamp: A. Black ink stamp "Flaxman Wade Heath England" (1a)
B. Ink stamp'"Flaxman Wade Heath England" with impressed No 331 (1b)

No.	Name	Description	Size	U.S. $	Can. $	U.K. £
1a	Jumbo Jim	Light brown	180 x 105	250.00	350.00	175.00
1b	Jumbo Jim	Turquoise blue	180 x 105	250.00	350.00	175.00

Laughing Rabbit

Backstamp: Black ink stamp "Flaxman Wade Heath England"

No.	Name	Description	Size	U.S. $	Can. $	U.K. £
1a	Laughing Rabbit, Large	Orange	175 x 75	135.00	180.00	90.00
1b	Laughing Rabbit, Large	Bright green	175 x 75	135.00	180.00	90.00
2a	Laughing Rabbit, Medium	Brown	160 x 70	110.00	150.00	75.00
2b	Laughing Rabbit, Medium	Green	160 x 70	110.00	150.00	75.00
2c	Laughing Rabbit, Medium	Blue	160 x 70	110.00	150.00	75.00
3a	Laughing Rabbit, Small	Beige	140 x 65	110.00	140.00	70.00
3b	Laughing Rabbit, Small	Blue	140 x 65	110.00	140.00	70.00
3c	Laughing Rabbit, Small	Green	140 x 65	110.00	140.00	70.00
4	Old Buck Rabbit	Brown	165 x 128	220.00	300.00	150.00

Pongo

Pongo was in production from 1935 to 1939 and was reissued for a short time in the late 1940s.

Backstamp: **A.** Black ink stamp "Flaxman Ware Hand Made Pottery By Wadeheath England"
B. Black ink stamp "Wadeheath Ware England"
C. Black ink stamp " Wade Heath England," 1938-1940s

No.	Name	Description	Size	U.S. $	Can. $	U.K. £
1a	Pongo, Large	Lilac; mauve nose	140 x 128	120.00	170.00	85.00
1b	Pongo, Large	Blue; mauve nose	140 x 128	120.00	170.00	85.00
1c	Pongo, Large	Mottled blue/orange	140 x 128	120.00	170.00	85.00
1d	Pongo, Large	Orange; mauve nose	140 x 128	120.00	170.00	85.00
1e	Pongo, Large	Orange	145 x 150	120.00	170.00	85.00
1f	Pongo, Large	Green	145 x 150	120.00	160.00	80.00
2a	Pongo, Medium	Lilac; mauve nose	128 x 115	120.00	160.00	80.00
2b	Pongo, Medium	Blue; mauve nose	128 x 115	120.00	160.00	80.00
2d	Pongo, Medium	Mottled blue/orange	128 x 115	120.00	160.00	80.00
2d	Pongo, Medium	Orange; mauve nose	128 x 115	120.00	160.00	80.00
2e	Pongo, Medium	Turquoise; black eyes, nose	128 x 115	120.00	160.00	80.00
3	Pongo, Miniature	Blue	105 x 95	100.00	125.00	65.00
4a	Pongo, Small	Lilac; mauve nose	115 x 100	75.00	100.00	50.00
4b	Pongo, Small	Blue; mauve nose	115 x 100	75.00	100.00	50.00
4c	Pongo, Small	Orange; mauve nose	115 x 100	75.00	100.00	50.00
4d	Pongo, Small	Green; blue eyes, nose	120 x 110	75.00	100.00	50.00
4e	Pongo, Small	Mauve	120 x 110	75.00	100.00	50.00

MICKEY MOUSE

1935

A rare model of Mickey Mouse was produced by the Wadeheath Pottery at the same time as a children's toy Mickey Mouse tea set. This model was first advertised along with the toy tea set in March 1935.

Backstamp: Black ink stamp "Wadeheath Ware by Permission Walt Disney Mickey Mouse Ltd Made in England" (1935)

No.	Description	Size	U.S. $	Can. $	U.K. £
1a	Black and white body; yellow hands and shoes; blue shorts; brown suitcase	90	1,900.00	2,600.00	1,300.00
1b	Black and white body; yellow gloves; green shorts; orange shoes; brown suitcase	90	1,900.00	2,600.00	1,300.00
1c	Black and white body; yellow gloves; blue shorts; orange shoes; brown suitcase	90	1,900.00	2,600.00	1,300.00
1d	Black and white body; yellow gloves; orange shorts and shoes; brown suitcase	95	1,900.00	2,600.00	1,300.00

DONALD DUCK

1937

Backstamp: Black ink stamp "WadeHeath England" with lion (1934-1937)

No.	Description	Size	U.S. $	Can. $	U.K. £
1	White body; yellow beak/legs; blue hat and coat; red bow tie	127	1,200.00	1,600.00	800.00

HIAWATHA
1937

"Hiawatha" was produced with a cellulose glaze, so it is difficult to find in mint condition.

Size: 100 x 50 mm.
Backstamp: Black hand-painted "'Hiawatha' Wade England"

No.	Description	U.S. $	Can. $	U.K. £
1a	Yellow feather; red trousers	260.00	350.00	175.00
1b	Red feather; blue trousers	260.00	350.00	175.00

PLUTO

1937-1938

Pluto models may have the impressed shape number 205.

Size: 100 x 162 mm.
Backstamp: Black ink stamp "Wadeheath by permission of Walt Disney, England"

No.	Description	U.S.$	Can.$	U.K.£
1a	Orange-brown; black ears, nose, eyes	300.00	375.00	185.00
1b	Grey; black ears, nose, eyes	300.00	375.00	185.00

PLUTO'S PUPS
1937

Pluto's quintuplet puppies, the Quinpuplets, were from the Walt Disney cartoon film of the same name. In the film they were not given names, but one pup reappeared in a 1942 Disney cartoon as Pluto Junior.

Backstamp: A. Black ink stamp "Flaxman Wadeheath England" (3a)
B. Black ink stamp "Wadeheath by permission of Walt Disney, England" (1a, 1b, 1c, 2, 3b, 3c, 3d, 3e, 3f, 4a, 4b, 5)

No.	Name	Description	Size	U.S. $	Can. $	U.K. £
1a	Pup Lying on Back	Orange	62 x 112	360.00	400.00	200.00
1b	Pup Lying on Back	Beige	62 x 112	360.00	400.00	200.00
1c	Pup Lying on Back	Green	62 x 112	360.00	400.00	200.00
2	Pup Sitting	Grey; blue ears, eyes, nose	100 x 62	360.00	400.00	200.00
3a	Pup Sitting, Front Paws Up	Beige	95 x 85	360.00	400.00	200.00
3b	Pup Sitting, Front Paws Up	Light blue; dark blue ears, eyes	95 x 85	360.00	400.00	200.00
3c	Pup Sitting, Front Paws Up	Light grey; dark blue ears, eyes	95 x 85	360.00	400.00	200.00
3d	Pup Sitting, Front Paws Up	Grey; blue ears, eyes, nose	95 x 85	360.00	400.00	200.00
3e	Pup Sitting, Front Paws Up	Orange	95 x 85	360.00	400.00	200.00
3f	Pup Sitting, Front Paws Up	Orange; blue ears, eyes, nose	95 x 85	360.00	400.00	200.00
4a	Pup Lying, Head on Paws	Orange	62 x 112	360.00	400.00	200.00
4b	Pup Lying, Head on Paws	Beige	62 x 112	360.00	400.00	200.00
5	Pup Standing, Licking	Grey; blue ears, eyes, nose	100 x 62	360.00	400.00	200.00

SAMMY SEAL

1937

Backstamp: Black ink stamp "Wadeheath England by permission Walt Disney"

No.	Description	Size	U.S. $	Can. $	U.K. £
1a	Beige	150 x 150	360.00	400.00	200.00
1b	Grey; black eyes, nose	150 x 150	360.00	400.00	200.00
1c	Pink; black eyes, nose	150 x 150	360.00	400.00	200.00
1d	Orange	150 x 150	360.00	400.00	200.00
1e	Orange; black eyes, nose	150 x 150	360.00	400.00	200.00
1f	Off white; brown eyes	150 x 150	360.00	400.00	200.00
1g	White; black eyes, nose	150 x 150	360.00	400.00	200.00
2	Orange; black eyes, nose	110 x 110	300.00	350.00	150.00

SNOW WHITE AND THE SEVEN DWARFS

1938

STYLE ONE

The George Wade Pottery held a Walt Disney licence to produce Disney models, and the Wade Heath Royal Victoria Pottery issued this first *Snow White* set to coincide with the release of the Walt Disney film, *Snow White and the Seven Dwarfs*. These models were produced with a cellulose glaze.

Backstamp: A. Black hand-painted "Wade [name of model]," plus red ink stamp with a leaping deer and "Made in England" (1)
B. Black hand-painted "Wade [name of model]," plus red ink stamp "Made in England" (2, 3, 4, 6, 7, 8, 9)
C. Unmarked (5)

No.	Name	Description	Size	U.S. $	Can .$	U.K. £
1	Snow White	Yellow dress; red bodice	180 x 65	450.00	600.00	300.00
2	Bashful	Orange coat; blue trousers	100 x 45	235.00	240.00	170.00
3	Doc	Orange jacket; maroon trousers	110 x 55	235.00	240.00	170.00
4	Dopey	Red coat; green trousers	110 x 45	235.00	240.00	170.00
5	Grumpy	Maroon jacket; green trousers	100 x 60	235.00	240.00	170.00
6	Happy	Orange jacket; red trousers	125 x 55	235.00	240.00	170.00
7	Sleepy	Orange-brown jacket; blue trousers	100 x 35	235.00	240.00	170.00
8	Sneezy	Blue jacket; red trousers	100 x 35	235.00	240.00	170.00
—	Set (8 pieces)			2,500.00	3,500.00	1,200.00

SNOW WHITE AND THE SEVEN DWARFS

1981-1984

STYLE TWO

This issue of *Snow White and the Seven Dwarfs*, modelled by Alan Maslankowski, was first offered through mail order by Harpers Direct Mail Marketing just before Christmas 1981, then distributed in stores during the next spring.

Snow White, First Version

Snow White, Second Version

Backstamp: **A.** Black and gold label "© Walt Disney Productions Wade England" (1a, 8)
B. Black transfer "© Walt Disney Productions Wade England" (1b, 2-8)
C. Black transfer "Wade Made in England" (1a, 2, 4, 6)

No.	Name	Description	Size	U.S. $	Can. $	U.K. £
1a	Snow White	Head straight; smiling; pink spots on sleeves; light blue bodice; pale yellow skirt	95 x 100	185.00	250.00	125.00
1b	Snow White	Head back; pink stripes on sleeves; light blue bodice with pink heart; pale yellow skirt	95 x 100	185.00	250.00	125.00
2	Bashful	Orange coat; grey hat; beige shoes	80 x 45	155.00	200.00	100.00
3	Doc	Blue coat; grey trousers; beige hat, shoes	80 x 50	200.00	270.00	135.00
4	Dopey	Beige coat; red hat; pale blue shoes	80 x 50	155.00	200.00	100.00
5	Grumpy	Red coat; beige hat; brown shoes	75 x 45	155.00	200.00	100.00
6	Happy	Brown vest; beige hat; blue trousers	85 x 50	155.00	200.00	100.00
7	Sleepy	Pale green coat, shoes; orange hat	80 x 50	120.00	160.00	80.00
8	Sneezy	Navy coat; blue trousers; brown hat, shoes	80 x 45	155.00	200.00	100.00
—	Set (8)			1,000.00	1,500.00	500.00

DOPEY

1939

This cellulose model of Dopey is a different model than the one used for the 1938 Snow White set. He was the only model produced in an intended Snow White set for F.W. Woolworth, England during Christmas 1939, but with the onset of World War II the order for the rest of the models was cancelled.

Backstamp: None

No.	Description	Size	U.S. $	Can. $	U.K. £
1	Mauve hat; yellow coat; brown shoes	110 x 53	400.00	525.00	200.00

SNOW WHITE AND THE SEVEN DWARFS DERIVATIVES

BROOCHES

Circa 1938

Miniature lapel brooches were produced in the cellulose glaze used by the Wadeheath pottery during the mid-late 1930s, one of Snow White's face and full figure brooches of the dwarfs. The brooches have only been found in Canada and the USA. They were probably produced for Walt Disney staff during the North American promotion of the film *Snow White and the* Seven Dwarfs. They have an unusual "Wade Burslem England" backstamp, which adds to the belief that they were a special promotion.

Backstamp: Embossed "[name of character] Made in England Wade Burslem England"

No.	Name	Description	Size	U.S. $	Can. $	U.K. £
1	Snow White	Black hair and eyes; red bowand mouth	40		Very Rare	
2	Bashful	Green hat; orange coat; blue trousers; brown shoes	35		Very Rare	
3	Doc	Green hat; orange coat; maroon trousers; yellow belt buckle; blue shoes	35		Very Rare	
4	Grumpy	Orange hat; orange-brown coat; blue trousers; orange brown shoes	37		Very Rare	
5	Happy	Light blue hat; brown coat; green trousers; red-brown shoes	35		Very Rare	
6	Sleepy	Green hat; brown coat; purple trousers; red shoes	35		Very Rare	
7	Sneezy	Green hat; blue coat; orange-red trousers; orange shoes	35		Very Rare	

COMIC ANIMALS AND BIRDS

From the late 1940s to the 1950s, the Wade Heath Royal Victoria Pottery and the George Wade Pottery produced a large series of small animal models, some described as comic or novelty. Because the two potteries produced the same models using the same moulds and both used the "Wade England" mark, it is hard to tell which models were made in which pottery. But it is believed that models stamped "Wade England" in green, brown or black were produced in the Royal Victoria Pottery before 1953, and those models transfer printed with a black or blue "Wade England" mark were produced in the George Wade Pottery in the early to mid 1950s. The *Comic Families* models have creamy beige background glazes with dark coloured clothing and are also found in white with pastel blue and grey markings.

During this period whenever Sir George Wade would come across surplus models, he would say, "Stick 'em on something." The figures would be sent to the Wade Heath Pottery, where they were joined onto surplus bramble-ware mustard pots (minus their lids) or basket-ware egg cups, then mounted on a moulded leaf-shaped base to make a novelty bowl. The finished product was then repainted and called a "Stick-em-on-Something Posy Bowl."

For ease of reference, the models are listed in alphabetical order, not in order of issue.

COMIC DUCK FAMILY

1950s

The *Comic Duck Family* was designed by Robert Barlow. The original price for "Mr. Duck" and "Mrs. Duck" was 2/6d each. "Dack" and "Dilly" each sold for 1/6d.

Backstamp: A. Unmarked (1a, 2a, 2b)
            B. Black transfer print "Wade England" (1b, 1c, 2a, 2b, 3, 4)

No.	Name	Description	Size	U.S. $	Can. $	U.K.£
1a	Mr. Duck	White; beige beak, tail, feet; blue cap, tie; small eyes	70 x 38	190.00	250.00	125.00
1b	Mr. Duck	White; yellow beak, feet; orange-red cap; small eyes	70 x 38	190.00	250.00	125.00
1c	Mr. Duck	White/beige; blue cap, tie, base; large black eyes	70 x 38	190.00	250.00	125.00
2a	Mrs. Duck	White; yellow beak, feet, bonnet; small eyes	70 x 37	190.00	250.00	125.00
2b	Mrs. Duck	White/beige; blue bonnet, basket, base; large black eyes	70 x 37	190.00	250.00	125.00
3	Dack	White; yellow beak, feet; blue cap; small eyes	40 x 28	160.00	240.00	120.00
4	Dilly	White; yellow beak, feet; orange tam; small eyes	40 x 27	160.00	240.00	120.00

COMIC FROG FAMILY

Circa 1948 - 1952

Mrs. Frog

Backstamp: Black ink stamp "Wade England"

No.	Name	Description	Size	U.S. $	Can. $	U.K.£
1	Mr. Frog	Dark green; bowler hat; cigar	40 x 58	180.00	240.00	120.00
2	Mrs. Frog	Dark green; bonnet; umbrella	40 x 58	180.00	240.00	120.00
3	Boy Frog	Dark green; rugby ball	28 x 38	180.00	240.00	120.00
4	Girl Frog	Dark green; bunch of flowers	28 x 38	180.00	240.00	120.00

COMIC PENGUIN FAMILY

Circa 1948 - 1955

The *Comic Penguin Family* was produced in pastels and in dark colours. Before the 1950s these models were stamped "Wade England" and afterwards were printed with a "Wade England" mark. "Mr. Penguin" and "Mrs. Penguin" are also found as salt and pepper pots. The original price of "Mr. Penguin" and "Mrs. Penguin" was 2/6d each. "Benny" and "Penny" each sold for 1/6d.

Backstamp: **A.** Black ink stamp "Wade England" (1b, 3)
B. Black transfer "Wade England" (1a, 4, 6, 7)
C. Unmarked (2, 5)

No.	Name	Description	Size	U.S. $	Can. $	U.K. £
1a	Mr. Penguin	White/grey; pale blue cap, scarf; black umbrella	90 x 40	180.00	240.00	120.00
1b	Mr. Penguin	White; blue cap, scarf; black umbrella	90 x 40	180.00	240.00	120.00
2	Mr. Penguin	Black/white; dark blue cap, scarf; yellow beak, hands, feet	65 x 40	180.00	240.00	120.00
3	Mrs. Penguin	White/grey penguin, shawl; black bag	85 x 40	180.00	240.00	120.00
4	Benny	White/grey; blue tam; black book	55 x 25	180.00	240.00	120.00
5	Penny	White/grey; blue bonnet; black penguin doll	50 x 25	180.00	240.00	120.00

COMIC PENGUIN FAMILY DERIVATIVES

SALT AND PEPPER POTS

Circa 1948

Backstamp: **A.** Black ink stamp "Wade England" (1, 2)
   B. Black transfer "Wade England" (1, 2)
   C. Unmarked (3, 4, 5)

No.	Name	Description	Size	U.S. $	Can. $	U.K. £
1	Mr. Penguin Pepper Pot	Black/white; maroon cap, scarf, umbrella	90 x 40	140.00	190.00	95.00
2	Mr. Penguin Pepper Pot	Black/white; blue cap, scarf	65 x 40	140.00	190.00	95.00
3	Mr. Penguin Pepper Pot	Pale green	75 x 40	180.00	240.00	120.00
4	Mrs. Penguin Salt Pot	Black/white; maroon shawl, handbag	85 x 40	140.00	190.00	95.00
5	Mrs. Penguin Salt Pot	Pale green	65 x 40	180.00	240.00	120.00

COMIC PIG FAMILY

"Mr. Pig" and "Mrs. Pig" were produced in cream with dark coloured clothing.

Photograph not available
at press time

Backstamp: Black ink stamp "Wade England"

No.	Name	Description	Size	U.S. $	Can. $	U.K. £
1	Mr. Pig	Cream; maroon tie, jacket	90 x 32	100.00	125.00	65.00
2	Mrs. Pig	Cream; dark yellow hat	80 x 30	100.00	125.00	65.00
3	Boy Pig	Unknown	Unknown		Rare	
4	Girl Pig	Unknown	Unknown		Rare	

COMIC PIG FAMILY DERIVATIVES

SALT AND PEPPER POTS

Circa 1948

The "Mr. Pig Salt Pot" and "Mrs. Pig Pepper Pot" were issued as a cruet set, both on an oval tray. The ink stamp on these models is a type used before the 1950s.

Size: 90 x 32 mm.
Backstamp: Black ink stamp "Wade England"

No.	Name	Description	U.S. $	Can. $	U.K. £
1	Mr. Pig Salt Pot	Cream; maroon tie, jacket	120.00	155.00	70.00
2	Mrs. Pig Pepper Pot	Cream; dark yellow hat	120.00	155.00	70.00
—	Set (2) with Tray		220.00	290.00	145.00

COMIC RABBIT FAMILY

Circa 1948 - 1955

Before the 1950s these models were produced in cream with dark coloured clothing; in the 1950s they were made in white with pastel markings. The original prices were 2/6d each for "Mr. Rabbit" and for "Mrs. Rabbit," and 1/6d each for "Fluff" and for "Puff."

Backstamp: **A.** Black ink stamp "Wade England" (1a, 2a, 3a, 4a)
B. Black transfer "Wade England" (1c, 2b, 3b, 4b)
C. Unmarked (1b, 1d)

No.	Name	Description	Size	U.S. $	Can. $	U.K. £
1a	Mr. Rabbit	Cream; dark yellow jacket	90 x 40	140.00	200.00	100.00
1b	Mr. Rabbit	Cream; black jacket	90 x 40	140.00	200.00	100.00
1c	Mr. Rabbit	White; blue jacket	90 x 40	140.00	200.00	100.00
1d	Mr. Rabbit	Bright yellow all over	90 x 40	180.00	240.00	120.00
2a	Mrs. Rabbit	Cream; maroon bonnet; yellow basket	90 x 40	140.00	200.00	100.00
2b	Mrs. Rabbit	White; grey ear tips; blue bonnet, basket	90 x 40	140.00	200.00	100.00
3a	Fluff	Cream; dark blue shawl	40 x 30	160.00	200.00	100.00
3b	Fluff	White; grey ear tips; blue/grey shawl	40 x 30	160.00	200.00	100.00
4a	Puff	Cream; dark yellow jacket	40 x 30	160.00	200.00	100.00
4b	Puff	White; grey ear tips; blue jacket	40 x 30	160.00	200.00	100.00

COMIC RABBIT FAMILY DERIVATIVES

SALT AND PEPPER POTS

Circa 1948

The "Mr. Rabbit Salt Pot" and "Mrs. Rabbit Pepper Pot" were issued as a cruet set, both standing on an oval tray.

Backstamp: Black ink stamp "Wade England"

No.	Name	Description	Size	U.S. $	Can. $	U.K. £
1	Mr. Rabbit Salt Pot	Cream; black hat; yellow jacket	90 x 40	90.00	120.00	60.00
2	Mrs. Rabbit Pepper Pot	Cream; maroon hat; yellow ribbon	90 x 40	90.00	120.00	60.00
—	Set (2) with Tray				Rare	

COMIC RABBIT (LITTLE LAUGHING BUNNY)

Circa 1948 - 1952

There are a number of variations in the size of the "Little Laughing Bunny," due to the die being retooled when worn. The colour of the grey models is also not consistent because the models were decorated in two different potteries. The original price was 1/-.

A poem by one of the Wade Heath figure casters in a spring 1954 *Jolly Potter* magazine refers to the "Comic Rabbit" as the "Little Laughing Bunny."

Backstamp: **A.** Black ink stamp "Wade England" (1a, 1b, 1c
            B. Black transfer print "Wade England" (1d)
            C. Blue transfer print "Wade England" (1d)
            D. Brown ink stamp (1e, 1f, 1g, 1h, 1i, 1j)

No.	Description	Size	U.S. $	Can. $	U.K. £
1a	Pale grey; brown ears, mouth; black eyes	63 x 38	75.00	100.00	50.00
1b	Pale grey; brown ears, mouth; red eyes	63 x 38	75.00	100.00	50.00
1c	White; brown ears, toes	63 x 38	75.00	100.00	50.00
1d	Dark grey; red mouth	63 x 38	75.00	100.00	50.00
1e	Beige; red mouth; black eyes; white stomach	65 x 40	75.00	100.00	50.00
1f	Dark grey; red mouth; black eyes	63 x 40	75.00	100.00	50.00
1g	Pale grey; red mouth; black eyes	63 x 40	75.00	100.00	50.00
1h	Pale grey; brown striped ears; red mouth; black eyes	63 x 40	75.00	100.00	50.00
1i	Pink; red mouth; black eyes	70 x 40	75.00	100.00	50.00
1j	White; brown striped ears; red mouth; black eyes	65 x 40	75.00	100.00	50.00

COMIC RABBIT DERIVATIVES

ART DECO ASHTRAY

Circa 1948

The Art Deco shaped ashtray is similar in shape to a model produced by Sylvac in the late 1940s which would have an impressed "Sylvac" and a design No 1532 on the base. Although the illustrated model does not have a Wade mark it has a registered design No. of 827631.

Size: 92 mm.
Backstamp: Ink stamp "Regd 827631 Made in England"

No.	Description	U.S. $	Can. $	U.K. £
1	Beige rabbit; grey ashtray	120.00	150.00	75.00

ASHTRAY

Circa 1948

Size: 110 x 100 mm.
Backstamp: Green-brown ink stamp "Wade England"

No.	Description	U.S. $	Can. $	U.K. £
1	Dark grey rabbit; yellow S-shaped ash tray	120.00	150.00	75.00

POSY BOWL

Circa 1948

Size: 85 x 80 mm.
Backstamp: Green-brown ink stamp "Wade England"

No.	Description	U.S. $	Can.$	U.K. £
1a	Blue; bramble-ware mustard pot	135.00	180.00	90.00
1b	Green; bramble-ware mustard pot	135.00	180.00	90.00
1c	Yellow; bramble-ware mustard pot	135.00	180.00	90.00

COMIC DONKEYS

Circa 1948 - 1952

The *Comic Donkeys* set is a pair of comic figures, one happy and one sad, which were produced in the Wade Pottery between the late 1940s and the early 1950s. The original price was 2/6d each.

Size: 110 x 55 mm.
Backstamp: Black ink stamp "Wade England"

No.	Name	Description	U.S. $	Can. $	U.K. £
1	Cheerful Charlie	Beige; coffee mane, tail, hooves	220.00	300.00	150.00
2	Doleful Dan	Beige; coffee mane, tail, hooves	220.00	300.00	150.00

COMIC DONKEYS DERIVATIVES

Circa 1948

SALT POT

Backstamp: Green-brown ink stamp "Wade England"

No.	Name	Description	Size	U.S. $	Can. $	U.K. £
1	Cheerful Charlie	Pink; beige mane, tail, hooves	110 x 55	115.00	300.00	150.00

POSY BOWLS

Cheerful Charlie

Doleful Dan

Size: 105 x 105 mm.
Backstamp: Green-brown ink stamp "Wade England"

No.	Name	Description	U.S. $	Can. $	U.K. £
1a	Cheerful Charlie	Multi-coloured egg-cup posy bowl	125.00	170.00	85.00
1b	Cheerful Charlie	Blue egg-cup posy bowl	110.00	150.00	75.00
1c	Cheerful Charlie	Cream egg-cup posy bowl	110.00	150.00	75.00
2a	Doleful Dan	Multi-coloured egg-cup posy bowl	125.00	170.00	85.00
2b	Doleful Dan	Blue egg-cup posy bowl	110.00	150.00	75.00
2c	Doleful Dan	Green egg-cup posy bowl	110.00	150.00	75.00

KISSING BUNNIES

Circa 1948-1950s

Kissing Bunnies, large eyes

Kissing Bunnies, small eyes

Backstamp: Black transfer print "Wade England"

No.	Description	Size	U.S. $	Can. $	U.K. £
1a	White bunny; grey bunny; large eyes	64 x 80	110.00	150.00	75.00
1b	White bunny; beige bunny; large eyes	64 x 80	110.00	150.00	75.00
1c	White bunny; grey ears, tail; brown bunny; white tail; small eyes	64 x 80	110.00	150.00	75.00
1d	White bunny; grey bunny; white tail; large eyes	64 x 80	110.00	150.00	75.00
1e	White bunny; grey tail; grey bunny; large eyes	64 x 80	110.00	150.00	75.00

KISSING BUNNIES DERIVATIVES

Circa 1948

ASHTRAY

This ashtray is similar in design to a model produced by Sylvac in the late 1940s known as an "Angular ashtray with Kissing Rabbits,"and carrying an impressed design No. of 1532.

Backstamp: Ink stamp "Made in England Reg No 824 (the rest of the numbers are missing

No.	Name	Description	Size	U.S. $	Can. $	U.K. £
1	Kissing Bunnies	White & brown bunnies; light green tray	85	110.00	150.00	75.00

POSY BOWL

Size: 70 x 87 mm.
Backstamp: Green-brown ink stamp "Wade England"

No.	Name	Description	U.S. $	Can. $	U.K. £
1a	Kissing Bunnies	Cream; bramble-ware mustard pot	110.00	150.00	75.00
1b	Kissing Bunnies	Green; bramble-ware mustard pot	110.00	150.00	75.00
1c	Kissing Bunnies	Blue; bramble-ware mustard pot	110.00	150.00	75.00
1d	Kissing Bunnies	White bunnies; black markings; large eyes; multi-coloured bramble-ware mustard pot,flower, base	145.00	170.00	85.00

FAIRY TALE AND NURSERY RHYME FIGURES

Circa 1948 - 1958

At the end of World War II the giftware restrictions on potteries were lifted. Although there was plenty of work available to replace war-damaged industrial wares, a few novelty figurines were produced by the Wade Heath Royal Victoria Pottery and by the George Wade Pottery.

Before 1953 these models were produced in the Royal Victoria Pottery and were marked with a green ink stamp. Models produced in 1953 and after, in either the Royal Victoria Pottery or in the George Wade Pottery, were marked with black transfers.

All the nursery rhyme and fairy tale models were coloured in delicate shades of pastel blues, whites and greys. Because they were produced in both potteries and dies were replaced when worn, there are slight variations in size and in hair colour.

WYNKEN, BLYNKEN, NOD AND I'VE A BEAR BEHIND

Circa 1948 - 1958

This set of four nursery rhyme characters was based on the poem "Wynken, Blynken and Nod," by American writer Eugene Field: "Wynken, Blynken and Nod one night; sailed off in a wooden shoe; Sailed on a river of crystal light into a sea of dew."

The poem does not include the character I've a Bear Behind; this was purely a whim of the Wade modeller. Green moss covers the feet of some models, so their slippers cannot be seen.

FIRST VERSION, FLOWER BASE

Backstamp: A. Green ink stamp "[Name of model] Wade England" (1a, 1b, 2, 3, 4)
B. Black transfer print "Wade England" and green ink stamp "Wade England [model name]" (4)

No.	Name	Description	Size	U.S. $	Can. $	U.K. £
1a	Wynken	Brown hair; blue suit	75 x 40	220.00	290.00	145.00
1b	Wynken	Blond hair; blue suit	71 x 38	220.00	290.00	145.00
2a	Blynken	Blond hair; blue suit	58 x 40	220.00	290.00	145.00
2b	Blynken	Brown hair; blue suit	58 x 40	220.00	290.00	145.00
3	Nod	Blond hair; blue suit	70 x 40	220.00	290.00	145.00
4	I've a Bear Behind	Blond hair; blue suit	70 x 40	220.00	290.00	145.00

Backstamp: Black transfer "Wade England [name of model]"

No.	Name	Description	Size	U.S. $	Can. $	U.K. £
1	Wynken	Blond hair; blue suit	75 x 40	185.00	250.00	125.00
2a	Blynken	Blond hair; blue suit	58 x 40	185.00	250.00	125.00
2b	Blynken	Light brown hair; blue suit	58 x 40	185.00	250.00	125.00
3	Nod	Light brown hair; blue suit	70 x 40	205.00	270.00	135.00
4	I've a Bear Behind	Light brown hair; blue suit	70 x 40	205.00	270.00	135.00

TINKER, TAILOR, SOLDIER, SAILOR

1953 - Circa 1958

Tinker, Tailor, Soldier, Sailor is a series of eight little boys dressed in adult clothes, depicting the characters from a 1940s children's rhyme.

Backstamp: Black transfer "Wade [name of model] England"

No.	Name	Description	Size	U.S. $	Can. $	U.K. £
1a	Tinker	Blue suit; white/grey cap; grey base	55 x 45	300.00	400.00	200.00
1b	Tinker	Pale blue suit; grey checkered cap; grey base	55 x 45	300.00	400.00	200.00
2	Tailor	Blue suit; grey trousers, base	55 x 45	300.00	400.00	200.00
3	Soldier	Blue suit, base; white/grey hat	80 x 45	300.00	400.00	200.00
4a	Sailor	Blue suit, base; white/grey hat	90 x 45	300.00	400.00	200.00
4b	Sailor	Pale blue suit; white/grey hat	90 x 45	300.00	400.00	200.00
5	Rich Man	Blue coat; grey hat, trousers; blue-green base	90 x 45	300.00	400.00	200.00
6a	Poor Man	Blue suit, base; grey hat	75 x 45	300.00	400.00	200.00
6b	Poor Man	Pale blue suit; grey hat	75 x 45	300.00	400.00	200.00
7	Beggar Man	Blue suit; white/blue scarf; blue-green base	65 x 45	300.00	400.00	200.00
8a	Thief	Blue suit; grey mask; blue-green base	80 x 45	300.00	400.00	200.00
8b	Thief	Pale blue suit; grey mask; blue-green base	80 x 45	300.00	400.00	200.00

NURSERY RHYMES

1953 - Circa 1958

Although Wade may have intended to add to this series each year, only two *Nursery Rhymes* characters were produced.

Backstamp: Black transfer "Wade [name of model] England"

No.	Name	Description	Size	U.S. $	Can. $	U.K. £
1a	Little Jack Horner	Blue shorts; dark blue braces	70 x 42	550.00	600.00	300.00
1b	Little Jack Horner	Grey trousers, braces	70 x 42	550.00	600.00	300.00
1c	Little Jack Horner	White shirt, trousers	70 x 42	550.00	600.00	300.00
2	Little Miss Muffet	Blonde hair; blue dress; pink petticoat	72 x 66	550.00	600.00	300.00

THE BUTCHER, THE BAKER AND THE CANDLESTICK MAKER

1953 - Circa 1958

Backstamp: **A.** Black transfer "Wade England [name of model]" (1, 2a, 2b, 3)
B. Blue transfer "Wade England [name of model]" (2a, 2b)

No.	Name	Description	Size	U.S. $	Can. $	U.K. £
1	The Butcher	Blue/white apron; grey trousers	95 x 40	300.00	400.00	200.00
2a	The Baker	Blue/white shirt; blue trousers	95 x 30	300.00	400.00	200.00
2b	The Baker	White shirt; blue trousers	95 x 30	300.00	400.00	200.00
3a	The Candlestick Maker	Black coat; grey trousers; yellow candlestick	110 x 25	375.00	500.00	250.00
3b	The Candlestick Maker	Black coat; grey trousers; beige candlestick	110 x 25	375.00	500.00	250.00
3c	The Candlestick Maker	Green coat; grey trousers; beige candlestick	110 x 25	375.00	500.00	250.00

GOLDILOCKS AND THE THREE BEARS

1953 - Circa 1958

Goldilocks and the Three Bears is a set of four models based on the children's fairy tale. It is believed that these models were intended for export only, because they are named "Poppa Bear" and "Mama Bear," which are North American expressions, instead of "Father Bear" and "Mother Bear," as they would be called in Britain.

Backstamp: Black transfer "Wade England [name of model]"

No.	Name	Description	Size	U.S. $	Can. $	U.K. £
1	Goldilocks	Blonde; blue/white skirt; pink petticoat, bonnet	100 x 60	375.00	500.00	250.00
2	Poppa Bear	Light brown; blue jacket; grey waistcoat	95 x 30	375.00	500.00	250.00
3	Mama Bear	Light brown; blue-grey dress	100 x 65	375.00	500.00	250.00
4	Baby Bear	Brown; blue dungarees	50 x 30	375.00	500.00	250.00

FIRST WHIMSIES

1954-1961

Following the end of World War II, the massive program to replace war-damaged houses and factories created a heavy demand for industrial ceramics, but by the early 1950s this demand had slackened, and new products had to be produced in order to avoid worker layoffs in the George Wade Potteries. With many years of experience making small pressed articles for industrial use, coupled with a unique ability in specialist tool-making, it was decided to manufacture a range of miniature animals.

The first set of five models was produced in 1954 and was designed for children to spend their pocket money on. When Mr. Wade's secretary referred to the models as "whimsical," the series was named *Whimsies* (and later referred to as *First Whimsies*).

The original models were packaged and sold in sets of five pieces for 5/9d. Only those models on bases wide enough for a Wade stamp were marked; free-standing models with open-cast legs generally had no room for marks. All boxes were marked "Wade Whimsies," but once the unmarked figures were removed from their boxes, there was no way to tell they were Wade.

Whimsies models had their first showing at the British Industries Fair in 1954. At first the reaction of dealers and wholesalers to the five tiny models was discouraging. But the following day, when the public was allowed into the show, they quickly changed their attitude when they saw the growing numbers of children and parents queuing to buy *Whimsies*.

For the next six years, Wade produced and sold nine sets of five and one set of four miniature animal models. Today these *First Whimsies* are highly sought after by collectors all over the world.

ENGLISH ANIMALS

Set 1 1954-1958

Backstamp: A. Embossed "Wade" (1, 2)
B. Unmarked (3, 4, 5)

No.	Name	Description	Size	U.S. $	Can. $	U.K. £
1	Leaping Fawn	White; green base	40 x 40	45.00	40.00	20.00
2	Horse	Light brown; green/brown base	35 x 50	45.00	40.00	20.00
3	Spaniel with Ball	White; grey rump, tail	25 x 40	30.00	40.00	20.00
4	Poodle	Light brown; white markings	35 x 35	45.00	50.00	25.00
5	Squirrel	Light grey	25 x 50	25.00	35.00	18.00

Note: Whimsie animals are arranged in issue order.

ENGLISH ANIMALS

Set Two 1954 -1958

Backstamp: **A.** Black and gold label "Genuine Wade Porcelain Made in England" (1, 3)
B. Unmarked (1, 2, 3, 4, 5)

No.	Name	Description	Size	U.S. $	Can. $	U.K. £
1	Bull	Brown legs; green base	45 x 55	80.00	100.00	50.00
2	Lamb	Brown muzzle, front legs; green base	45 x 25	50.00	65.00	25.00
3	Kitten	Grey face, paws, tail; blue bow	15 x 40	95.00	125.00	40.00
4	Hare	Light grey/white, white base	30 x 45	38.00	50.00	22.00
5	Dachshund	Beige	35 x 45	90.00	125.00	40.00

ENGLISH COUNTRY ANIMALS

Set Three 1955-1958

Backstamp: **A.** Unmarked (1, 2, 3)
B. Embossed "Wade" (4, 5)

No.	Name	Description	Size	U.S. $	Can. $	U.K. £
1	Badger	Grey; black/white face	30 x 40	35.00	45.00	22.00
2	Fox Cub	Light brown	35 x 35	70.00	95.00	35.00
3	Stoat	Grey tail; red eyes	20 x 35	55.00	70.00	35.00
4	Shetland Pony	Grey mane; green base	35 x 40	35.00	45.00	20.00
5	Retriever	Brown; white legs; green/white base	30 x 40	30.00	40.00	20.00

AFRICAN JUNGLE ANIMALS

Set Four 1955-1958

Backstamp: **A.** Unmarked (1, 5)
B. Black ink stamp "Wade Made in England" (2, 3, 4)

No.	Name	Description	Size	U.S. $	Can. $	U.K. £
1	Lion	Light brown	30 x 35	50.00	65.00	28.00
2	Crocodile	Green-brown	15 x 40	70.00	90.00	35.00
3	Monkey and Baby	Brown; green stump	45 x 25	35.00	45.00	20.00
4	Rhinoceros	Grey; green base	45 x 45	35.00	45.00	20.00
5	Baby Elephant	Grey	40 x 40	55.00	75.00	28.00

HORSES

Set Five 1956-1959

This is the only *First Whimsies* set of four figures and, despite its title, it includes a dog.

Backstamp: Embossed "Wade"

No.	Name	Description	Size	U.S. $	Can. $	U.K. £
1a	Mare	Light brown; brown tail, mane; green base	45 x 40	45.00	60.00	28.00
1b	Mare	White; brown mane, tail, hooves; green base	45 x 40	45.00	60.00	28.00
2a	Foal	Light brown; brown mane, tail; green base	40 x 40	45.00	60.00	28.00
2b	Foal	Dark brown; green base	40 x 40	45.00	60.00	28.00
2c	Foal	White; brown mane, tail, hooves; green base	45 x 40	45.00	60.00	28.00
3	Colt	Light brown; brown mane, tail; green base	40 x 40	45.00	60.00	28.00
4	Beagle	Brown patches; green base	20 x 20	60.00	80.00	35.00

POLAR ANIMALS

Set Six 1956-1959

The original price was 6/6d for the set.

Backstamp: Unmarked

No.	Name	Description	Size	U.S. $	Can. $	U.K. £
1	King Penguin	Black back, head, flippers; yellow beak, feet	35 x 20	45.00	60.00	28.00
2	Husky	Fawn/white; grey ears, muzzle	30 x 25	45.00	60.00	28.00
3	Polar Bear	Grey muzzle; blue base	45 x 45	45.00	60.00	25.00
4	Baby Seal	Light grey; white base	25 x 25	30.00	40.00	20.00
5a	Polar Bear Cub	White; brown eyes, nose, claws	20 x 30	40.00	50.00	25.00
5b	Polar Bear Cub	Pink; brown eyes, nose, claws	20 x 30	40.00	50.00	25.00

PEDIGREE DOGS

Set Seven 1957-1961

The original price was 6/6d for a box of five models.

Backstamp: Unmarked

No.	Name	Description	Size	U.S. $	Can. $	U.K. £
1	Alsatian	Grey/brown, green-brown base	35 x 40	30.00	40.00	20.00
2	West Highland Terrier	White	25 x 30	45.00	60.00	25.00
3	Corgi	Beige/white	25 x 30	40.00	50.00	25.00
4	Boxer	Brown; grey face; brown-green base	35 x 40	35.00	45.00	22.00
5	Saint Bernard	Brown/white	40 x 45	55.00	75.00	28.00

ZOO ANIMALS

Set Eight 1957-1961

Two panda figures were issued by Wade, one larger than the other. The smaller one, with a black band across its chest, is the right model for this set; the larger, 35 by 25 millimetre figure is out of proportion to the other models in the set. The larger model may have been produced first, then found to be too large and was set aside for possible use in special offers or premiums. Whether or not it was actually used in a premium set or simply sold off is not known. The original price per box was 5/9d.

Backstamp: Unmarked

No.	Name	Description	Size	U.S. $	Can. $	U.K. £
1	Llama	Grey face; brown-green base	45 x 30	40.00	50.00	20.00
2	Lion Cub	Brown; white chest	25 x 25	35.00	45.00	20.00
3a	Giant Panda, Small	Black/white; black band on chest	30 x 18	35.00	45.00	20.00
3b	Giant Panda, Large	Black/white	35 x 25	35.00	45.00	20.00
4	Bactrian Camel	Light brown; dark brown humps; green base	40 x 40	40.00	50.00	25.00
5	Cockatoo	Yellow crest; grey base	30 x 30	55.00	75.00	25.00

NORTH AMERICAN ANIMALS

Set Nine 1958-1961

The "Grizzly Cub," model 4a, is the figure issued as part of this set. Models 4b and 4c were issued at a later time. The original issue price was 6/6d per set.

Backstamp: **A.** Unmarked (1, 2, 4a, 4b, 4c, 5)
B. Embossed "Wade" (3)
C. Embossed "Wade England" (3)

No.	Name	Description	Size	U.S. $	Can. $	U.K. £
1	Snowy Owl	Brown eyes, claws	28 x 30	50.00	65.00	32.00
2	Racoon	Grey/black, white base	30 x 30	40.00	50.00	22.00
3	Grizzly Bear	Brown/white; green base	50 x 25	50.00	65.00	32.00
4a	Grizzly Cub	Light brown, green base	25 x 25	35.00	45.00	20.00
4b	Grizzly Cub	Brown; pink ears	25 x 30	35.00	45.00	20.00
4c	Grizzly Cub	White; pink ears	25 x 25	40.00	50.00	28.00
5	Cougar	Brown; white face, feet	20 x 45	50.00	65.00	32.00

FARM ANIMALS

Set Ten 1959-1961

These are the hardest of all *First Whimsies* models to find. This was the last set made and was only in production for a short time.

The "Shire Horse" and "Swan" in this set have been unlawfully reproduced and sold as authentic *First Whimsies*. The "Shire Horse" fake is slightly larger, it leans backwards in an ungainly way (most will not stand) and its nose is longer. It does not have the appearance of a real horse, but looks more like a caricature. The counterfeit "Swan" has a thicker neck and shorter beak, and the detailing of the feathers is not as fine as on the original.

The original price was 5/9d per boxed set.

Backstamp: Unmarked

No.	Name	Description	Size	U.S. $	Can. $	U.K. £
1	Pig	Pink; green base	20 x 35	75.00	100.00	38.00
2	Italian Goat	Grey; white face, chest; green base	30 x 30	75.00	100.00	38.00
3a	Foxhound	Beige patches; green base	25 x 45	75.00	100.00	38.00
3b	Foxhound	Light brown patches; green/white base	25 x 45	75.00	100.00	38.00
4a	Shire Horse	Creamy beige; brown mane and tail	50 x 50	250.00	340.00	125.00
4b	Shire Horse	White; grey mane; brown hooves	50 x 40	245.00	325.00	115.00
4c	Shire Horse	Red brown; cream mane; cream / black hooves	50 x 50	250.00	340.00	125.00
5	Swan	Yellow beak; black tip	25 x 35	195.00	260.00	90.00

FIRST WHIMSIES DERIVATIVES

ZOO LIGHTS (CANDLE HOLDERS)

1957-1960

George Wade's policy of using unsold models by adding them to new items produced many different "Stick-em-on-Somethings," such as *Zoo Lights*, *Whimtrays* and *Disney Lights*. Luckily for collectors, single models of *First Whimsies* animals, which were eluding capture in their original form, were attached to an oval base with a candle holder on the back to become *Zoo Lights*. Almost all the *First Whimsies* animals are on *Zoo Lights*. The candle holders come in black, yellow, blue and pink, and all the animals are in their original colour glazes.

The *Zoo Lights* were first issued prior to Christmas 1957 as *Animal Candlesticks* (with the exception of the "Camel," "Llama" and "Panda," which were issued in August 1958), and were discontinued in January 1960. They are listed in alphabetical order.

Backstamp: Embossed "Wade Porcelain Made in England"

No.	Name	Description	Size	U.S. $	Can. $	U.K. £
1a	Alsatian	Grey/brown; black holder	47 x 48	38.00	50.00	18.00
1b	Alsatian	yellow holder	47 x 48	38.00	50.00	18.00
1c	Alsatian	blue holder	47 x 48	38.00	50.00	18.00
1d	Alsatian	pink holder	47 x 48	38.00	50.00	18.00
2a	Baby Seal	Light grey; black holder	35 x 48	38.00	50.00	18.00
2b	Baby Seal	yellow holder	35 x 48	38.00	50.00	18.00
2c	Baby Seal	blue holder	35 x 48	38.00	50.00	18.00
2d	Baby Seal	pink holder	35 x 48	38.00	50.00	18.00
3a	Bactrian Camel	Light brown; black holder	52 x 48	38.00	50.00	18.00
3b	Bactrian Camel	yellow holder	52 x 48	38.00	50.00	18.00
3c	Bactrian Camel	blue holder	52 x 48	38.00	50.00	18.00
3d	Bactrian Camel	pink holder	52 x 48	38.00	50.00	18.00
4a	Badger	Grey/black/white; black holder	40 x 48	38.00	50.00	18.00
4b	Badger	yellow holder	40 x 48	38.00	50.00	18.00
4c	Badger	blue holder	40 x 48	38.00	50.00	18.00
4d	Badger	pink holder	40 x 48	38.00	50.00	18.00
5a	Boxer	Brown; black holder	45 x 48	38.00	50.00	18.00
5b	Boxer	yellow holder	45 x 48	38.00	50.00	18.00
5c	Boxer	blue holder	45 x 48	38.00	50.00	18.00
5d	Boxer	pink holder	45 x 48	38.00	50.00	18.00
6a	Cockatoo	Yellow crest; black holder	44 x 48	38.00	50.00	18.00
6b	Cockatoo	yellow holder	44 x 48	38.00	50.00	18.00
6c	Cockatoo	blue holder	44 x 48	38.00	50.00	18.00
6d	Cockatoo	pink holder	44 x 48	38.00	50.00	18.00
7a	Corgi	Beige/white; black holder	37 x 48	38.00	50.00	18.00
7b	Corgi	yellow holder	37 x 48	38.00	50.00	18.00
7c	Corgi	blue holder	37 x 48	38.00	50.00	18.00
7d	Corgi	pink holder	37 x 48	38.00	50.00	18.00

No.	Name	Description	Size	U.S.$	Can.$	U.K.£
8a	Giant Panda, Small	Black/white; black holder	40 x 48	38.00	50.00	18.00
8b	Giant Panda, Small	yellow holder	40 x 48	38.00	50.00	18.00
8c	Giant Panda, Small	blue holder	40 x 48	38.00	50.00	18.00
8d	Giant Panda, Small	pink holder	40 x 48	38.00	50.00	18.00
9a	Grizzly Bear	Brown/white; black holder	60 x 48	38.00	50.00	18.00
9b	Grizzly Bear	yellow holder	60 x 48	38.00	50.00	18.00
9c	Grizzly Bear	blue holder	60 x 48	38.00	50.00	18.00
9d	Grizzly Bear	pink holder	60 x 48	38.00	50.00	18.00
10a	Hare	Light grey/white; black holder	40 x 48	38.00	50.00	18.00
10b	Hare	yellow holder	40 x 48	38.00	50.00	18.00
10c	Hare	blue holder	40 x 48	38.00	50.00	18.00
10d	Hare	pink holder	40 x 48	38.00	50.00	18.00
11a	Husky	Fawn/white; black holder	44 x 48	38.00	50.00	18.00
11b	Husky	yellow holder	44 x 48	38.00	50.00	18.00
11c	Husky	blue holder	44 x 48	38.00	50.00	18.00
11d	Husky	pink holder	44 x 48	38.00	50.00	18.00
12a	King Penguin	Black/white; black holder	44 x 48	38.00	50.00	18.00
12b	King Penguin	yellow holder	44 x 48	38.00	50.00	18.00
12c	King Penguin	blue holder	44 x 48	38.00	50.00	18.00
12d	King Penguin	pink holder	44 x 48	38.00	50.00	18.00
13a	Lion Cub	Brown; black holder	37 x 48	38.00	50.00	18.00
13b	Lion Cub	yellow holder	37 x 48	38.00	50.00	18.00
13c	Lion Cub	blue holder	37 x 48	38.00	50.00	18.00
13d	Lion Cub	pink holder	37 x 48	38.00	50.00	18.00
14a	Llama	Grey face; black holder	55 x 48	38.00	50.00	18.00
14b	Llama	yellow holder	55 x 48	38.00	50.00	18.00
14c	Llama	blue holder	55 x 48	38.00	50.00	18.00
14d	Llama	pink holder	55 x 48	38.00	50.00	18.00
15a	Mare	Light brown; black holder	55 x 48	38.00	50.00	18.00
15b	Mare	yellow holder	55 x 48	38.00	50.00	18.00
15c	Mare	blue holder	55 x 48	38.00	50.00	18.00
15d	Mare	pink holder	55 x 48	38.00	50.00	18.00
15e	Mare	White; royal blue holder	55 x 48	38.00	50.00	18.00
16a	Polar Bear Cub	White; black holder	35 x 48	38.00	50.00	18.00
16b	Polar Bear Cub	yellow holder	35 x 48	38.00	50.00	18.00
16c	Polar Bear Cub	blue holder	35 x 48	38.00	50.00	18.00
16d	Polar Bear Cub	pink holder	35 x 48	38.00	50.00	18.00
17a	Poodle	Light brown; black holder	44 x 48	38.00	50.00	18.00
17b	Poodle	yellow holder	44 x 48	38.00	50.00	18.00
17c	Poodle	blue holder	44 x 48	38.00	50.00	18.00
17d	Poodle	pink holder	44 x 48	38.00	50.00	18.00
18a	Retriever	Brown/white; black holder	40 x 48	38.00	50.00	18.00
18b	Retriever	yellow holder	40 x 48	38.00	50.00	18.00
18c	Retriever	blue holder	40 x 48	38.00	50.00	18.00
18d	Retriever	pink holder	40 x 48	38.00	50.00	18.00
19a	Spaniel	White; black holder	35 x 48	38.00	50.00	18.00
19b	Spaniel	yellow holder	35 x 48	38.00	50.00	18.00
19c	Spaniel	blue holder	35 x 48	38.00	50.00	18.00
19d	Spaniel	pink holder	35 x 48	38.00	50.00	18.00
20a	Squirrel	Light grey; black holder	35 x 48	38.00	50.00	18.00
20b	Squirrel	yellow holder	35 x 48	38.00	50.00	18.00
20c	Squirrel	blue holder	35 x 48	38.00	50.00	18.00
20d	Squirrel	pink holder	35 x 48	38.00	50.00	18.00
21a	West Highland Terrier	White; black holder	35 x 48	38.00	50.00	18.00
21b	West Highland Terrier	yellow holder	35 x 48	38.00	50.00	18.00
21c	West Highland Terrier	blue holder	35 x 48	38.00	50.00	18.00
21d	West Highland Terrier	pink holder	35 x 48	38.00	50.00	18.00

WHIMTRAYS

1958-1965

Whimtrays are small round dishes with a *First Whimsies* animal on the back edge of the tray. The issue date was January 1958 (except for the "Bactrian Camel," "Cockatoo," "Giant Panda," "Llama" and "Lion Cub" *Whimtrays*, which were issued in August 1958), and they originally sold for 2/6d each. The trays come in black, blue, yellow and pink.

The following *Whimtrays* are listed in alphabetical order.

Backstamp: Embossed "Whimtrays—Wade Porcelain Made in England"

No.	Name	Description	Size	U.S. $	Can. $	U.K. £
1a	Alsatian	Grey/brown; black tray	55 x 75	30.00	40.00	15.00
1b	Alsatian	blue tray	55 x 75	30.00	40.00	15.00
1c	Alsatian	yellow tray	55 x 75	30.00	40.00	15.00
1d	Alsatian	pink tray	55 x 75	30.00	40.00	15.00
2a	Bactrian Camel	Light brown; black tray	60 x 75	30.00	40.00	15.00
2b	Bactrian Camel	blue tray	60 x 75	30.00	40.00	15.00
2c	Bactrian Camel	yellow tray	60 x 75	30.00	40.00	15.00
2d	Bactrian Camel	pink tray	60 x 75	30.00	40.00	15.00
3a	Baby Seal	Grey; black tray	40 x 75	30.00	40.00	15.00
3b	Baby Seal	blue tray	40 x 75	30.00	40.00	15.00
3c	Baby Seal	yellow tray	40 x 75	30.00	40.00	15.00
3d	Baby Seal	pink tray	40 x 75	30.00	40.00	15.00
4a	Boxer	Brown; black tray	45 x 75	30.00	40.00	15.00
4b	Boxer	blue tray	45 x 75	30.00	40.00	15.00
4c	Boxer	yellow tray	45 x 75	30.00	40.00	15.00
4d	Boxer	pink tray	45 x 75	30.00	40.00	15.00
5a	Cockatoo	Yellow crest; black tray	50 x 75	30.00	40.00	15.00
5b	Cockatoo	blue tray	50 x 75	30.00	40.00	15.00
5c	Cockatoo	yellow tray	50 x 75	30.00	40.00	15.00
5d	Cockatoo	pink tray	50 x 75	30.00	40.00	15.00
6a	Corgi	Beige/white; black tray	45 x 75	30.00	40.00	15.00
6b	Corgi	blue tray	45 x 75	30.00	40.00	15.00
6c	Corgi	yellow tray	45 x 75	30.00	40.00	15.00
6d	Corgi	pink tray	45 x 75	30.00	40.00	15.00
7a	Giant Panda	Black/white; black tray	50 x 75	30.00	40.00	15.00
7b	Giant Panda	blue tray	50 x 75	30.00	40.00	15.00
7c	Giant Panda	yellow tray	50 x 75	30.00	40.00	15.00
7d	Giant Panda	pink tray	50 x 75	30.00	40.00	15.00
8a	Giant Panda, Small	Black/white; black tray	45 x 75	30.00	40.00	15.00
8b	Giant Panda, Small	blue tray	45 x 75	30.00	40.00	15.00
8c	Giant Panda, Small	yellow tray	45 x 75	30.00	40.00	15.00
8d	Giant Panda, Small	pink tray	45 x 75	30.00	40.00	15.00

No.	Name	Description	Size	U.S.$	Can.$	U.K.£
9a	Grizzly Bear	Brown/white; black tray	65 x 75	30.00	40.00	15.00
9b	Grizzly Bear	blue tray	65 x 75	30.00	40.00	15.00
9c	Grizzly Bear	yellow tray	65 x 75	30.00	40.00	15.00
9d	Grizzly Bear	pink tray	65 x 75	30.00	40.00	15.00
10a	Grizzly Cub	Brown; black tray	45 x 75	30.00	40.00	15.00
10b	Grizzly Cub	blue tray	45 x 75	30.00	40.00	15.00
10c	Grizzly Cub	yellow tray	45 x 75	30.00	40.00	15.00
10d	Grizzly Cub	pink tray	45 x 75	30.00	40.00	15.00
11a	Hare	Light grey/white; black tray	50 x 75	30.00	40.00	15.00
11b	Hare	blue tray	50 x 75	30.00	40.00	15.00
11c	Hare	yellow tray	50 x 75	30.00	40.00	15.00
11d	Hare	pink tray	50 x 75	30.00	40.00	15.00
12a	Husky	Fawn/white; black tray	50 x 75	30.00	40.00	15.00
12b	Husky	blue tray	50 x 75	30.00	40.00	15.00
12c	Husky	yellow tray	50 x 75	30.00	40.00	15.00
12d	Husky	pink tray	50 x 75	30.00	40.00	15.00
13a	King Penguin	Black/white; black tray	50 x 75	30.00	40.00	15.00
13b	King Penguin	blue tray	50 x 75	30.00	40.00	15.00
13c	King Penguin	yellow tray	50 x 75	30.00	40.00	15.00
13d	King Penguin	pink tray	50 x 75	30.00	40.00	15.00
14a	Lion Cub	Brown; black tray	45 x 75	30.00	40.00	15.00
14b	Lion Cub	blue tray	45 x 75	30.00	40.00	15.00
14c	Lion Cub	yellow tray	45 x 75	30.00	40.00	15.00
14d	Lion Cub	pink tray	45 x 75	30.00	40.00	15.00
15a	Llama	Grey face; black tray	65 x 75	30.00	40.00	15.00
15b	Llama	blue tray	65 x 75	30.00	40.00	15.00
15c	Llama	yellow tray	65 x 75	30.00	40.00	15.00
15d	Llama	pink tray	65 x 75	30.00	40.00	15.00
16a	Mare	Light brown; black tray	55 x 75	30.00	40.00	15.00
16b	Mare	blue tray	55 x 75	30.00	40.00	15.00
16c	Mare	yellow tray	55 x 75	30.00	40.00	15.00
16d	Mare	pink tray	55 x 75	30.00	40.00	15.00
17a	Monkey and Baby	Brown; black tray	65 x 75	30.00	40.00	15.00
17b	Monkey and Baby	blue tray	65 x 75	30.00	40.00	15.00
17c	Monkey and Baby	yellow tray	65 x 75	30.00	40.00	15.00
17d	Monkey and Baby	pink tray	65 x 75	30.00	40.00	15.00
18a	Polar Bear	White; black tray	65 x 75	30.00	40.00	15.00
18b	Polar Bear	blue tray	65 x 75	30.00	40.00	15.00
18c	Polar Bear	yellow tray	65 x 75	30.00	40.00	15.00
18d	Polar Bear	pink tray	65 x 75	30.00	40.00	15.00
19a	Polar Bear Cub	White; black tray	40 x 75	30.00	40.00	15.00
19b	Polar Bear Cub	blue tray	40 x 75	30.00	40.00	15.00
19c	Polar Bear Cub	yellow tray	40 x 75	30.00	40.00	15.00
19d	Polar Bear Cub	pink tray	40 x 75	30.00	40.00	15.00
20a	Racoon	Grey/black; black tray	50 x 75	30.00	40.00	15.00
20b	Racoon	blue tray	50 x 75	30.00	40.00	15.00
20c	Racoon	yellow tray	50 x 75	30.00	40.00	15.00
20d	Racoon	pink tray	50 x 75	30.00	40.00	15.00
21a	Snowy Owl	White; black tray	44 x 75	30.00	40.00	15.00
21b	Snowy Owl	blue tray	44 x 75	30.00	40.00	15.00
21c	Snowy Owl	yellow tray	44 x 75	30.00	40.00	15.00
21d	Snowy Owl	pink tray	44 x 75	30.00	40.00	15.00
22a	Spaniel	White; black tray	45 x 75	30.00	40.00	15.00
22b	Spaniel	blue tray	45 x 75	30.00	40.00	15.00
22c	Spaniel	yellow tray	45 x 75	30.00	40.00	15.00
22d	Spaniel	pink tray	45 x 75	30.00	40.00	15.00
23a	Squirrel	Light grey; black tray	45 x 75	30.00	40.00	15.00
23b	Squirrel	blue tray	45 x 75	30.00	40.00	15.00
23c	Squirrel	yellow tray	45 x 75	30.00	40.00	15.00
23d	Squirrel	pink tray	45 x 75	30.00	40.00	15.00

No.	Name	Description	Size	U.S.$	Can.$	U.K.£
24a	Swan	White; black tray	40 x 75	100.00	135.00	55.00
24b	Swan	blue tray	40 x 75	100.00	135.00	55.00
24c	Swan	yellow tray	40 x 75	100.00	135.00	55.00
24d	Swan	pink tray	40 x 75	100.00	135.00	55.00
25a	West Highland Terrier	White; black tray	40 x 75	30.00	40.00	15.00
25b	West Highland Terrier	blue tray	40 x 75	30.00	40.00	15.00
25c	West Highland Terrier	yellow tray	40 x 75	30.00	40.00	15.00
25d	West Highland Terrier	pink tray	40 x 75	30.00	40.00	15.00

MARE AND COLT DISH

1963

The "Mare and Colt Dish" has two models from the *First Whimsies Horses*, set 5, on the rim of a figure-eight shaped dish. The original price was 6/6d. This dish is rare.

Size: 110 x 20 mm.
Backstamp: Embossed "Wade Porcelain Made in England"

No.	Description	U.S. $	Can. $	U.K. £
1	Light brown horses; black dish	60.00	80.00	40.00

MINIKINS

1955-1958

Minikins were issued in three separate series, with four different-shaped *Minikins* in each. They were sold to the retailer in boxes of 48 models (12 of each shape). *Minikins* were modelled by William Harper

The models are completely covered in white glaze, with decorative motifs on their bodies, different coloured ears and six eye styles. The combinations of eye expression, ear colour and body decoration could produce a total of 48 styles of *Minikins* in each set.

None of the *Minikins* was marked. Advertisements show that series B was offered for sale for Christmas 1956, and the demise of series C is mentioned in Wade's August 1958 "Wholesalers Newsletter." The original price was 1/- each.

MINIKINS SHOP COUNTER PLAQUE

1955-1958

This small half circular plaque would have been used by the retailer in his shop display for Minikins and was not made for general sale. The wording on the plaque is "Porcelain Wade Minikins Made in England."

Backstamp: None

No.	Description	Size	U.S. $	Can. $	U.K. £
1	White; black lettering	28	300.00	400.00	150.00

CATS AND RABBITS

Series A 1955-1958

Cat Walking

Size: 20 x 38 mm.
Backstamp: Unmarked

No.	Description	U.S. $	Can. $	U.K. £
1a	White; blue ears, tail; black/brown eyes	30.00	40.00	14.00
1b	White; yellow ears, tail; black/brown eyes	30.00	40.00	14.00
1c	White; yellow ears, tail; black/green eyes	30.00	40.00	14.00

Cat Standing

Size: 30 x 17 mm.
Backstamp: Unmarked

No.	Description	U.S. $	Can. $	U.K. £
2a	Brown; black eyes, nose	30.00	40.00	14.00
2b	White; green ears; black eyes, nose; blue patches	30.00	40.00	14.00
2c	White; green ears; black eyes; blue patches	30.00	40.00	14.00
2d	White; green ears; black/green eyes; blue patches	30.00	40.00	14.00
2e	White; yellow ears; black eyes; green starburst	30.00	40.00	14.00
2f	White; yellow ears; black eyes; red starburst	30.00	40.00	14.00
2g	White; yellow ears; black/green eyes; blue starburst	30.00	40.00	14.00
2h	White; yellow ears; black/green eyes; green daisy	30.00	40.00	14.00

Rabbit Sitting

Size: 30 x 18 mm.
Backstamp: Unmarked

No.	Description	U.S. $	Can. $	U.K. £
3a	Brown; turquoise ears; black eyes, nose	30.00	40.00	14.00
3b	White; blue ears, nose; small black eyes	30.00	40.00	14.00
3c	White; green ears; eyes open; red nose; blue patch	30.00	40.00	14.00
3d	White; green ears; winking eyes; red nose; blue patch	30.00	40.00	14.00
3e	White; green/yellow ears; eyes open; red nose	30.00	40.00	14.00
3f	White; green/yellow ears; winking eyes; red nose	30.00	40.00	14.00
3g	White; turquoise ears, nose; small black eyes	30.00	40.00	14.00

Narrow-eared Rabbit

Size: 30 x 18 mm.
Backstamp: Unmarked

No.	Description	U.S. $	Can. $	U.K. £
4a	White; green ears; large black/brown eyes; black nose; blue patch	30.00	40.00	14.00
4b	White; yellow ears; large black eyes; red nose; blue patch;	30.00	40.00	14.00
4c	White; yellow ears; large black/brown eyes; black nose; blue patch	30.00	40.00	14.00
4d	White; yellow ears; large black eyes; red nose; blue OXO design	30.00	40.00	14.00
4e	White; yellow ears; large black eyes; red nose; green OXO design	30.00	40.00	14.00
4f	White; yellow ears; large black/brown eyes; red nose; green/red OXO design	30.00	40.00	14.00

MOUSE, RABBIT, BULL AND COW

Series B 1956-1958

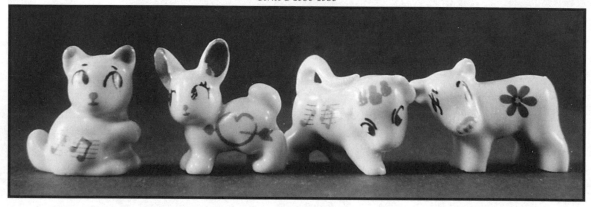

Mouse

Size: 25 x 23 mm.
Backstamp: Unmarked

No.	Description	U.S. $	Can. $	U.K. £
1a	Brown; small black eyes, nose	30.00	40.00	14.00
1b	Brown; small black eyes, nose; dark blue patch	30.00	40.00	14.00
1c	White all over	25.00	35.00	12.00
1d	White; small black eyes, nose; blue patch	30.00	40.00	14.00
1e	White; green ears, nose; large black eyes; orange daisy (front); green daisy (back)	30.00	40.00	14.00
1f	White; green ears, nose; large black eyes; orange/green notes (front); orange daisy (back)	30.00	40.00	14.00
1g	White; green ears, nose; large black eyes; red/green L-plate (back and front)	30.00	40.00	14.00
1h	White; pink ears; large black eyes; green nose; blue/red notes (front); blue daisy (back)	30.00	40.00	14.00
1i	White; pink ears; large black eyes; green nose; blue heart/green arrow (front); blue daisy (back)	30.00	40.00	14.00
1j	White; yellow ears; large black eyes; orange nose; blue/green notes (front); red/blue notes (back)	30.00	40.00	14.00
1k	White; yellow ears; large black eyes; orange nose; green daisy front; green heart/ blue arrow back	30.00	40.00	14.00
1l	White; yellow ears; large black eyes; blue nose; red L (front); orange L (back)	30.00	40.00	14.00
1m	White; yellow ears; large black eyes; orange nose; orange daisy (front); orange/blue notes (back)	30.00	40.00	14.00

Wide-eared Rabbit

Narrow-eared Rabbit (left) Wide-eared Rabbit (right)

Size: 25 x 20 mm.
Backstamp: Unmarked

No.	Description	U.S. $	Can. $	U.K. £
2a	White; green ears; blue nose; red/green flower (front); red heart/blue arrow (back)	30.00	40.00	14.00
2b	White; green ears; red nose; red heart/green arrow (front); blue heart/green arrow (back)	30.00	40.00	14.00
2c	White; pink ears; black nose; orange daisy (front); orange L (back)	30.00	40.00	14.00
2d	White; pink ears; black nose; red L-plate (front and back)	30.00	40.00	14.00
2e	White; yellow ears; blue/green notes (front); green heart/blue arrow (back)	30.00	40.00	14.00
2f	White; yellow ears; red heart/blue arrow (front and back)	30.00	40.00	14.00

Bull

Size: 20 x 25 mm.
Backstamp: Unmarked

No.	Description	U.S. $	Can. $	U.K. £
3a	Brown; small black eyes, nose; black spot (front and back)	30.00	40.00	14.00
3b	Brown; small black eyes, nose; black spot/yellow X (back and front)	30.00	40.00	14.00
3c	White; small black eyes, nose; black spot (front and back)	30.00	40.00	14.00
3d	White; large black/blue eyes; black nose; black spot/yellow X (front and back)	30.00	40.00	14.00
3e	White; green hair; large black eyes, nose; green daisy (front); red/green L-plate (back)	30.00	40.00	14.00
3f	White; green hair; black eyes, nose; green heart/blue arrow (front); orange heart/green arrow (back)	30.00	40.00	14.00
3g	White; green hair; large black eyes, nose; orange daisy (front); black daisy (back)	30.00	40.00	14.00
3h	White; green hair; black eyes, nose; red/blue notes (front); orange heart/blue arrow (back)	30.00	40.00	14.00
3i	White; green hair; large black eyes, nose; red/blue notes (front); red/green L-plate (back)	30.00	40.00	14.00
3j	White; yellow hair; black eyes, nose; blue/green notes (front); blue heart/yellow arrow (back)	30.00	40.00	14.00
3k	White; yellow hair; black eyes, nose; blue/green notes (front); red/green L-plate (back)	30.00	40.00	14.00
3l	White; yellow hair; large black eyes; red heart / blue arrow front; red L back	30.00	40.00	14.00
3m	White; yellow hair; large brown eyes; blue & yellow flower; red musical notes with green lines	30.00	40.00	14.00

Cow

Size: 22 x 20 mm.
Backstamp: Unmarked

No.	Description	U.S. $	Can. $	U.K. £
4a	White; green ears; black eyes; blue nose; orange daisy (front); blue daisy (back)	30.00	40.00	14.00
4b	White; green ears; black eyes; blue nose; orange/green notes (front) orange heart & blue arrow (back)	30.00	40.00	14.00
4c	White; pink ears; black eyes; red nose; red flower (front); red heart/green arrow (back)	30.00	40.00	14.00
4d	White; yellow ears; black eyes; blue nose; orange/blue notes (front); orange heart/green arrow (back)	30.00	40.00	14.00
4e	White; yellow ears; black eyes; blue nose; red heart/arrow (front); yellow daisy (back)	30.00	40.00	14.00
4f	White; yellow ears; black eyes; red nose; blue daisy (front); orange L (back)	30.00	40.00	14.00
4g	White; yellow ears; black eyes; red nose; blue daisy (front); red/blue notes (back)	30.00	40.00	14.00
4h	White; yellow ears; black eyes; red nose; green daisy (front); red flower (back)	30.00	40.00	14.00
4i	White; yellow ears; black eyes; red nose; blue heart/green arrow (front);blue daisy (back)	30.00	40.00	14.00

PELICAN, FAWN, DOG AND DONKEY

Series C 1957-1958

Pelican

Size: 30 x 15 mm.
Backstamp: Unmarked

No.	Description	U.S. $	Can. $	U.K. £
1a	White; black/blue eyes; blue wings, feet, anchor	30.00	40.00	15.00
1b	White; black/blue eyes; green wings, feet; blue anchor	30.00	40.00	15.00
1c	White; black/blue eyes; pink wings, feet; blue anchor	30.00	40.00	15.00
1d	White; black/blue eyes; yellow wings, feet; blue anchor	30.00	40.00	15.00
1e	White; black/blue eyes; green wings, feet; black waistcoat; red bowtie	30.00	40.00	15.00
1f	White; black/blue eyes; pink wings, feet; black waistcoat; red bowtie	30.00	40.00	15.00
1g	White; black/blue eyes; yellow wings, feet; black waistcoat; red bowtie	30.00	40.00	15.00
1h	White; black/blue eyes; yellow wings, feet; blue waistcoat; red bowtie	30.00	40.00	15.00

Fawn

Size: 28 x 20mm.
Backstamp: Unmarked

No.	Description	U.S. $	Can. $	U.K.
2a	White; green ears, tail; black/blue eyes; yellow flower	25.00	40.00	15.00
2b	White; green ears, tail; black/yellow eyes; yellow heart; red arrow	25.00	40.00	15.00
2c	White; pink ears, tail; black/blue eyes; blue flowers/heart/notes	25.00	40.00	15.00
2d	White; pink ears; black/blue eyes; yellow flower	25.00	40.00	15.00
2e	White; pink ears; black/yellow eyes; yellow flower	25.00	40.00	15.00
2f	White; yellow ears, tail; black/blue eyes; blue flowers/heart/notes	25.00	40.00	15.00
2g	White; yellow ears, tail; black/yellow eyes; red flower	25.00	40.00	15.00

Dog

Size: 28 x 15 mm.
Backstamp: Unmarked

No.	Description	U.S. $	Can. $	U.K. £
3a	White; blue ears; small black/blue eyes; blue collar	30.00	40.00	16.00
3b	White; blue/green ears; small black/blue eyes; orange flowers; blue collar	30.00	40.00	16.00
3c	White; green ears; large black/blue eyes; red/green collar	30.00	40.00	16.00
3d	White; green ears; small black/blue eyes; orange/red flowers; no collar	30.00	40.00	16.00
3e	White; green ears; small black/blue eyes; red/green collar	30.00	40.00	16.00
3f	White; pink ears; small black/blue eyes; orange/pink collar	30.00	40.00	16.00
3g	White; yellow ears; small black/blue eyes; orange/yellow collar	30.00	40.00	16.00

Donkey

Size: 35 x 20 mm.
Backstamp: Unmarked

No.	Description	U.S. $	Can. $	U.K. £
4a	White; green ears; large black/blue eyes; pink/blue garland	30.00	40.00	16.00
4b	White; green ears; large black/blue eyes; red flower (front)	30.00	40.00	16.00
4c	White; pink ears; large black/blue eyes; red flower (front)	30.00	40.00	16.00
4d	White; pink ears; large black/blue eyes; red/yellow flower garland	30.00	40.00	16.00
4e	White; pink ears; large black/yellow eyes; red/yellow garland	30.00	40.00	16.00
4f	White; yellow ears; large black/blue eyes; red flower (front)	30.00	40.00	16.00
4g	White; yellow ears; large black/blue eyes; pink/blue garland	30.00	40.00	16.00
4h	White; yellow ears; large black/yellow eyes; red/yellow garland	30.00	40.00	16.00

VARIOUS NOVELTY MODELS

1955-1960

The issue date for these models is late 1955. Although Wade advertisements suggest that they were in production for five years, they are hard to find and are considered rare.

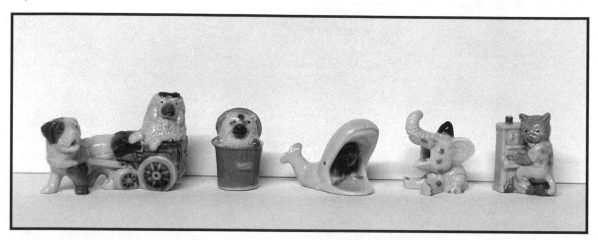

Backstamp: **A.** Embossed "Wade" (1, 2)
B. Unmarked (3, 4, 5)
C. Black and gold label "Wade England" (3, 4, 5)

No.	Name	Description	Size	U.S. $	Can. $	U.K. £
1	Bernie and Poo	One white/brown; one white/blue	55 x 75	170.00	225.00	80.00
2	Dustbin Cat	White; grey dustbin	45 x 25	200.00	260.00	80.00
3	Jonah in the Whale	Blue jacket; white whale	40 x 40	200.00	260.00	80.00
4	Jumbo Jim	Blue hat, tears	45 x 25	215.00	280.00	120.00
5a	Kitten on the Keys	Grey cat; white blue spotted shirt; white trousers	30 X 35	235.00	310.00	130.00
5b	Kitten on the Keys	White	30 x 35	235.00	310.00	130.00

LUCKY LEPRECHAUNS

1956-1959, Circa 1960, 1980s

This set of three *Lucky Leprechauns* was first issued in 1956 by Wade (Ulster) Ltd. When the models were originally shipped to retailers, they were packaged in decorative display boxes of 24 models, with hat colours of white, yellow, orange, red, maroon, blue or green. Also included was a porcelain shamrock leaf to use as a price display. On it was printed "Lucky Leprechauns Made in Ireland By Wade Co. Armagh 1/11d each." Many of these shamrock plaques have survived and are sought by collectors. The *Lucky Leprechauns* set was reissued in the mid 1960s and again in the 1980s.

FIRST VERSION — BROWN FACES, PAPER LABEL

1956-1959

Originally the models each had a black and gold label on the base. The label is easily washed off and if it is missing it is difficult to tell which version the figure comes from. As a general guide, the 1956-1959 models have brown faces, whereas the faces of later figures are flesh coloured.

Backstamp: A. Black and gold label "Made in Ireland by Wade Co. Armagh" (1-3)
B. Unmarked (1-3)

No.	Name	Description	Size	U.S. $	Can. $	U.K. £
1a	Cobbler	Dark green hat; grey coat; boots; blue trousers	37 x 30	30.00	40.00	14.00
1b	Cobbler	Maroon hat; grey coat, boots; blue trousers	37 x 30	30.00	40.00	14.00
1c	Cobbler	Orange hat; grey coat, boots; blue trousers	37 x 30	30.00	40.00	14.00
1d	Cobbler	Red hat; grey coat, boots; blue trousers	37 x 30	30.00	40.00	14.00
1d	Cobbler	White hat; grey coat, boots; blue trousers	37 x 30	30.00	40.00	14.00
2a	Tailor	Blue hat; white coat; blue trousers; grey boot	38 x 19	30.00	40.00	14.00
2b	Tailor	Dark green hat; white coat; blue trousers; grey boot	38 x 19	30.00	40.00	14.00
2c	Tailor	Red hat; white coat; blue trousers; grey boot	38 x 19	30.00	40.00	14.00
3a	Crock O' Gold	Maroon hat; blue coat; grey trousers; brown boots	34 x 25	30.00	40.00	14.00
3b	Crock O' Gold	Orange hat; blue coat; grey trousers; brown boots	34 x 25	30.00	40.00	14.00
3c	Crock O' Gold	Red hat; blue coat; grey trousers; brown boots	34 x 25	30.00	40.00	14.00
3d	Crock O' Gold	Dark yellow hat; blue coat; grey trousers; brown boots	34 x 25	30.00	40.00	14.00
3e	Crock O' Gold	Yellow hat; green coat; grey trousers; brown boots	34 x 25	30.00	40.00	14.00

SECOND VERSION — FLESH COLOURED FACES, WITHOUT BACKSTAMPS

1960s

This boxed set of three *Lucky Leprechauns* had no labels and were unmarked. Once removed from their box, there is no indication of the year of issue or of the maker. The reissued models have flesh-coloured faces, which distinguish them from the original 1956-1959 version.

Backstamp: Unmarked

No.	Name	Description	Size	U.S. $	Can. $	U.K. £
1a	Cobbler	Green hat; light grey coat, boots; pale blue trousers	38 x 31	20.00	25.00	10.00
1b	Cobbler	Orange hat; light grey coat, boots; pale blue trousers	38 x 31	20.00	25.00	10.00
1c	Cobbler	Red hat; light grey coat, boots; pale blue trousers	38 x 31	20.00	25.00	10.00
1d	Cobbler	Yellow hat; light grey coat, boots pale blue trousers	38 x 31	20.00	25.00	10.00
2a	Tailor	Pale blue hat, trousers; white coat; grey boot	39 x 20	20.00	25.00	10.00
2b	Tailor	Green hat; white coat; pale blue trousers; grey boot	39 x 20	20.00	25.00	10.00
2c	Tailor	Red hat; white coat; pale blue trousers; grey boot	39 x 20	20.00	25.00	10.00
2d	Tailor	Yellow hat; white coat; pale blue trousers; grey boot	39 x 20	20.00	25.00	10.00
3a	Crock O' Gold	Blue hat; pale blue grey coat; light grey trousers; brown boots with or without brown stripe	34 x 26	20.00	25.00	10.00
3b	Crock O' Gold	Green hat; pale blue grey coat; light grey trousers; brown boots with or without brown stripe	34 x 26	20.00	25.00	10.00
3c	Crock O' Gold	Red hat; pale blue grey coat; light grey trousers; brown boots with or without brown stripe	34 x 26	20.00	25.00	10.00
3d	Crock O' Gold	Yellow hat; pale blue grey coat; light grey trousers; brown boots with or without brown stripe	34 x 26	20.00	25.00	10.00
—	Boxed set (3)			75.00	85.00	25.00

THIRD VERSION — FLESH COLOURED FACES, WITH BACKSTAMP

1971-1976

See previous page for
photograph

Backstamp: A. Small black ink stamp "Made in Ireland" (1a)
B. Large black ink stamp "Made in Ireland" (1b, 2a, 2b, 3a, 3b, 3c)

No.	Name	Description	Size	U.S. $	Can. $	U.K. £
1a	Cobbler	Red hat; grey coat, boots; pale blue trousers	38 x 31	15.00	20.00	10.00
1b	Cobbler	White hat; dark grey coat, boots; dark blue trousers	38 x 31	15.00	20.00	10.00
2a	Tailor	Blue hat / trousers; white coat; grey boot	39 x 20	15.00	20.00	10.00
2b	Tailor	Yellow hat; white coat; blue trousers; grey boot	39 x 20	15.00	20.00	10.00
3a	Crock O' Gold	Blue hat; blue coat; light grey trousers; brown boots with or without brown stripe	34 x 26	15.00	20.00	10.00
3b	Crock O' Gold	Red hat; blue coat; light grey trousers; brown boots with or without brown stripe	34 x 26	15.00	20.00	10.00
3c	Crock O' Gold	Yellow hat; blue coat; light grey trousers; brown boots with or without brown stripe	34 x 26	15.00	20.00	10.00

LUCKY LEPRECHAUN SHAMROCK PLAQUE

1956-1959

Backstamp: None

No.	Description	Size	U.S. $	Can. $	U.K. £
1	White/green; black lettering	100 x 48	200.00	265.00	100.00

LUCKY LEPRECHAUNS DERIVATIVES

PIN TRAYS

The *Lucky Leprechauns* models used on these pin trays were issued by Wade (Ulster) Ltd. from 1956 to 1959. The pin tray in which the Lucky Leprechaun sits was originally produced as a "pin tray" (plain) and as a "butter pat" (with transfer printed decorations) see *The Charlton Standard Catalogue of Wade Decorative Ware, Vol 2* and *The Charlton Standard Catalogue of Wade Tableware, Vol. 3*.

There are two styles of pin trays:
Style One: Recessed Centre Tray Irish Wade Shape No I.P.619, early 1950s backstamp
Style Two: Flat Centre Tray, 1971-1976 backstamp

STYLE ONE TRAYS — FIRST AND SECOND VERSION LUCKY LEPRACHAUNS, 1956-1960s
STYLE TWO TRAYS —SECOND AND THIRD VERSION LUCKY LEPRACHAUNS, 1960s-1970s

There are no price differentials between Style One or Style Two trays or between Version One, Two or Three leprachauns.

Size: 45 x 75 mm.
Colour: Blue-green trays
Backstamp: Embossed Circular "Irish Porcelain Made in Ireland" around a central shamrock with letter T (early 1950s)

No.	Name	Description	U.S. $	Can. $	U.K. £
1a	Cobbler	Dark green hat; grey coat, boots; blue trousers	27.00	32.00	10.00
1b	Cobbler	Orange hat; grey coat, boots; blue trousers	27.00	32.00	10.00
1c	Cobbler	Maroon hat; grey coat, boots; blue trousers	27.00	32.00	10.00
1d	Cobbler	White hat; grey coat, boots; blue trousers	27.00	32.00	10.00
2a	Tailor	Blue hat; white coat; blue trousers; grey boot	27.00	32.00	10.00
2b	Tailor	Dark green hat; white coat; blue trousers; grey boot	27.00	32.00	10.00
2c	Tailor	Maroon hat; white coat; blue trousers; grey boot	27.00	32.00	10.00
3a	Crock O' Gold	Maroon hat; blue coat; grey trousers; brown boots	27.00	32.00	10.00
3b	Crock O' Gold	Orange hat; blue coat; grey trousers; brown boots	27.00	32.00	10.00
3c	Crock O' Gold	Dark yellow hat; blue coat; grey trousers; brown boots	27.00	32.00	10.00

Backstamp: Embossed circular "Made in Ireland Irish Porcelain Wade Eire Tir A Dheanta" IP 619
with shamrock and crown in centre

No.	Name	Description	U.S. $	Can. $	U.K. £
1a	Cobbler	Green hat; light grey coat, boots; pale blue trousers	27.00	32.00	14.00
1b	Cobbler	Orange hat; light grey coat, boots; pale blue trousers	27.00	32.00	14.00
1c	Cobbler	Red hat; light grey coat, boots; pale blue trousers	27.00	32.00	14.00
1d	Cobbler	Yellow hat; light grey coat, boots; pale blue trousers	27.00	32.00	14.00
2a	Tailor	Pale blue hat, trousers; white coat; grey boot	27.00	32.00	14.00
2b	Tailor	Green hat; white coat; pale blue trousers; grey boot	27.00	32.00	14.00
2c	Tailor	Red hat; white coat; pale blue trousers; grey boot	27.00	32.00	14.00
2d	Tailor	Yellow hat; white coat; pale blue trousers; grey boot	27.00	32.00	14.00
3a	Crock O' Gold	Blue hat; pale blue grey coat; light grey trousers; brown boots with or without brown stripe	27.00	32.00	14.00
3b	Crock O' Gold	Green hat; pale blue grey coat; light grey trousers; brown boots with or without brown stripe	27.00	32.00	14.00
3c	Crock O' Gold	Red hat; pale blue grey coat; light grey trousers; brown boots with or without brown stripe	27.00	32.00	14.00
3d	Crock O' Gold	Yellow hat; pale blue grey coat; light grey trousers; brown boots with or without brown stripe	27.00	32.00	14.00

BUTTER DISH — SECOND VERSION COBBLER AND TAILOR

The George Wade butter dish was first produced from 1955 to 1959, with a model of a squirrel, rabbit or the 1956 *Hat Box* "Jock" on the back rim. In the 1970s the dish was combined with surplus Irish Wade *Lucky Leprechauns* to produce novelty butter dishes.

Backstamp: Embossed "Wade England"

No.	Name	Description	Size	U.S. $	Can. $	U.K. £
1a	Tailor	Green hat; yellow dish	65 x 80	30.00	40.00	20.00
1b	Tailor	Blue hat; yellow dish	65 x 80	30.00	40.00	20.00
1c	Tailor	Red hat; yellow dish	65 x 80	30.00	40.00	20.00
2a	Cobbler	Green hat; yellow dish	65 x 80	30.00	40.00	20.00
2b	Cobbler	Blue hat; yellow dish	65 x 80	30.00	40.00	20.00

LUCKY LEPRECHAUNS ON PLINTHS

THIRD VERSION LUCKY LEPRECHAUNS ON MARBLE PLINTHS

Circa 1975-1985

These models were taken from the reissued 1974-1985 *Lucky Leprechauns* set and mounted on a block of Connemara marble. They were intended for the tourist trade.

Size: 58 x 52 mm.
82 x 79 mm. (trio)
Backstamp: Gold label "Lucky Irish Leprechauns, Made in Ireland"

No.	Name	Description	U.S. $	Can. $	U.K. £
1a	Cobbler	Light brown stool; beige shoe	15.00	20.00	10.00
2a	Tailor	Blue hat; grey trousers, shoes	15.00	20.00	10.00
2b	Tailor	Yellow hat; grey trousers, shoes	15.00	20.00	10.00
3a	Crock o' Gold	Yellow hat, coins; grey jacket, trousers	15.00	20.00	10.00
3b	Crock o' Gold	Red hat; yellow coins; grey jacket, trousers	15.00	20.00	10.00
3c	Crock o' Gold	Blue hat; yellow coins; grey jacket, trousers	15.00	20.00	10.00
4	Trio of models	Cobbler: red hat; tailor: blue hat; leprechaun: grey	20.00	25.00	15.00

COBBLER AND COTTAGE ON MARBLE PLINTH

1970s

The cobbler and the reissued "Shamrock Cottage" (1974-1985) were combined and mounted on a rectangular marble base.

Photograph not available
at press time

Size: Unknown
Backstamp: None

No.	Name	Description	U.S. $	Can. $	U.K. £
1	Cobbler and Cottage	Beige stool; white shoes; yellow roof; blue windows; dark brown peat		Rare	

TAILOR AND COTTAGE ON PORCELAIN "IRELAND" PLINTH

1970s

The reissued "Tailor" and the reissued "Shamrock Cottage" (1974-1985) were combined by Wade Ireland and placed on a porcelain outline of the map of Ireland to form this unusual and sought-after souvenir model. It was discontinued in 1979.

Size: 65 x 140 mm.
Backstamp: Embossed "Made in Ireland"

No.	Name	Description	U.S. $	Can. $	U.K. £
1a	Tailor	Blue hat; grey trousers, shoes; grey-green base	120.00	160.00	90.00
1b	Tailor	Yellow hat; grey trousers, shoes; grey-green base	120.00	160.00	90.00
1c	Tailor	Blue hat, trousers, grey shoes, grey-green base	120.00	160.00	90.00

LUCKY FAIRY FOLK

FIRST VERSION, BROWN FACES, 1956-1960

   Lucky Fairy Folk, produced by Wade (Ulster) Ltd., is a set of three models sitting on the backs of a rabbit and a pig and on top of an acorn. Each figure was sold separately in a cylindrical-shaped acetate packet, with a multi-coloured string handle. On the end of the string was a black foil label, which read "Made in Ireland By Wade Co. Armagh" in gold lettering. The models themselves are not marked, so once removed from the packet, there is no indication of which pottery they were from. On the first issue models the colour of the face is beige brown and the snout and toes on the pigs was originally grey and was then changed to beige.

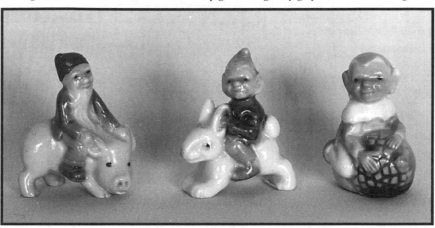

Backstamp: Unmarked

No.	Name	Description	Size	U.S. $	Can. $	U.K. £
1a	Leprechaun on Pig	Dark green hat; grey coat; blue trousers; white boots; pig has grey snout and toes	45 x 35	55.00	75.00	30.00
1b	Leprechaun on Pig	Orange hat; blue coat; grey trousers; pig has grey snout and toes	45 x 35	55.00	75.00	30.00
1c	Leprechaun on Pig	Red hat; blue coat; grey trousers; white boots; pig has beige snout and toes	45 x 35	55.00	75.00	30.00
1d	Leprechaun on Pig	Red hat; blue coat, boots; grey trousers; pig has beige snout and toes	45 x 35	55.00	75.00	30.00
2a	Pixie on Rabbit	Dark green hat; dark blue coat; grey trousers; blue boots; white rabbit	40 x 32	75.00	100.00	50.00
2b	Pixie on Rabbit	Red hat; dark blue coat; grey trousers; blue boots; white rabbit	40 x 32	75.00	100.00	50.00
2c	Pixie on Rabbit	Dark yellow hat; dark blue coat; grey trousers; blue boots; white rabbit	40 x 32	75.00	100.00	50.00
3a	Pixie on Acorn	Blue hat, boots; white trousers; grey coat	40 x 30	75.00	100.00	36.00
3b	Pixie on Acorn	Dark green hat; white trousers; grey coat	40 x 30	75.00	100.00	36.00
3c	Pixie on Acorn	Orange hat; white trousers; grey coat; blue boots	40 x 30	75.00	100.00	36.00
3d	Pixie on Acorn	Red hat; white trousers; grey coat; blue boots	40 x 30	75.00	100.00	36.00
3e	Pixie on Acorn	Dark yellow hat; white trousers; grey coat; blue boots	40 x 30	75.00	100.00	36.00
3f	Pixie on Acorn	White hat, trousers; grey coat; blue boots	40 x 30	75.00	100.00	36.00

The difference between this version and the first version issued in 1956 is the colour of the Leprechauns face.

Photograph not available
at press time

Size: 45 x 35 mm.
Backstamp: Unmarked

No.	Name	Description	U.S. $	Can. $	U.K. £
1	Leprechaun On A Pig	Red hat; flesh face, hands; blue coat, boots; beige trousers; pig has light beige snout and toes	55.00	75.00	30.00

LUCKY FAIRY FOLK DERIVATIVE

PIXIE ON ACORN BUTTER DISH

1970s

Size: 65 x 80 mm.
Backstamp: Embossed "Wade England"

No.	Description	U.S.$	Can.$	U.K.£
1a	Green hat; yellow dish	75.00	100.00	30.00
1b	Yellow hat, dish	75.00	100.00	30.00
1c	Red hat; yellow dish	75.00	100.00	30.00
1d	Blue hat; yellow dish	75.00	100.00	30.00

SNIPPETS

1956-1957

Snippets models are thin, flat outlines of a figure with a rectangular porcelain box on the back, which enables the model to stand. It was a new idea by Wade, one which was not very successful at the time. Only two sets of three models were produced. Because of this and the fact that they are easily broken, these models are rare.

SAILING SHIPS

Set 1 1956

Set 1 was a set of three 15th, 16th and 17th century sailing ships, modelled as an outline of the ships and enamelled in bright colours. The three ships are in graduated sizes.

Backstamp: **A.** Black transfer "Wade Snippet No. 1 Mayflower Carried 102 Pilgrims to North America 1620 Real Porcelain — Made In England" (1)
 B. Black transfer "Wade Snippet No. 2 Santa Maria Flag ship of Columbus 1492 Real Porcelain — Made In England" (2)
 C. Black transfer "Wade Snippet No. 3 Revenge Flag ship of Sir Richard Grenville 1591 Real Porcelain — Made in England" (3)

No.	Name	Description	Size	U.S. $	Can. $	U.K. £
1	The Mayflower	Brown; yellow sails; red flags; blue/white waves	58 x 60	65.00	85.00	45.00
2	The Santa Maria	Brown; green sails; red/yellow flags; blue/white waves	45 x 50	65.00	85.00	45.00
3	The Revenge	Brown; red sails; yellow flags; blue/white waves	35 x 45	65.00	85.00	45.00
—	Set (3)			200.00	250.00	130.00

HANSEL AND GRETEL

Set 2 1957

Set 2 comprises three characters from the fairy tale,"Hansel and Gretel."

Backstamp: A. Black transfer "Wade Snippet No. 4 Hansel — Real Porcelain — Made in England" (4a, 4b)
B. Black transfer "Wade Snippet No. 5 Gretel — Real Porcelain — M ade in England" (5)
C. Black transfer "Wade Snippet No. 6 Gingy — Real Porcelain — Made in England" (6)

No.	Name	Description	Size	U.S. $	Can. $	U.K. £
1a	Hansel	Yellow stockings; grey-blue trousers, jacket; red shirt, toadstools	64 x 42	165.00	250.00	110.00
1b	Hansel	Green stockings; grey-blue trousers, jacket; red shirt, toadstools	64 x 42	165.00	250.00	110.00
2	Gretel	Yellow pigtail, apron; blue shoe; green grass; red toadstools	56 x 42	165.00	250.00	110.00
3	Gingy the Bear	Brown/beige; red toadstools	32 x 20	180.00	275.00	135.00
—	Set (3)			500.00	700.00	350.00

FLYING BIRDS

1956-1961

Wade produced two sets in the *Flying Birds* series, "Swallows" and "Swifts." They were issued in white, with either green, yellow, blue or beige wings and heads. These models were first produced in England, then their production was moved to Wade (Ulster) Ltd. The *Flying Birds* series was sold in boxed sets of three models of the same colour. The "Swifts" models were the last production run and are harder to find.

FIRST ISSUE, WADE ENGLAND

SWALLOWS

Set 1 1956-1960

The original price for a set of three "Swallows" was 5/9d, which was later increased to 5/11d.

Size: 65 x 68 mm.
Backstamp: Unmarked

No.	Description	U.S. $	Can. $	U.K. £
1a	Beige wings, tail	20.00	26.00	12.00
1b	Blue wings, tail	20.00	26.00	12.00
1c	Green wings, tail	20.00	26.00	12.00
1d	Grey wings, tail	20.00	26.00	12.00
1e	Salmon pink wings, tail	20.00	26.00	12.00
1f	Yellow wings, tail	25.00	30.00	15.00
—	Boxed set (3)	45.00	60.00	35.00
—	Boxed set (3—yellow)	65.00	85.00	40.00

SWIFTS

Set 2 1958-1959

The original price for three "Swifts" was 6/11d.

Size: 86 x 76 mm.
Backstamp: Unmarked

No.	Description	U.S. $	Can. $	U.K. £
1a	Blue wings, tail	28.00	38.00	24.00
1b	Green wings, tail	28.00	38.00	24.00
1c	Grey wings, tail	28.00	38.00	24.00
1d	Yellow wings, tail	28.00	38.00	24.00
1e	Beige wings, tail	28.00	38.00	24.00
—	Boxed set (3)	80.00	100.00	60.00

SECOND ISSUE, WADE ULSTER

Following the production of the *Flying Birds* series in the George Wade Pottery, the models were made by Wade (Ulster) Ltd. As with the George Wade production, two sets were made. In this case, however, the numbers of the sets were reversed. Set 1 was now the "Swifts;" set 2 was the "Swallows."

SWIFTS

Set 1 1960-1961

The original price for three "Swifts" was 6/11d.

Size: 86 x 76 mm.
Backstamp: Unmarked

No.	Description	U.S. $	Can. $	U.K. £
1a	Blue head, wings	28.00	38.00	24.00
1b	Yellow head, wings	28.00	38.00	24.00
—	Boxed set (3)	90.00	120.00	55.00

SWALLOWS

Set 2 1960-1961

On the front of the original box was printed, "Flying Birds Made in Ireland by Wade Co. Armagh, The Mourne Range of Porcelain Miniatures." "The Mourne Range of Wade Porcelain Miniatures" is on the end of the box and inside is "No. 2 The Mourne Range of Porcelain Miniatures, Made in Ireland by Wade Co. Armagh." The original price for a box of three "Swallows" was 5/11d per boxed set.

Size: 65 x 68 mm.
Backstamp: Unmarked

No.	Description	U.S. $	Can. $	U.K. £
1a	Beige wings, tail	20.00	26.00	12.00
1b	Blue wings, tail	20.00	26.00	12.00
1c	Green wings, tail	20.00	26.00	12.00
1d	Grey wings, tail	20.00	26.00	12.00
1e	Yellow wings, tail	20.00	26.00	12.00
—	Boxed set (3)	80.00	100.00	50.00

SHAMROCK POTTERY SERIES

1956–1961, 1977-1984

In 1956 Wade Ireland introduced a small series of models known as the Shamrock Pottery Series. It consisted of the "Pink Elephant," "Irish Comical Pig," "Shamrock Cottage," "Pixie Dish" and the "Donkey and Cart Posy Bowl." The "Shamrock Cottage," "Pixie Dish" and "Donkey and Cart Posy Bowl" were reissued between 1977 and the early 1980s. (For "Donkey and Cart Posy Bowl," see *The Charlton Standard Catalogue of Wade, Volume Two: Decorative Ware*).

PINK ELEPHANT

1956-1961

The *Pink Elephant*, made by Wade (Ulster) Ltd., is found with several different slogans on its back associated with the consumption of too much alcohol. Some have names on them of places of interest. Originally these models sold for 2/6d each.

Size: 40 x 80 mm.
Backstamp: Green transfer print "Shamrock Pottery Made in Ireland"

No.	Description	U.S. $	Can. $	U.K. £
1a	"Bournemouth;" pink; orange nostrils, tail	65.00	85.00	38.00
1b	"Devil's Bridge;" pink; green nostrils, tail	65.00	85.00	38.00
1c	"Henley on Thames;" pink; green nostrils, tail	65.00	85.00	38.00
1d	"Isle of Wight;" pink; orange nostrils, tail	65.00	85.00	38.00
1e	"Never Again;" pink; green nostrils, tail	65.00	85.00	38.00
1f	"Never Again;" pink; orange nostrils, tail	65.00	85.00	38.00
1g	"Never Mix Em!;" pink; green nostrils, tail	65.00	85.00	38.00
1h	"Oh! My Head;" pink; green nostrils, tail	65.00	85.00	38.00
1i	"Old Smithy Godshill," pink; green nostrils, tail	65.00	85.00	38.00
1j	Pale pink	65.00	85.00	38.00
1k	"Ramsgate;" pink; orange nostrils, tail	65.00	85.00	38.00
1l	"Salisbury;" pink; green nostrils, tail	65.00	85.00	38.00
1m	"Stick to Water;" pink; green nostrils, tail	65.00	85.00	38.00

IRISH COMICAL PIG

1956-1961

The *Irish Comical Pig*, made by Wade (Ulster) Ltd., is found in several different combinations of back patterns and nose and tail colours. The original selling price was 2/6d each. The places of interest named on the back are written in black lettering.

Size: 45 x 65 mm.
Backstamp: Green transfer print "Shamrock Pottery Made in Ireland"

No.	Name	Description	U.S. $	Can. $	U.K. £
1a	Shamrocks	White; green nostrils, tail, shamrocks	75.00	95.00	38.00
1b	Canterbury	Green nostrils, tail	75.00	95.00	38.00
1c	Daisy Pattern	Green/orange daisy; orange nostrils; yellow tail	75.00	95.00	38.00
1d	Daisy Pattern	Green/orange daisy;yellow nostrils, tail	75.00	95.00	38.00
1e	Daisy Pattern	Green/orange daisy; green nostrils, tail	75.00	95.00	38.00
1f	Eastbourne	Green nostrils; yellow tail	75.00	95.00	38.00
1g	Henley on Thames	Green nostrils; yellow tail	75.00	95.00	38.00
1h	Hunstanton	Green nostrils; yellow tail	75.00	95.00	38.00
1i	Isle of Wight	Green nostrils; yellow tail	75.00	95.00	38.00
1j	Loop Pattern	Orange loops; green stars, lines; brown eyes; green nostrils, tail	75.00	95.00	38.00
1k	Old Smithy Godshill	Green nostrils, tail	75.00	95.00	38.00
1l	Penmaenmawr	Green nostrils yellow tail	75.00	95.00	38.00
1m	Stratford-Upon-Avon	Green nostrils, tail	75.00	95.00	38.00
1n	Stratford-Upon-Avon	Green nostrils; yellow tail	75.00	95.00	38.00
1o	Windermere	Green nostrils; yellow tail	75.00	95.00	38.00
1p	York	Green nostrils; yellow tail	75.00	95.00	38.00

SHAMROCK COTTAGE

The "Shamrock Cottage" was a slipcast, hollow model of an Irish cottage, produced by Wade (Ulster) Ltd. It was sold in a box decorated with a shamrock design and labelled "Shamrock Pottery" and "Ireland's own Pottery." The original selling price was 2/6d.

FIRST VERSION

Light Brown Peat, Green Base

1956-1961, 1977-Early 1980s

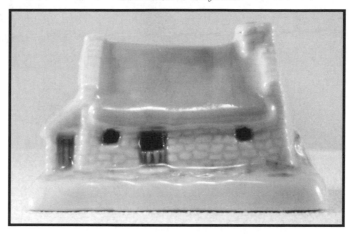

Size: 45 x 40 mm.
Backstamp: Impressed "Shamrock Pottery Made in Ireland"

No.	Description	U.S. $	Can. $	U.K. £
1	Yellow roof; blue doors, windows; light brown peat; green base	45.00	60.00	25.00

Dark Brown Peat, Mottled Green Base

1977-1984

This reissued "Shamrock Cottage" is the same as the 1956-1961 model, except that the colour of the peat pile at the back of the cottage is now a darker shade of brown. It has also been found with names of places of interest printed in black letters on the front rim of the base.

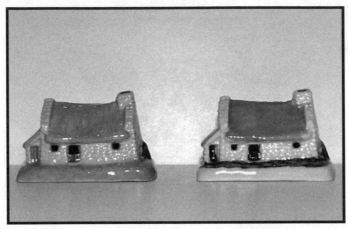

First Version (left), Second Version (right)

Size: 45 x 40 mm.
Backstamp: Impressed "Shamrock Pottery Made in Ireland"

No.	Description	U.S. $	Can. $	U.K. £
1a	Dark yellow roof; dark blue doors; dark brown peat; mottled green and white base; "Belfast" on rim	45.00	60.00	25.00
1b	Dark yellow roof; dark blue doors; dark brown peat; mottled green and white base; "Hawkshead" on rim	45.00	60.00	25.00
1c	Yellow roof; blue doors, windows; dark brown peat; mottled green and white base	45.00	60.00	25.00
1d	Yellow roof; blue doors; dark brown peat; mottled green and white base; "The Giant's Causeway" on rim	45.00	60.00	25.00
1e	Yellow roof; blue doors; dark brown peat; mottled green and white base; "Windermere" on rim	45.00	60.00	25.00

PIXIE DISH

1957-1959

The George Wade Pottery's 1957 oak leaf dish was issued with the 1956-1959 "Leprechaun Crock o' Gold" to produce this particular dish. The original selling price was 2/11d.

Size: 40 x 100 mm.
Backstamp: Embossed "Shamrock Pottery"

No.	Name	Description	U.S. $	Can. $	U.K. £
1a	Crock o' Gold	Orange hat; blue jacket; brown boots; green leaf	30.00	40.00	10.00
1b	Crock o' Gold	Yellow hat; blue jacket; brown boots; green leaf	30.00	40.00	10.00
1c	Crock o' Gold	Maroon hat; blue jacket; brown boots; green leaf	30.00	40.00	10.00

HAT BOX SERIES

These charming Walt Disney cartoon characters were sold in round, striped cardboard boxes which resemble hat boxes, from which this series takes its name. The boxes each had a colour print of the enclosed model on the lid. There are 26 models in this long-running series. The last ten models had only a short production run and are considered scarce. The hardest of all to find are the models from *The Sword in the Stone*, especially the Merlin models.

Three variations of "Jock" can be found. When first produced in 1956, he was not wearing a coat. After Wade was advised that he wore one in the film, he was made with a blue tartan coat in early 1957. Later that year the coat was changed to green tartan.

The original price for all the models was 2/11d, except for the figures from *The Sword in the Stone*, which sold for 3/6d. The films from which the models were taken are as follows:

Film	Model	Date of Issue
Lady and the Tramp	Lady	January 1956
	Jock, Blue Coat	Early 1957
	Jock, Green Coat	Late 1957
	Jock, No Coat	January 1956
	Tramp	January 1956
	Trusty	January 1956
	Peg	February 1957
	Scamp	February 1957
	Dachie	January 1958
	Si	August 1958
	Am	August 1958
	Boris	February 1960
	Toughy	February 1960
Bambi	Bambi	December 1957
	Flower	December 1957
	Thumper	December 1957
Dumbo	Dumbo	December 1957
Fantasia	Baby Pegasus	January 1958
101 Dalmatians	The Colonel	September 1961
	Sergeant Tibbs	September 1961
	Rolly	September 1961
	Lucky	September 1961
The Sword in the Stone	Madam Mim	Autumn 1962
	Merlin as a Turtle	Autumn 1962
	Archimedes	Autumn 1962
	Merlin as a Hare	Autumn 1962
	The Girl Squirrel	Autumn 1962
	Merlin as a Caterpillar	Autumn 1962

HAT BOX — FIRST ISSUE

1956-1965

Set One

Backstamp: **A.** Unmarked (1-6)
B. Black and gold "Wade England" label (1-6)
C. Blue transfer "Wade England" (1, 3, 6)

No.	Name	Description	Size	U.S. $	Can. $	U.K. £
1	Lady	Beige; light brown ears; blue collar	40 x 35	35.00	45.00	18.00
2a	Jock, No Coat	Blue-grey	40 x 25	40.00	55.00	25.00
2b	Jock, Blue Tartan	Blue coat	40 x 25	40.00	55.00	25.00
2c	Jock, Green Tartan	Green coat; purple mouth	40 x 25	35.00	45.00	18.00
3	Tramp, Standing	Grey/white; red tongue	50 x 50	85.00	115.00	40.00
4a	Trusty	Brown; brown nose	55 x 35	38.00	50.00	25.00
4b	Trusty	Brown; black nose	55 x 35	38.00	50.00	25.00
5	Peg	Yellow fringe; red nose, mouth	40 x 35	30.00	40.00	18.00
6	Scamp	Grey; mauve ears, mouth; brown toes	40 x 35	35.00	45.00	18.00

Set Two

Backstamp: **A.** Unmarked (7-16)
B. Black and gold "Wade England" label (7-16)

No.	Name	Description	Size	U.S. $	Can. $	U.K. £
7	Bambi	Beige; tan/white patches; dark brown eyes	40 x 35	25.00	35.00	15.00
8	Flower	Black/white; blue eyes; red tongue	40 x 25	70.00	95.00	28.00
9a	Thumper	Blue-grey; pink cheeks; red mouth	60 x 35	40.00	55.00	24.00
9b	Thumper	Blue-gray; white cheeks; red mouth	60 x 35	40.00	55.00	24.00
10	Dumbo	Grey/white; pink ears	40 x 38	90.00	120.00	36.00
11	Baby Pegasus	Blue-grey; blue eyes; pink nose, mouth	40 x 30	100.00	135.00	40.00
12	Dachie	Brown; dark brown ears; red mouth	60 x 30	40.00	55.00	24.00
13	Si	Beige; black tail, legs, ears; blue eyes	60 x 30	75.00	100.00	30.00
14	Am	Beige; black tail, legs, ears; eyes closed	60 x 25	50.00	65.00	28.00
15	Boris	Grey; white chest, tail tip; pink in ears	60 x 28	70.00	95.00	36.00
16	Toughy	Brown; white chest, face; red tongue	55 x 30	90.00	120.00	55.00

Set Three

Backstamp: **A.** Unmarked (17-26)
B. Black and gold "Wade England" label (17-26)

No.	Name	Description	Size	U.S. $	Can. $	U.K. £
17	The Colonel	Beige/white; black streak across eye	50 x 34	90.00	120.00	55.00
18	Sergeant Tibbs	Beige; white chest, nose, paws; blue in ears	55 x 30	90.00	120.00	55.00
19	Rolly	White; black spots; red collar; sitting	40 x 30	90.00	120.00	55.00
20	Lucky	White; black spots, ears; red collar; standing	30 x 35	140.00	185.00	60.00
21	Madam Mim	Honey/brown; black neck, wing tips	30 x 28	240.00	300.00	100.00
22	Merlin as a Turtle	Brown-grey; black/white eyes	30 x 45	325.00	450.00	165.00
23	Archimedes	Brown head, back, wings, log	50 x 35	150.00	200.00	75.00
24	Merlin as a Hare	Blue; white tail, chest	55 x 35	215.00	285.00	100.00
25	The Girl Squirrel	Beige; honey brown tail	50 x 30	100.00	135.00	80.00
26	Merlin as a Caterpillar	White/pink/mauve; black/yellow eyes	20 x 45	275.00	365.00	120.00

HAT BOX FIRST ISSUE DERIVATIVES

BUTTER DISH

From 1955 to 1956, the George Wade Pottery produced a butter dish, to which "Jock" was later added on the back rim.

Photograph not available
at press time

Size: 65 x 80 mm.
Backstamp: Embossed "Wade England"

No.	Name	Description	U.S.$	Can.$	U.K.£
1a	Jock	No coat; blue dish	50.00	70.00	25.00
1b	Jock	No coat; grey dish	50.00	70.00	25.00
1c	Jock	Blue coat, dish	50.00	70.00	25.00
1d	Jock	Green coat; blue dish	50.00	70.00	25.00

CARD TRUMPS

Photograph not available
at press time

Backstamp: Raised "Bouldray Wade Porcelain 2 Made in England"

No.	Name	Description	Size	U.S. $	Can. $	U.K. £
1	Merlin as a Hare	Brass frame; blue tray; blue/grey Merlin; white plastic cards	90 x 75	100.00	135.00	60.00

DISNEY LIGHTS (CANDLE HOLDERS)

Circa 1960

This set is similar in appearance to the 1959-1960 *Zoo Lights*, but the triangular base is much larger, thicker and heavier, and it has an original issue *Hat Box* model (style 9 has a *First Whimsies* "Panda") sitting on the front edge of the candle holder. The holders are all black and were made for cake-size candles, which stand in a hole on the back edge. These models are rarely found. Examples other than those listed below are believed to exist.

Flower (3)

Lady (5)

Backstamp: Embossed "Wade"

No.	Name	Description	Size	U.S. $	Can. $	U.K. £
1	Bambi	Beige; black holder	60 x 50	90.00	120.00	48.00
2	Dumbo	White/pink; black holder	60 x 50	120.00	150.00	75.00
3	Flower	Black/white; black holder	60 x 50	120.00	150.00	75.00
4	Jock	Blue-grey/white; green coat; black holder	60 x 50	90.00	120.00	48.00
5	Lady	Beige/white; black holder	60 x 50	90.00	120.00	48.00
6	Lucky	White; black spots, holder	50 x 50	120.00	150.00	75.00
7	Rolly	White; black spots, holder	60 x 50	120.00	150.00	75.00
8	Thumper	Blue-grey/white; black holder	80 x 50	90.00	120.00	48.00
9	Panda, Large	Black/white; black base	55 x 50	68.00	80.00	30.00

The only

magazine

for collectors!

A monthly magazine for collecting enthusiasts. From affordable antiques like Royal Doulton, to modern collectables such as Lilliput, Wade, Disneyana or sports memorabilia, Collect it! covers it - and gives you extensive valuation listings and a fact file to back up any collection.

Available at major newsagents. For more information and subscriptions call: +44 1344 868280 or fax +44 1344 861777. Email: collectit@dial.pipex.com

Collect it!

Collect it! launched in response to a need - the need for a magazine for the collector in everyone!

Collect it! has already established itself in the UK as THE magazine for collectors. Covering subjects from McDonalds toys and cigarette packets, to Wade, Lilliput, Royal Doulton and Moorcroft, all in a full colour glossy magazine.

Antiques worth fortunes are out of the range of all but the very few. What people want to read about are the bargains they can find at prices they can afford and the values of the things they already have. Collect it! covers all of these, with articles on future collectables, affordable antiques and memorabilia.

Available at major newsagents in the UK, USA, Canada, Australia, New Zealand and Japan, Collect it! has become indispensable to anyone with a general interest in spotting the antiques of tomorrow.

For further information and the cost of a year's subscription,

call: +44 1344 868 280

TITLE .... FULL NAME ....

ADDRESS ....

....

....

DAYTIME TEL NO .... ZIPCODE ....

☐ I enclose a cheque for .... made payable to Collect it Ltd.

☐ Please debit £................:.................... from my   ☐ Mastercard   ☐ Visa

CARD NUMBER: ▢▢▢▢ ▢▢▢▢ ▢▢▢▢ ▢▢▢▢

EXPIRY DATE .... / ....

SIGNATURE .... DATE ....

Collect it Ltd, P.O. Box 3658, Bracknell, Berkshire RG12 7XZ, Great Britain.

HAT BOX — SECOND ISSUE

1981-1985

In spring 1981 George Wade and Son renewed its licence with Walt Disney Productions Ltd. and reissued six models from the Walt Disney *Hat Box* series, using the original moulds.

At first glance the reissues are hard to distinguish from the earlier figures. The sizes of these first six models are the same as for the original *Hat Box* characters, and there is only a slight variation in colour.

Four new models from the Disney film, *The Fox and the Hound* —"Tod," "Copper," "Chief" and "Big Mama"—were added in February 1982. In 1985 the last two models in the set—a new "Tramp" and a reissued "Peg" — were issued.

The models were sold in round plastic hat box-shaped containers and later in oblong cardboard boxes, except for "Tramp" and "Peg," which came in cardboard boxes only.

Backstamp: Black and gold label "Walt Disney Productions Wade England"

No.	Name	Description	Size	U.S. $	Can. $	U.K. £
1	Lady	Dark brown ears; light blue collar	40 x 35	25.00	35.00	16.00
2	Jock, Green Tartan	Green coat; pink mouth; orange collar	40 x 25	32.00	42.00	18.00
3	Scamp	Pink mouth, ears; facial markings flat	40 x 35	30.00	40.00	16.00
4	Dachsie	Light brown ears; pink mouth	60 x 30	30.00	40.00	16.00
5	Bambi	Light brown eyes	40 x 35	30.00	40.00	16.00
6	Thumper	Pink mouth, cheeks; pale orange flower	60 x 35	30.00	40.00	16.00
7	Tod	Red-brown; dark brown paws	45 x 50	50.00	65.00	37.00
8	Copper	Beige; brown patch, ears; white chest, paws	45 x 50	30.00	40.00	16.00
9	Chief	Grey; white chest; black eyes; red tongue	50 x 20	30.00	40.00	16.00
10	Big Mama	Beige head, back, wings; orange beak	45 x 45	38.00	50.00	22.00
11	Tramp, Sitting	Grey; red tongue	47 x 30	50.00	65.00	25.00
12	Peg	Beige fringe; brown nose; pink mouth	40 x 35	26.00	35.00	16.00

Note: Prices listed are for pieces only or pieces in cardboard boxes. Models found in their original plastic box will command a premium of 10-20% above list price.

DISNEY MONEY BOXES

1962

This series comprises a set of five money boxes in the shape of a dog kennel, with an original issue *Hat Box* figure standing in front of the entrance. The coin slot is in the kennel roof. The issue date for these money boxes was spring 1962, and they originally sold for 9/11d.

Size: 95 x 105 mm.
Backstamp: Unmarked

No.	Name	Description	U.S. $	Can. $	U.K. £
1	Lady	Beige; blue kennel	200.00	265.00	125.00
2	Jock, No Coat	Blue-grey; blue kennel	200.00	265.00	125.00
3	Scamp	Grey; blue kennel	200.00	265.00	125.00
4	Rolly	White; blue kennel	200.00	265.00	125.00
5	Lucky	White; blue kennel	200.00	265.00	125.00

DRUM BOX SERIES

1957-1959

In the advertising literature of the time, Wade called this set the *Animal Band*, later changing it to the *Drum Box* series. The set consists of five comical animals, four playing a musical instrument and the fifth, "Dora" the donkey, is the soprano. They were sold in round cardboard drum-design boxes, from which the series got its name. The original price for each model was 3/11d. They were issued in May 1957 and discontinued in spring 1959.

Backstamp: Unmarked

No.	Name	Description	Size	U.S. $	Can. $	U.K. £
1	Jem	Red collar; grey trousers; black tie, eye patch	45 x 25	100.00	135.00	50.00
2	Clara	White dress; yellow stripes; brown cello	50 x 25	100.00	135.00	50.00
3	Harpy	Blue dress; mauve/white harp	45 x 28	100.00	135.00	50.00
4	Trunky	White shirt, trousers; black tie	50 x 35	110.00	140.00	55.00
5	Dora	White dress; red hem; yellow base	55 x 25	160.00	210.00	80.00

TREASURES SET

1957-1959

The *Treasures* set was the first in an intended series, but unfortunately for collectors, the rest of it was never put into production. It consists of a set of five white elephants in varying sizes, with bright pink blankets decorated with orange, yellow, blue and green flowers. Early advertising material calls the set *Elephant Chains* and *Elephant Train*.

The original price for a box of five elephants was 10/6d.

Backstamp: Blue transfer "Wade England"

No.	Name	Description	Size	U.S. $	Can. $	U.K. £
1	Large Elephant	White; pink blanket; howdah and mahout; blue turban	47 x 63	150.00	200.00	70.00
2	Medium Elephant	White; pink blanket; gold tassel	35 x 57	150.00	200.00	65.00
3	Small Elephant	White; pink blanket; gold tassel	28 x 54	150.00	200.00	65.00
4	Tiny Elephant	White; pink blanket; gold tassel	24 x 45	150.00	200.00	60.00
5	Miniature Elephant	White; pink blanket; gold tassel	20 x 39	150.00	200.00	60.00
		Boxed set of 5		1,200.00	1,500.00	400.00

ALPHABET AND LONDON TRAINS

1958-1961

The *Alphabet Train* comprises a miniature engine pulling six carriages and was intended to be educational, as well as fun, for children to play with. The carriages have various numbers on their roofs and letters of the alphabet on both sides. The *London Train* has a single letter on the roof of each carriage (forming the name *London*), with scenes of Tower Bridge, St. Paul's Cathedral, Trafalgar Square, Piccadilly Circus, Big Ben or Westminster Abbey on each side.

The issue date for both sets was August 1958, and they originally sold for 6/11d. They were discontinued in January 1959. The trains are very rare. As they are only seen in complete sets, no individual prices are given below.

Size: 27 x 205 mm.
Backstamp: Unmarked

No.	Name	Description	U.S. $	Can. $	U.K. £
1a	Alphabet Set: Engine, Tender, 6 Carriages	Blue engine	900.00	1,200.00	450.00

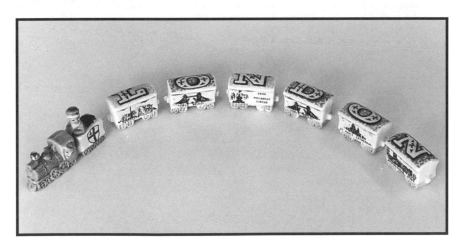

No.	Name	Description	U.S. $	Can. $	U.K. £
1b	London Set: Engine, Tender, 6 Carriages	Grey engine	1,000.00	1,500.00	600.00

THE NODDY SET
Style One

The *Noddy* set consists of four characters created by the English children's writer Enid Blyton. A pilot test for the new series was started in July 1958. Only four models were issued, with an original price of 3/11d each. Production was discontinued in autumn 1961.

Backstamp: Unmarked

No.	Name	Description	Size	U.S. $	Can. $	U.K. £
1	Noddy	Red shirt, shoes; blue hat, trousers, bows	70 x 35	300.00	375.00	145.00
2	Big Ears	Blue jacket; yellow trousers; red hat	170 x 35	225.00	300.00	100.00
3	Mr. Plod	Blue uniform, helmet; yellow buttons	160 x 35	170.00	225.00	85.00
4	Miss Fluffy Cat	Brown coat, collar; yellow hat; red bag	60 x 35	80.00	105.00	50.00

THE NODDY SET DERIVATIVES

TOADSTOOL COTTAGE MONEY BOXES

Circa 1961

Following Wade's policy of using up unsold stock by converting it into better-selling lines (as with *First Whimsies* on candle holders and *Whimtrays*), "Big Ears" and "Noddy" from the *Noddy* set were placed on toadstool cottage money boxes, with a coin slot in the back rim of the roof. This series had a very limited production run and is extremely rare. The issue date is unknown, but it was probably soon after the *Noddy* set was finished in 1960. These models originally had black and gold foil labels.

Size: 110 x 120 mm.
Backstamp: **A.** Black and gold foil label "Genuine Wade Porcelain made in England"
B. Unmarked

No.	Name	Description	U.S. $	Can. $	U.K. £
1a	Big Ears	Brown roof with white spots; yellow chimney, flowers; blue windows, door; green grass	375.00	500.00	185.00
1b	Big Ears	Brown roof with white spots; yellow chimney, flowers; blue windows; brown door; green grass	375.00	500.00	185.00
2	Noddy	Brown roof with white spots; yellow chimney, flowers; blue windows, door; green grass	400.00	525.00	200.00

THE TORTOISE FAMILY

1958-1988

Wade's first tortoise, the "Large (Father)," was issued in January 1958, and it proved so popular that the following January Wade introduced two more, the "Medium (Mother)" and "Small (Baby)," which were sold as a pair. These three models were so successful that they were produced almost continuously for the next thirty years. Considered by Wade as their best-selling line, this family of tortoises is in plentiful supply. The original price for the "Large (Father)" was 4/6d; the pair of "Medium (Mother)" and "Small (Baby)" cost 4/9d.

In 1973 the "Jumbo" tortoise was added to the family. It was modelled differently from the other tortoises, however, and resembles a turtle. Because it was not in production for as long as the rest of the *Tortoise Family*, it is harder to find.

The "Large (Father)" and the "Jumbo" tortoises are the only ones in this series to have lift-off shells. The numbers 1 through 8 were embossed on the bases of model 3, which refer to the production tool used to press the model. Production tools usually lasted for one to three years before having to be replaced; therefore, the models with the lowest numbers should be the oldest.

Two variations have been found in the Father Tortoise model, both types are backstamped with an impressed 'Wade Porcelain Made in England' but Type Two may have been produced in the Wade Ireland pottery.

Type One: The body of the tortoise has an open back with a slot in it and there is a slotted projection on the tail which fits into the open slot on the base, there are small pads on the bottom of the feet. Type One has embossed mould Nos 1 and 5.

Type Two: The tortoise has a closed back and there is a projection just below the tail which holds the shell in place, the bottom of the feet are smooth. Type Two has an embossed mould No 4.

Type One   Type Two

Baby, Mother, and Father

Jumbo Tortoise

Backstamp: A. Embossed "Wade Porcelain Made in England No. 3" (1, 2, 3)
B. Embossed "Wade Made in England" (4)

No.	Name	Description	Size	U.S. $	Can. $	U.K. £
1a	Small (Baby)	Brown/blue	25 x 45	10.00	15.00	5.00
1b	Small (Baby)	Green/blue	25 x 45	35.00	45.00	30.00
1c	Small (Baby)	Green	25 x 45	35.00	45.00	30.00
2a	Medium (Mother)	Brown/blue	35 x 75	10.00	15.00	5.00
2b	Medium (Mother)	Green/blue	35 x 75	35.00	45.00	30.00
2c	Medium (Mother)	Green	35 x 75	35.00	45.00	30.00
3a	Large (Father)	Beige;/blue	50 x 105	15.00	20.00	8.00
3b	Large (Father)	Brown/blue	50 x 105	15.00	20.00	8.00
3c	Large (Father)	Green/blue	50 x 105	15.00	20.00	8.00
3d	Large (Father)	Green	50 x 105	15.00	20.00	8.00
4	Jumbo	Beige/blue	65 x 150	75.00	100.00	30.00

THE TORTOISE FAMILY DERIVATIVES

ASH BOWLS

1958-1984

The tortoise ash bowls are large and round, with a scintillite, high-gloss finish. An embossed reptile-skin design covers the inside, and a model from the *Tortoise Family* set is fixed to the inside curve of the bowl. The ash bowl with the "Medium (Mother)" tortoise was issued in January 1958 for 12/6d. The ash bowl with the "Small (Baby)" tortoise was produced from 1975 to 1984.

Backstamp: A. Impressed "Wade Porcelain Made in England" (1a, 1b, 1c)
          B. Large embossed "Wade Made in England" (2a, 2b, 2c)

No.	Description	Size	U.S. $	Can. $	U.K. £
1a	Ash bowl with "Medium (Mother)" tortoise; brown/blue	55 x 183	55.00	70.00	30.00
1b	Ash bowl with "Medium (Mother)" tortoise; green/blue	55 x 183	55.00	70.00	30.00
2a	Ash bowl with "Small (Baby)" tortoise; brown/blue	45 x 145	45.00	60.00	28.00
2b	Ash bowl with "Small (Baby)" tortoise; green/blue	45 x 145	45.00	60.00	28.00

FOOTED OBLONG BOWL

1976

The round tortoise ash bowls were such a successful line that Wade introduced a new oblong bowl in 1976. This bowl had feet and was embossed with a reptile-skin design and finished with a scintillite, high-gloss finish. The "Medium (Mother)" tortoise figure was used on this bowl.

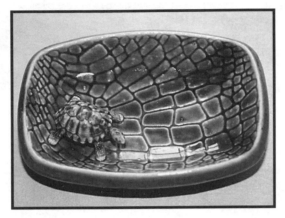

Size: 150 x 100 mm.
Backstamp: Large embossed "Wade Made in England"

No.	Description	U.S. $	Can. $	U.K. £
1	"Medium (Mother)" tortoise;" beige/blue	60.00	80.00	30.00

SOUVENIR TORTOISES

Circa 1976

Wade retooled the "Medium (Mother)" tortoise from the *Tortoise Family* series by cutting a recess in the back of the model and inserting the name of a British colony resort in embossed letters in the top shell.

Size: 35 x 75 mm.
Backstamp: Embossed "Wade Porcelain Made in England"

No.	Name	Description	U.S.$	Can.$	U.K.£
1	Bahamas	"Bahamas" on shell; brown; blue markings	30.00	40.00	15.00
2	Bermuda	"Bermuda" on shell; brown; blue markings	30.00	40.00	15.00
3	Bermuda Triangle	"Bermuda Triangle" on shell; brown; blue markings	30.00	40.00	15.00
4	Devil's Hole, Bermuda	"Devil's Hole, Bermuda" on shell; brown; blue markings	30.00	40.00	15.00

Note: See page 192 for a commissioned set of tortoises for *Ciba Geigy* that is another derivative of the *Tortoise Family*.

THE BRITISH CHARACTER SET

1959

The *British Character* set, also known to collectors as London characters, includes four models: the "Pearly King," "Pearly Queen," "Lawyer" and the Billingsgate "Fish Porter." They were produced for only one year and are rarely seen and highly sought after.

Backstamp: A. Unmarked (1-4)
B. Black and gold label "Genuine Wade Porcelain" (1-4)

No.	Name	Description	Size	U.S. $	Can. $	U.K. £
1	Pearly King	White pearlised suit, cap: yellow brim	68 x 28	160.00	210.00	100.00
2a	Pearly Queen	White pearlised dress, jacket; yellow ribbon; lower hat brim black	68 x 38	200.00	265.00	100.00
2b	Pearly Queen	Blue/pink pearlised dress; lower hat brim pink	68 x 38	200.00	265.00	100.00
3	Lawyer	White wig; black gown, shoes; brown base	68 x 28	250.00	330.00	145.00
4	Fish Porter	Blue trousers; green tie; blue base	75 x 28	250.00	330.00	145.00

POGO

1959

"Pogo" is based on a 1940s possum character featured in American newspapers and comics. The model was produced by Wade (Ulster) Ltd. and modelled by William Harper, who worked for the George Wade Pottery during the 1950s.

Size: 85 x 30 mm.
Backstamp: Black ink stamp "Pogo Copyright, Walt Kelly, Made in Ireland 1959"

No.	Description	U.S. $	Can. $	U.K. £
1	Grey; blue jacket; blue/pink bird	500.00	660.00	350.00

MABEL LUCIE ATTWELL FIGURES

1959-1961

Manufactured under licence to designs by Mabel Lucie Attwell, these two figures of "Sam" and "Sarah," with their pet dogs, were produced to test the public's reaction to a change of style. Apparently they were not very popular at the time, perhaps due to the high retail price of 6/11d. Subsequently these models, which are sought after by Wade and by Mabel Lucie Attwell collectors, are in high demand.

The issue date for "Sam" and "Sarah" was October 1959, and they were discontinued in summer 1961. Their original price was 6/11d each.

Backstamp: Embossed Raised "Wade Porcelain-Mabel Lucie Attwell © Made in England"

No.	Name	Description	Size	U.S. $	Can. $	U.K. £
1	Sam	Ginger hair; yellow shirt; grey dog	78 x 85	250.00	300.00	130.00
2a	Sarah	Green shoes; blue/white dress; white/black dog	75 x 100	250.00	300.00	130.00
2b	Sarah	Red shoes; blue/white dress; white/black dog	75 x 100	250.00	300.00	130.00
2c	Sarah	Blue shoes; blue/white dress; white/black dog	75 x 100	250.00	300.00	130.00

BENGO AND HIS PUPPY FRIENDS, TV PETS

1959-1965

TV Pets was based on a popular British television cartoon series called "Bengo and his Puppy Friends," created by William Timym, an Austrian refugee who owned a boxer puppy named Bengo.

The issue date for "Bengo," "Simon," "Pepi" and "Fifi" was May 1959; "Mitzi" and "Chee-Chee" came into production in September 1959; and "Bruno" and "Droopy" were issued in February 1961. At the beginning of 1965, the last two puppies joined the series, the same year the series came to an end, making a total of ten models in the set. The last two models are difficult to find, as they were only in production for a few months at most. The original price was 3/11d each.

Backstamp: **A.** Unmarked (1-10)
B. Black and gold label "Genuine Wade Porcelain Made in England" (1-10)

No.	Name	Description	Size	U.S. $	Can. $	U.K. £
1	Bengo (Boxer)	Light brown/white; grey muzzle	55 x 50	70.00	90.00	35.00
2	Simon (Dalmatian)	White; black spots	60 x 40	75.00	95.00	25.00
3	Pepi (Chihuahua)	Tan patches; large black eyes; red mouth	55 x 35	90.00	120.00	35.00
4	Fifi (Poodle)	Grey-blue head, ears, legs; red bow	55 x 35	55.00	75.00	24.00
5	Chee-Chee (Pekinese)	Beige; white face, chest, paws	60 x 35	65.00	85.00	32.00
6	Mitzi (Kitten)	Blue-grey/white; pink mouth	50 x 50	75.00	95.00	35.00
7	Bruno Junior (Saint Bernard)	Brown rump, head, ears; red tongue	55 x 35	100.00	135.00	45.00
8	Droopy Junior (Basset Hound)	Light brown; white chest; grey ear tips	55 x 40	105.00	140.00	50.00
9	Percy (Afghan)	Beige; orange patches; grey face	65 x 30	105.00	140.00	50.00
10	Whisky (Corgi)	Beige; white face, chest, paws; red tongue	55 x 65	200.00	265.00	90.00

DISNEY BLOW UPS

1961-1965

Disney Blow Ups is a set of ten characters from the Disney films *Lady and the Tramp* and *Bambi*. They are referred to as blow ups because they are larger slip-cast versions of the miniature *Hat Box Series* which preceded them. "Tramp," "Jock," "Thumper" and "Dachie" are the hardest of these models to find.

Name	Issue Price	Issue Date
Tramp	17/6d	January 1961
Lady	15/-	January 1961
Bambi	13/6d	January 1961
Scamp	12/6d	January 1961
Si	15/-	Autumn 1961
Am	15/-	Autumn 1961
Thumper	12/6d	Autumn 1961
Trusty	17/6d	Autumn 1961
Jock	13/6d	Autumn 1962
Dachie	15/-	Autumn 1962

Backstamp: **A.** Black transfer "Wade Porcelain—Copyright Walt Disney Productions—Made in England" (1-10)
B. Black transfer "Wade Porcelain—Copyright Walt Disney Productions—Made in Ireland" (7)

No.	Name	Description	Size	U.S. $	Can. $	U.K. £
1	Tramp	Grey; white face, neck, chest; red tongue	160 x 105	375.00	500.00	190.00
2	Lady	Beige; honey ears; blue collar	110 x 140	275.00	350.00	175.00
3	Bambi	Beige; white spots; pink ears; red tongue	110 x 120	180.00	240.00	95.00
4	Scamp	Grey; pink ears; white/maroon paws	110 x 115	225.00	300.00	95.00
5	Si	Brown; black/lilac ears; blue eyes; red mouth	140 x 110	225.00	300.00	120.00
6	Am	Brown; black/lilac ears; black nose, tail, legs	147 x 85	225.00	300.00	120.00
7	Thumper	Blue; white/yellow, white/red flowers	130 x 80	500.00	665.00	300.00
8	Trusty	Beige; red-brown ears; gold medallion	135 x 80	300.00	375.00	165.00
9	Jock	Grey; pink/mauve ears; gold medallion	100 x 115	550.00	750.00	300.00
10	Dachie	Beige; brown ears, eyes; red tongue	125 x 105	550.00	750.00	300.00

HAPPY FAMILIES

The *Happy Families* series was first issued from 1961 to 1965 and consisted of a mother animal and her two babies. The original five sets were sold in boxes with "Happy Families" printed in large letters in different colours on the front.

The first three *Happy Families* were the *Hippo Family* (3/11d), the *Tiger Family* (4/6d) and the *Giraffe Family* (4/11d), were modelled by Leslie McKinnon and issued in the autumn and winter of 1961. They proved to be so popular that in spring 1962, Wade issued two more families, the *Rabbit Family* and the *Mouse Family*.

In 1978 four sets were reissued using the original moulds, and the only way to distinguish them from the earlier models is by a slight variation in colour. By 1984 four more families had been added—the *Frog Family*, *Pig Family*, *Elephant Family* and *Owl Family*. In spring 1987, the last year of the series, the *Dog Family* and *Cat Family* joined the series, making a total of ten sets issued from 1978 to 1987.

The reissued *Happy Families* series was sold in blue-green boxes with giraffes, rabbits, mice and hippos printed on them. The boxes were changed again in 1984 to white with pastel-coloured jungle scenes.

At some time during the late 1980s, Wade sold off its remaining stock of *Happy Families* to Tesco Stores, a British discount company. The Tesco Stores box had a rigid cellophane top, front and sides; the base and back were cardboard. There is no reference to Wade on these boxes.

HIPPO FAMILY

First Issue 1961-1965

Backstamp: Unknown

No.	Name	Description	Size	U.S. $	Can. $	U.K. £
1	Mother	Dark/dull blue eyes	35 x 50	10.00	15.00	5.00
2	Baby, Asleep	Eyes shut	20 x 25	8.00	10.00	4.00
3	Baby, Awake	Dark/dull blue eyes	28 x 25	8.00	10.00	4.00
—	Set (3) Boxed			25.00	35.00	10.00

Second Issue 1978-1987

Backstamp: Black transfer "Wade Made in England"

No.	Name	Description	Size	U.S. $	Can. $	U.K. £
1a	Mother	Smoky blue; blue tear; brown eyes	35 x 50	10.00	15.00	5.00
1b	Mother	Reddish pink; white face; black eyes; red mouth	28 x 65	10.00	15.00	5.00
2	Baby, Asleep	Smoky blue; blue tear; brown eyes	20 x 25	8.00	10.00	4.00
3a	Baby, Awake	Smoky blue; blue tear; brown eyes	28 x 25	8.00	10.00	4.00
3b	Baby, Awake	Reddish pink; white face; black eyes; red mouth	28 x 65	8.00	10.00	4.00
—	Set (3) Boxed			25.00	35.00	15.00

HIPPO FAMILY DERIVATIVES

HIPPO MOTHER BLOW UP

The hippo "Mother" is the only one of the *Happy Families* models reported in a blow-up size. Perhaps it was a prototype model, which was not issued because of high production costs.

Photograph not available
at press time

Size: Unknown
Backstamp: Unmarked

No.	Description	U.S.$	Can.$	U.K.£
1	Pale blue; blue eyes	Extremely rare		

TIGER FAMILY

1961-1965

This set was not reissued, so it is rare and highly sought after.

Backstamp: Unmarked

No.	Name	Description	Size	U.S. $	Can. $	U.K. £
1	Mother	Beige; brown stripes; green eyes; red tongue	40 x 40	80.00	105.00	30.00
2	Baby, Sleeping	Beige; brown stripes; green eyes; red tongue	10 x 30	50.00	65.00	25.00
3	Baby, Awake	Beige; brown stripes; green eyes; red tongue	10 x 30	50.00	65.00	25.00
—	Set (3) Boxed			170.00	225.00	80.00

GIRAFFE FAMILY

First Issue 1961-1965

Except for a slight variation in eyelid and horn colour, the original and reissued models are hard to distinguish from each other.

Backstamp: A. Unmarked (1-3)
          B. Black and gold label "Genuine Wade Porcelain Made in England" (1-3)
          C. Brown ink stamp "Wade England" with cricket (1-3)

No.	Name	Description	Size	U.S. $	Can. $	U.K. £
1	Mother	Beige; light blue eyelids; light grey horns	60 x 45	20.00	25.00	10.00
2	Baby, Sleeping	Beige; light blue eyelids; light grey horns	15 x 30	15.00	20.00	6.00
3	Baby, Awake	Beige; light blue eyelids; light grey horns	40 x 28	15.00	20.00	8.00
—	Set (3) Boxed			45.00	60.00	20.00

Second Issue 1978-1987

Backstamp: A. Unmarked (1-3)
          B. Brown transfer "Wade Made in England" (1-3)
          C. Black transfer "Wade Made in England" (1-3)

No.	Name	Description	Size	U.S. $	Can. $	U.K. £
1	Mother	Beige; turquoise eyelids; dark grey horns	60 x 45	20.00	25.00	10.00
2	Baby, Sleeping	Beige; turquoise eyelids; dark grey horns	15 x 30	15.00	20.00	6.00
3	Baby, Awake	Beige; turquoise eyelids; dark grey horns	40 x 28	15.00	20.00	8.00
—	Set (3) Boxed			43.00	60.00	20.00

RABBIT FAMILY

First Issue 1963-1965

Backstamp: **A.** Unmarked (1-3)
B. Black and gold label "Genuine Wade Porcelain Made in England" (1-3)

No.	Name	Description	Size	U.S. $	Can. $	U.K. £
1	Mother	White; turquoise patches	55 x 30	30.00	50.00	20.00
2	Baby, Sitting	White; turquoise patches	34 x 28	25.00	45.00	20.00
3	Baby, Standing	White; turquoise patches	30 x 35	25.00	45.00	20.00
—				80.00	150.00	55.00

Second Issue 1978-1984

Backstamp: **A.** Black transfer "Wade made in England" (1-3)
B. Unmarked (1-3)

No.	Name	Description	Size	U.S. $	Can. $	U.K. £
1	Mother	White; blue patches	55 x 30	15.00	20.00	8.00
2	Baby, Sitting	White; blue patches	34 x 28	10.00	15.00	5.00
3	Baby, Standing	White; blue patches	30 x 35	10.00	15.00	5.00
—	Set (3) Boxed			40.00	50.00	20.00

...ginal models have yellow tails, compared

wi...

E...

No.		Size	U.S. $	Can. $	U.K. £
1		28	40.00	60.00	20.00
2		28	35.00	50.00	20.00
3		30	35.00	50.00	20.00
—			100.00	125.00	50.00

Bac...

No.		U.S. $	Can. $	U.K. £
1		15.00	20.00	8.00
2		8.00	15.00	5.00
3		8.00	15.00	5.00
—		30.00	45.00	20.00

SUNLIGHT SOAP
A child can use it.

FROG FAMILY

1984-1987

Backstamp: **A.** Black transfer "Wade Made in England" (1-3)
B. Red transfer "Wade Made in England" (1-3)

No.	Name	Description	Size	U.S. $	Can. $	U.K. £
1	Mother	Brown; red-brown spots	25 x 45	15.00	20.00	8.00
2	Baby, Smiling	Brown; red-brown spot	20 x 30	10.00	15.00	5.00
3	Baby, Singing	Brown; red-brown spots	25 x 25	10.00	15.00	8.00
—	Set (3) Boxed			30.00	40.00	20.00

PIG FAMILY

1984-1987

Backstamp: **A.** Black transfer "Wade Made in England" (1-3)
B. Red transfer "Wade Made in England" (1-3)

No.	Name	Description	Size	U.S. $	Can. $	U.K. £
1a	Mother	Pink; black eyes; red mouth	28 x 65	15.00	20.00	9.00
1b	Mother	Reddish pink; white face; black eyes; red mouth	28 x 65	15.00	20.00	9.00
2	Baby, Asleep	Pink; blue eyelids	15 x 45	12.00	18.00	8.00
3a	Baby, Awake	Pink; black eyes; red mouth	18 x 40	12.00	18.00	8.00
3b	Baby, Awake	Reddish pink; white face; black eyes; red mouth	18 x 40	12.00	18.00	8.00
—	Set (3) Boxed			38.00	50.00	25.00

ELEPHANT FAMILY

1984-1987

Backstamp: Black transfer "Wade Made in England" (some with cricket in large C)

No.	Name	Description	Size	U.S. $	Can. $	U.K. £
1a	Mother	Blue; pink ears, mouth	35 x 70	15.00	20.00	8.00
1b	Mother	Grey; pink ears, mouth	35 x 70	15.00	20.00	8.00
2a	Baby, Trunk Up	Blue; pink ears, mouth	45 x 22	12.00	15.00	7.00
2b	Baby, Trunk Up	Grey; pink ears, mouth	45 x 22	12.00	15.00	7.00
3a	Baby, Trunk Down	Blue; pink ears, mouth	25 x 55	12.00	15.00	7.00
3b	Baby, Trunk Down	Grey; pink ears, mouth	25 x 55	12.00	15.00	7.00
—	Set (3) Boxed			25.00	35.00	20.00

OWL FAMILY

1984-1987

Backstamp: **A.** Black transfer "Wade Made in England" (1-3)
B. Red transfer "Wade Made in England" (1-3)

No.	Name	Description	Size	U.S. $	Can. $	U.K. £
1	Mother	Cream; beige head, back, wings	40 x 40	15.00	20.00	8.00
2	Baby, Wings Closed	Cream; beige head, back, wings	25 x 20	12.00	15.00	7.00
3	Baby, Wings Open	Cream; beige head, back, wings	25 x 32	12.00	15.00	7.00
—	Set (3) Boxed			25.00	35.00	20.00

DOG FAMILY

1987

Backstamp: A. Black transfer "Wade Made in England" (1-3)
B. Unmarked (1-3)

No.	Name	Description	Size	U.S. $	Can. $	U.K. £
1	Mother	Brown; white face, chest	55 x 35	15.00	20.00	10.00
2	Puppy, Standing	Brown; white face, chest	30 x 35	12.00	15.00	8.00
3	Puppy Lying	Brown; white face, chest	30 x 40	12.00	15.00	8.00
—	Set (3) Boxed			30.00	35.00	22.00

CAT FAMILY

1987

Backstamp: Black transfer "Wade Made in England"

No.	Name	Description	Size	U.S. $	Can. $	U.K. £
1	Mother	Grey/white; blue eyes; pink ear tips	45 x 35	15.00	20.00	10.00
2	Kitten, Sitting	Grey/white; blue eyes; pink ears	30 x 20	12.00	15.00	8.00
3	Kitten, Lying	Grey/white; blue eyes; pink ears	30 x 35	12.00	15.00	8.00
—	Set (3) Boxed			30.00	35.00	22.00

CHILD STUDIES

1962

Child Studies was a short-lived set of four children in national costumes, representing England, Ireland, Scotland and Wales. Each model stands on a circular base, which has an embossed flower design on it.

Their issue date was spring 1962, and they sold for an original price of 21/- each .

Backstamp: **A.** Unmarked (1-4)
              B. Blue transfer "Wade England" (1-4)

No.	Name	Description	Size	U.S. $	Can. $	U.K. £
1	English Boy	Yellow hair; black hat; red jacket; blue waistcoat; grassy base	120 x 40	450.00	600.00	300.00
2	Irish Girl	Green kilt; shamrock base	115 x 40	775.00	1,000.00	520.00
3	Scots Boy	Blue kilt; black tam, jacket; thistle base	120 x 40	450.00	600.00	300.00
4	Welsh Girl	Striped skirt; chequered shawl; daffodil base	135 x 40	450.00	600.00	300.00

HANNA-BARBERA CARTOON CHARACTERS
YOGI BEAR AND FRIENDS

1962-1963

Yogi Bear and Friends is a set of three cartoon characters that were popular on television from the late 1950s until the early 1960s. Their original price was 3/6d each.

Backstamp: Unmarked

No.	Name	Description	Size	U.S. $	Can. $	U.K. £
1	Yogi Bear	Beige; yellow/black hat; red tie	62 x 30	125.00	165.00	75.00
2a	Mr. Jinks	Pink; white/yellow/black face; blue bowtie	63 x 30	150.00	200.00	75.00
2b	Mr. Jinks	Yellow; white/yellow/black face; blue tie	63 x 30	150.00	200.00	75.00
3	Huckleberry Hound	Blue; white face; yellow bowtie	60 x 28	125.00	165.00	75.00

WALT DISNEY BULLDOGS

Circa 1968

Two model bulldogs have been found, possibly representing Pluto's arch enemy Butch and his nephew Bull. The models are slip cast. Both bulldogs are sitting and smiling; "Butch" scratches his ribs with his hind leg.

Photograph not available
at press time

Backstamp: Black print "Wade Porcelain Copyright Walt Disney Productions Made in England"

No.	Name	Description	Size	U.S. $	Can. $	U.K. £
1	Bull	Cream; grey muzzle, nose	85 x 100	300.00	400.00	150.00
2	Butch	Beige; grey muzzle, nose	90 x 110	300.00	400.00	150.00

POLAR BLOW UPS

1962-1963

The *Polar Blow Ups* set is a series of slightly modified blow ups of three of the *First Whimsies Polar Animals*, set 6: the "Polar Bear," "Polar Bear Cub" and "Seal Pup." They are slip-cast, hollow models, which because of high production costs, were never put into full production. Only a few hundred of these models are believed to exist. It is reported that a blow up of a "Mermaid," "Penguin," "Walrus," "Dolphin" and "Husky" have been seen and were produced at the same time, but no written or substantial visual evidence has confirmed this. They may have been prototypes, which never went into production.

Backstamp: A. Unmarked (1-8)
B. Black and gold label "Genuine Wade Porcelain Made in England" (1-3, 5-8)
C. Black and gold label "Made in Ireland by Wade Co. Armagh" (4)

No.	Name	Description	Size	U.S. $	Can. $	U.K. £
1	Polar Bear Mother	White/beige; pink tongue; blue/beige/white fish	150 x 120	375.00	500.00	185.00
2	Polar Bear Cub	White/beige; pink mouth	100 x 100	375.00	500.00	185.00
3	Seal	Greenish black; pink tongue	120 x 105	400.00	525.00	200.00
4	Walrus	Unknown	148 x 98	275.00	375.00	135.00
5	Husky	Beige/white	150 x 100	Unknown		
6	Mermaid	Unknown	Unknown	Unknown		
7	Penguin	Unknown	Unknown	Unknown		
8	Dolphin	Unknown	Unknown	Unknown		

ANGELS

1963

The *Angels* is a small series of models which were only produced for a short time. They were modelled in three different positions — standing, sitting and kneeling— and coloured in pastel shades of pink, green, yellow and blue. These figures are also found on angel dishes and on angel candle holders.The *Angels* originally sold for 1/11 each.

STANDING ANGEL

Size: 40 x 30 mm.
Backstamp: Unmarked

No.	Description	U.S. $	Can. $	U.K. £
1a	Pink dress; brown hair	100.00	135.00	50.00
1b	Pink dress; yellow hair	100.00	135.00	50.00
1c	Yellow dress; brown hair	100.00	135.00	50.00
1d	Yellow dress; yellow hair	100.00	135.00	50.00
1e	Green dress; brown hair	100.00	135.00	50.00
1f	Green dress; yellow hair	100.00	135.00	50.00
1g	Blue dress; brown hair	100.00	135.00	50.00
1h	Blue dress; yellow hair	100.00	135.00	50.00

SITTING ANGEL

Size: 40 x 30 mm.
Backstamp: Unmarked

No.	Description	U.S.$	Can.$	U.K.£
2a	Pink dress; brown hair	100.00	135.00	50.00
2b	Pink dress; yellow hair	100.00	135.00	50.00
2c	Yellow dress; brown hair	100.00	135.00	50.00
2d	Yellow dress; yellow hair	100.00	135.00	50.00
2e	Green dress; brown hair	100.00	135.00	50.00
2f	Green dress; yellow hair	100.00	135.00	50.00
2g	Blue dress; brown hair	100.00	135.00	50.00
2h	Blue dress; yellow hair	100.00	135.00	50.00

Size: 40 x 25 mm.
Backstamp: Unmarked

No.	Description	U.S.$	Can.$	U.K.£
3a	Pink dress; brown hair	100.00	135.00	50.00
3b	Pink dress; yellow hair	100.00	135.00	50.00
3c	Yellow dress; brown hair	100.00	135.00	50.00
3d	Yellow dress; yellow hair	100.00	135.00	50.00
3e	Green dress; brown hair	100.00	135.00	50.00
3f	Green dress; yellow hair	100.00	135.00	50.00
3g	Blue dress; brown hair	100.00	135.00	50.00
3h	Blue dress; yellow hair	100.00	135.00	50.00

ANGELS DERIVATIVES

DISHES

The dishes, similar to the *Whimtrays*, are black and the angel figure is positioned on the back rim. They originally sold for 2/11d each.

STANDING ANGEL DISH

Size: 40 x 75 mm.
Backstamp: Embossed "Angel Dish, Wade Porcelain, Made in England"

No.	Description	U.S. $	Can. $	U.K. £
1a	Pink dress; brown hair	80.00	100.00	40.00
1b	Pink dress; yellow hair	80.00	100.00	40.00
1c	Yellow dress; brown hair	80.00	100.00	40.00
1d	Yellow dress; yellow hair	80.00	100.00	40.00
1e	Green dress; brown hair	80.00	100.00	40.00
1f	Green dress; yellow hair	80.00	100.00	40.00
1g	Blue dress; brown hair	80.00	100.00	40.00
1h	Blue dress; yellow hair	80.00	100.00	40.00

SITTING ANGEL DISH

Size: 40 x 75 mm.
Backstamp: Embossed "Angel Dish, Wade Porcelain, Made in England"

No.	Description	U.S.$	Can.$	U.K.£
2a	Pink dress; brown hair	80.00	100.00	40.00
2b	Pink dress; yellow hair	80.00	100.00	40.00
2c	Yellow dress; brown hair	80.00	100.00	40.00
2d	Yellow dress; yellow hair	80.00	100.00	40.00
2e	Green dress; brown hair	80.00	100.00	40.00
2f	Green dress; yellow hair	80.00	100.00	40.00
2g	Blue dress; brown hair	80.00	100.00	40.00
2h	Blue dress; yellow hair	80.00	100.00	40.00

KNEELING ANGEL DISH

Size: 40 x 75 mm.
Backstamp: Embossed "Angel Dish, Wade Porcelain, Made in England"

No.	Description	U.S.$	Can.$	U.K.£
3a	Pink dress; brown hair	80.00	100.00	40.00
3b	Pink dress; yellow hair	80.00	100.00	40.00
3c	Yellow dress; brown hair	80.00	100.00	40.00
3d	Yellow dress; yellow hair	80.00	100.00	40.00
3e	Green dress; brown hair	80.00	100.00	40.00
3f	Green dress; yellow hair	80.00	100.00	40.00
3g	Blue dress; brown hair	80.00	100.00	40.00
3h	Blue dress; yellow hair	80.00	100.00	40.00

CANDLE HOLDERS

The angel models were mounted on the front of triangular-shaped candle holders (the same candle holders that were used for the 1960 *Disney Lights*). All the candle holders are black, and they were sold with a candy-twist candle for an original price of 2/11d each.

STANDING ANGEL CANDLE HOLDER

Size: 58 x 50 mm.
Backstamp: Embossed "Wade"

No.	Description	U.S. $	Can. $	U.K. £
1a	Pink dress; brown hair	120.00	160.00	60.00
1b	Pink dress; yellow hair	120.00	160.00	60.00
1c	Yellow dress; brown hair	120.00	160.00	60.00
1d	Yellow dress; yellow hair	120.00	160.00	60.00
1e	Green dress; brown hair	120.00	160.00	60.00
1f	Green dress; yellow hair	120.00	160.00	60.00
1g	Blue dress; brown hair	120.00	160.00	60.00
1h	Blue dress; yellow hair	120.00	160.00	60.00

SITTING ANGEL CANDLE HOLDER

Size: 58 x 50 mm.
Backstamp: Embossed "Wade"

No.	Description	U.S.$	Can.$	U.K.£
2a	Pink dress; brown hair	120.00	160.00	60.00
2b	Pink dress; yellow hair	120.00	160.00	60.00
2c	Yellow dress; brown hair	120.00	160.00	60.00
2d	Yellow dress; yellow hair	120.00	160.00	60.00
2e	Green dress; brown hair	120.00	160.00	60.00
2f	Green dress; yellow hair	120.00	160.00	60.00
2g	Blue dress; brown hair	120.00	160.00	60.00
2h	Blue dress; yellow hair	120.00	160.00	60.00

KNEELING ANGEL CANDLE HOLDER

Size: 58 x 50 mm.
Backstamp: Embossed "Wade"

No.	Description	U.S.$	Can.$	U.K.
3a	Pink dress; brown hair	120.00	160.00	60.00
3b	Pink dress; yellow hair	120.00	160.00	60.00
3c	Yellow dress; brown hair	120.00	160.00	60.00
3d	Yellow dress; yellow hair	120.00	160.00	60.00
3e	Green dress; brown hair	120.00	160.00	60.00
3f	Green dress; yellow hair	120.00	160.00	60.00
3g	Blue dress; brown hair	120.00	160.00	60.00
3h	Blue dress; yellow hair	120.00	160.00	60.00

FAWN MONEY BOX

Circa 1963

This figure is different from "Bambi," a *Disney Blow Up*, and has a coin slot in the back. It is believed that a few other *Disney Blow Ups* were remodelled as money boxes. There are unconfirmed reports of a "Lady Money Box," "Jock Money Box" and "Thumper Money Box," but no visual or written evidence has been found.

Because of high production costs, only a limited number of the "Fawn Money Box" were made.

Size: 120 x 105 mm.
Backstamp: **A.** Unmarked
B. Black transfer "Made in England"

No.	Description	U.S. $	Can. $	U.K. £
1	Brown; orange-brown patches	70.00	95.00	50.00

BENGO MONEY BOX

1965

Only one model from the *TV Pets* series was remodelled as a money box. Because the original model is standing and had no bulk in which to hold coins, it was unsuitable. A new model of a sitting Bengo was created with a round body to contain the money. The coin slot is in the dog's back.

Size: 150 x 140 mm.
Backstamp: Unmarked

No.	Description	U.S. $	Can. $	U.K. £
1	Beige; white on face, feet; yellow basket	325.00	425.00	160.00

KODIAK BEAR

Circa 1965

No one seems to be able to identify the series for which the "Kodiak Bear" was produced or why it was made. It may have been a prototype model produced for the first Red Rose Tea premiums, then rejected due to high production costs (its open arms required more fettling). As a result the "Kodiak Bear" was not put into full production, and any models produced may have been used up in miscellaneous premiums. A second variation of the bear is slightly smaller in size and has a small gap between his legs.

Size: 40 x 25 mm.
Backstamp: **A.** Embossed "Wade England"
            B. Unmarked

No.	Description	U.S. $	Can. $	U.K. £
1a	Beige brown; green base	60.00	75.00	20.00
1b	Brown; honey-brown face, chest, stomach	60.00	75.00	20.00
1c	Light brown; black nose; green base	60.00	75.00	20.00
1d	Red-brown	60.00	75.00	20.00

WHIMSIES DOGS AND PUPPIES

1969-1982

This *Dogs and Puppies* series was advertised and labelled on the boxes as *Whimsies*. The models are of a mother dog and her two puppies, which were produced intermittently between 1969 and 1982. The mother dog was sold in one box and her two puppies in another. The boxes resemble books, and the inside of the lid has a description of the dog's breed printed on it. The first three sets were packaged in blue boxes, the last two sets in red. The original price was 7/6d per box.

ALSATIAN

Set 1 1969-1982

Backstamp: Black and gold label "Genuine Wade Porcelain Made in England"

No.	Name	Description	Size	U.S. $	Can. $	U.K. £
1	Mother	Brown/honey brown	60 x 75	25.00	35.00	8.00
2	Puppy, Sitting	Brown/honey brown	40 x 45	15.00	20.00	6.00
3	Puppy, Lying	Brown/honey brown	35 x 45	15.00	20.00	6.00

CAIRN

Set 2 1969-1982

Backstamp: Black and gold label "Genuine Wade Porcelain Made in England"

No.	Name	Description	Size	U.S. $	Can. $	U.K. £
1	Mother	Honey brown; brown ears, nose	65 x 70	25.00	35.00	8.00
2	Puppy, Standing	Honey brown; brown ears, nose	40 x 50	15.00	20.00	8.00
3	Puppy, Lying	Honey brown; brown ears, nose	35 x 50	15.00	20.00	8.00

RED SETTER

Set 3 1973-1982

Backstamp: Black and gold label "Genuine Wade Porcelain Made in England"

No.	Name	Description	Size	U.S. $	Can. $	U.K. £
1	Mother	Red-brown	60 x 75	25.00	35.00	8.00
2	Puppy, Lying Facing Right	Red-brown	40 x 45	15.00	20.00	6.00
3	Puppy, Lying Facing Left	Red-brown	40 x 45	15.00	20.00	6.00

CORGI

Set 4 1979-1982

Backstamp: Black and gold label "Genuine Wade Porcelain Made in England"

No.	Name	Description	Size	U.S. $	Can. $	U.K. £
1	Mother	Honey brown; brown ears, nose; green base	60 x 60	40.00	55.00	25.00
2	Puppy, Sitting	Honey brown; brown ears, nose; green base	45 x 40	30.00	40.00	18.00
3	Puppy, Lying	Honey brown; brown ears, nose; green base	30 x 45	30.00	40.00	18.00

YORKSHIRE TERRIER

Set 5 1979-1982

Backstamp: Black and gold label "Genuine Wade Porcelain Made in England"

No.	Name	Description	Size	U.S. $	Can. $	U.K. £
1	Mother	Black/brown; honey brown face, chest	55 x 70	50.00	70.00	30.00
2	Puppy, Sitting	Black/brown; honey brown face, chest	40 x 40	60.00	80.00	30.00
3	Puppy, Walking	Black/brown; honey brown face, chest	35 x 45	60.00	80.00	30.00

WHIMISIES DOG DERIVATIVES

DOG PIPE STANDS

1973-1981

The *Dog Pipe Stands* have a mother dog from the 1969-1982 *Dogs and Puppies* series on the back rim of a stand. The original price was 72p each.

Size: 60 x 115 mm.
Backstamp: Embossed "Wade England"

No.	Name	Description	U.S. $	Can. $	U.K. £
1	Alsatian	Brown/honey brown; green stand	30.00	40.00	12.00
2	Cairn	Honey brown; green stand	30.00	40.00	12.00
3	Red Setter	Red-brown; green stand	30.00	40.00	12.00
4	Corgi	Honey brown; green stand	35.00	45.00	15.00
5	Yorkshire Terrier	Black/brown; green stand	40.00	50.00	30.00

CAT AND PUPPY DISHES

1974-1981

The *Cat and Puppy Dishes* is a series of 11 basket dishes with the puppies from the 1969-1982 *Dogs and Puppies* series sitting in them. The only change is the addition of a new model and the first in the series, the "Tabby Cat." With the exception of style 1b, the baskets are coloured in mottled greys and browns. The puppy dishes were packaged in pastel boxes marked "Pup-in-a-Basket" in North America.

Backstamp: Embossed "Wade England"

No.	Name	Description	Size	U.S. $	Can. $	U.K. £
1a	Tabby Cat	Brown stripes	50 x 75	30.00	40.00	15.00
1b	Tabby Cat	Brown stripes; dark brown basket	50 x 75	30.00	40.00	15.00
2	Alsatian Puppy, Sitting	Brown/honey-brown	40 x 75	20.00	30.00	8.00
3	Alsatian Puppy, Lying	Brown/honey brown	35 x 75	20.00	30.00	8.00
4	Cairn Puppy, Standing	Honey brown	40 x 75	20.00	35.00	8.00
5	Cairn Puppy, Lying	Honey brown	35 x 75	20.00	35.00	8.00
6	Red Setter Puppy, Lying, Facing Right	Brown	40 x 75	20.00	30.00	8.00
7	Red Setter Puppy, Lying, Facing Left	Red-brown	40 x 75	20.00	30.00	8.00
8	Corgi Puppy, Sitting	Honey brown	45 x 75	30.00	40.00	15.00
9	Corgi Puppy, Lying	Honey brown	30 x 75	30.00	40.00	15.00
10	Yorkie Puppy, Sitting	Grey/brown	30 x 75	40.00	45.00	15.00
11	Yorkie Puppy, Standing	Grey/brown	35 x 75	40.00	45.00	15.00

ENGLISH WHIMSIES

1971-1984

In 1971, 25 of the original Red Rose Tea Canada models were individually boxed and sold by Wade as a retail line. Unlike their famous forerunners, *First Whimsies*, this series has five models per set, with each figure sold in its own numbered box. The boxes in each set were the same colour (for example, set 1 was dark blue, set 2 was red, etc.). An updated list of models was added to the back of the boxes each year.

A new set was usually issued annually, although on some occasions when demand was strong, two sets were issued per year. A further 35 new models were added to the 25 original Canadian models, making an English series of 60 models.

Note that the "Trout" as it was first issued was unmarked, and the back of the base differs slightly from the second issue, which is marked "Wade England" on the back rim. The "Hippo," "Bison" and "Pig" come in more than one size, due to the replacement of broken dies. In fact there can be slight size variations in all the models listed below.

The black "Zebra" was glazed dark grey with black stripes, but after the first production run through the kiln, it emerged looking black all over, with very few markings to show it was a zebra. The Wade management then decided to change the colour to beige. The black "Zebra" is very rare. The "Bullfrog" is the same model as the Red Rose Tea "Frog," but has been changed from green-yellow to brown. The "Kitten" can be found with or without a backstamp.

English Whimsies was offered as a pocket-money line to children for a price of 2/2d each.

Set 1 Dark Blue Box 1971

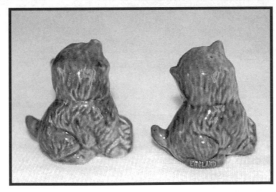

Without backstamp (left), With backstamp (right)

Backstamp: Embossed "Wade England"

No.	Name	Description	Size	U.S. $	Can. $	U.K. £
1	Fawn	Brown; blue ears	30 x 30	7.00	5.00	2.00
2	Rabbit	Beige; ears open	30 x 30	8.00	6.00	2.00
3	Mongrel	Dark brown back; light brown front	35 x 35	7.00	5.00	2.00
4a	Kitten	Dark/light brown; pink wool	30 x 30	6.00	8.00	2.00
4b	Kitten	Dark/light brown; red wool	30 x 30	6.00	8.00	2.00
5	Spaniel	Honey brown	35 x 35	8.00	5.00	2.00

Set 2 Red Box 1972

Backstamp: Embossed "Wade England"

No.	Name	Description	Size	U.S. $	Can. $	U.K. £
6	Duck	Blue/brown, yellow beak	30 x 40	9.00	7.00	2.00
7	Corgi	Honey brown	30 x 35	9.00	7.00	2.00
8	Beaver	Grey-brown; honey-brown face	35 x 45	8.00	6.00	2.00
9	Bushbaby	Brown; blue ears	30 x 30	6.00	4.00	2.00
10	Fox	Dark brown body, tail; fawn brown face, chest	30 x 30	7.00	7.00	2.00

Set 3 Dark Green Box 1972

Backstamp: **A.** Unmarked (15)
B. Embossed "Wade England" (11-15)

No.	Name	Description	Size	U.S. $	Can. $	U.K. £
11	Bear Cub	Grey; beige face	30 x 40	7.00	5.00	2.00
12	Otter	Beige; blue base	30 x 35	7.00	5.00	2.00
13	Setter	Brown; grey-green base	35 x 50	7.00	5.00	2.00
14	Owl	Dark brown; light brown chest, face	35 x 20	8.00	6.00	2.00
15	Trout	Brown; black patch; red tail; grey-green base	30 x 30	8.00	6.00	3.00

Set 4 Yellow Box 1973

Large Hippo (left), Small Hippo (right)

Backstamp: Embossed "Wade England"

No.	Name	Description	Size	U.S. $	Can. $	U.K. £
16	Lion	Light brown; dark brown head, mane	35 x 45	8.00	6.00	2.00
17	Elephant	Grey; black eyes	35 x 28	20.00	15.00	6.00
18	Giraffe	Beige	35 x 35	7.00	5.00	2.00
19	Chimpanzee	Dark brown; light brown face, patches	35 x 35	7.00	5.00	2.00
20a	Hippo	Large; honey brown	25 x 45	16.00	12.00	4.00
20b	Hippo	Small; honey brown	20 x 40	6.00	4.00	2.00

Set 5 Dark Red Box 1974

Backstamp: **A.** Embossed "Wade England" (21, 23, 25)
B. Embossed in recessed base "Wade England" (22)

No.	Name	Description	Size	U.S. $	Can. $	U.K. £
21	Squirrel	Grey; light brown head, legs; yellow acorn	35 x 30	7.00	5.00	2.00
22	Hedgehog	Dark brown; light brown face; black nose	23 x 40	9.00	7.00	2.00
23	Pine Martin	Honey brown	30 x 30	6.00	5.00	2.00
24	Field Mouse	Yellow-brown	35 x 25	12.00	11.00	3.00
25	Alsatian	Grey; tan face	30 x 40	9.00	7.00	2.00

Set 6 Light Blue Box 1975

Backstamp: Embossed "Wade England"

No.	Name	Description	Size	U.S. $	Can. $	U.K. £
26	Collie	Golden brown; green base	35 x 35	10.00	8.00	4.00
27	Cow	Honey brown	35 x 35	12.00	12.00	4.00
28a	Pig	Large; beige; green base	27 x 44	25.00	20.00	10.00
28b	Pig	Medium; beige; green base	25 x 40	15.00	10.00	5.00
28c	Pig	Small; beige; green base	25 x 35	15.00	10.00	5.00
29	Horse	Dark grey; green base	35 x 35	15.00	12.00	4.00
30	Lamb	Fawn brown; green base	30 x 25	8.00	10.00	4.00

Set 7 Orange Box 1976

Backstamp: Embossed "Wade England"

No.	Name	Description	Size	U.S. $	Can. $	U.K. £
31	Rhino	Grey; green base	25 x 35	8.00	6.00	4.00
32	Leopard	Yellow/brown; green base	17 x 45	6.00	8.00	4.00
33	Gorilla	Grey; grey-green base	35 x 25	8.00	8.00	4.00
34	Camel	Light brown; green base	35 x 35	9.00	11.00	4.00
35a	Zebra	Black; faint stripes	40 x 35	75.00	100.00	24.00
35b	Zebra	Light brown; green base	40 x 35	9.00	11.00	4.00

Set 8 Magenta Box 1977

Backstamp: Embossed "Wade England"

No.	Name	Description	Size	U.S. $	Can. $	U.K. £
36	Donkey	Light brown; green base	30 x 30	14.00	18.00	7.00
37	Barn Owl	Light brown; dark brown head, back; blue base	35 x 20	20.00	25.00	7.00
38	Cat	Light brown/ginger; grey-green base	40 x 17	20.00	25.00	7.00
39	Mouse	Beige; grey-blue base	40 x 25	12.00	16.00	7.00
40	Ram	White; grey face; green base	30 x 30	12.00	16.00	5.00

Set 9 Mid Blue Box 1978

Backstamp: **A.** Embossed "Wade England" (41, 42, 43, 45)
B. Embossed "Wade England" in recessed base (44)

No.	Name	Description	Size	U.S. $	Can. $	U.K. £
41	Dolphin	Grey-brown; blue base	30 x 40	25.00	35.00	15.00
42	Pelican	Brown; yellow beak; green base	45 x 40	20.00	25.00	6.00
43	Angel Fish	Dark grey; blue base	35 x 30	15.00	12.00	5.00
44	Turtle	Greenish grey	15 x 50	10.00	8.00	4.00
45	Seahorse	Yellow; grey base	50 x 17	20.00	25.00	7.00

Set 10 Light Green Box 1979

Backstamp: Embossed "Wade England"

No.	Name	Description	Size	U.S. $	Can. $	U.K. £
46	Kangaroo	Dark brown; light brown base	45 x 25	18.00	24.00	5.00
47	Orang-Utan	Ginger	30 x 30	5.00	7.00	4.00
48	Tiger	Yellow	35 x 25	15.00	20.00	5.00
49	Koala Bear	Yellow-brown; black nose; green base	35 x 25	20.00	25.00	9.00
50	Langur	Light brown; dark brown stump	35 x 30	5.00	7.00	4.00

Set 11 Dark Brown Box 1979

Large Bison (left), Small Bison (right)

Backstamp: **A.** Embossed "Wade England" (51a, 51b, 54, 55)
B. Embossed in recessed base "Wade England" (52, 53)

No.	Name	Description	Size	U.S. $	Can. $	U.K. £
51a	Bison	Large; honey brown; dark brown head, mane	32 x 45	14.00	10.00	4.00
51b	Bison	Small; honey brown; dark brown head, mane	28 x 40	7.00	5.00	4.00
52	Bluebird	Beige body, tail; blue wings, head	15 x 35	10.00	8.00	4.00
53	Bullfrog	Brown	15 x 30	25.00	32.00	10.00
54	Wild Boar	Light brown; green base	30 x 40	15.00	12.00	4.00
55	Racoon	Brown; grey-green base	25 x 35	15.00	12.00	4.00

Set 12 Deep Blue Box 1980

Backstamp: Embossed "Wade England"

No.	Name	Description	Size	U.S. $	Can. $	U.K. £
56	Penguin	Grey; white face, chest; yellow beak, feet	38 x 19	25.00	35.00	12.00
57	Seal Pup	Beige; blue base	25 x 37	20.00	30.00	7.00
58	Husky	Grey; grey/green base	35 x 30	20.00	30.00	9.00
59	Walrus	Light brown; grey base	30 x 30	12.00	15.00	3.00
60	Polar Bear	White; black nose; blue base	30 x 30	20.00	30.00	7.00

ENGLISH WHIMSIES DERIVATIVES

ENGLISH WHIMTRAYS, 1971-1984

These *Whimtrays* were made with models from the *English Whimsies* series.

Photograph not available
at press time

Size: 50 x 75 mm.
Backstamp: Embossed "'Whimtrays' Wade Porcelain Made in England"

No.	Name	Description	U.S. $	Can. $	U.K. £
1	Duck	Blue/brown; yellow beak; black tray	20.00	30.00	12.00
2	Fawn	Brown; blue ears; black tray	20.00	30.00	12.00
3	Trout	Brown; black patch; red tail; black tray	20.00	30.00	12.00

NURSERY FAVOURITES

1972-1981

Nursery Favourites is a series of 20 large nursery rhyme and storybook characters. It was issued in four sets of five models, and each set was sold in a different coloured box. The original selling price for each figure was 7/6d.

In 1990 and 1991, five *Nursery Favourites* were commissioned and reissued for Gold Star Gifthouse (see page 201).

Set 1 Dark Green Boxes 1972

Backstamp: Embossed "Wade England"

No.	Name	Description	Size	U.S. $	Can. $	U.K. £
1	Jack	Brown hair, waistcoat; green trousers	75 x 30	40.00	50.00	18.00
2	Jill	Green bonnet, dress	75 x 40	40.00	50.00	18.00
3	Little Miss Muffet	Yellow hair; grey-green dress	60 x 50	40.00	50.00	18.00
4	Little Jack Horner	Green jacket; yellow trousers; brown hair	70 x 40	40.00	50.00	18.00
5	Humpty Dumpty	Honey brown; green suit; red tie	65 x 43	40.00	50.00	18.00

Set 2 Blue Boxes 1973

Backstamp: Embossed "Wade England"

No.	Name	Description	Size	U.S. $	Can. $	U.K. £
6	Wee Willie Winkie	Yellow hair; grey nightshirt	75 x 35	35.00	50.00	16.00
7	Mary Had a Little Lamb	Blue bonnet, skirt; grey-blue jacket	75 x 40	35.00	50.00	16.00
8	Polly Put the Kettle On	Brown; pink cap, kettle	75 x 35	50.00	65.00	24.00
9	Old King Cole	Yellow/grey hat; blue-grey cloak	65 x 50	45.00	60.00	20.00
10	Tom Tom the Piper's Son	Grey hat, kilt; brown jacket	65 x 55	45.00	60.00	20.00

Set 3 Yellow Boxes 1974

Backstamp: Embossed "Wade England"

No.	Name	Description	Size	U.S. $	Can. $	U.K. £
11	Little Boy Blue	Blue cap, jacket, trousers	75 x 30	45.00	60.00	20.00
12	Mary Mary	Yellow hair; blue dress; pink shoes	75 x 45	55.00	75.00	30.00
13	The Cat and the Fiddle	Brown/grey cat; yellow fiddle	70 x 50	50.00	65.00	24.00
14	The Queen of Hearts	Pink crown, hearts; beige dress	75 x 48	55.00	75.00	32.00
15	Little Tommy Tucker	Yellow hair; blue pantaloons	75 x 30	40.00	55.00	20.00

Set 4 Purple Boxes 1976

Backstamp: Embossed "Wade England"

No.	Name	Description	Size	U.S. $	Can. $	U.K. £
16	The Three Bears	Grey; green base	70 x 60	55.00	75.00	30.00
17	Little Bo-Peep	Beige bonnet, dress; pink ribbon	70 x 40	80.00	100.00	40.00
18	Goosey Goosey Gander	Beige; pink beak; blue-brown steps	66 x 55	150.00	175.00	75.00
19	Old Woman in a Shoe	Blue bonnet, dress; brown roof, door	60 x 55	125.00	150.00	60.00
20	Puss in Boots	Beige; blue boots	70 x 30	50.00	60.00	25.00

M.G.M. CARTOON CHARACTERS
TOM AND JERRY

1973-1979

Only two models were issued in the *Tom and Jerry* series, courtesy of Metro-Goldwyn-Mayer. The original price for the set of two models was 95p.

Backstamp: Embossed "Wade England © M.G.M."

No.	Name	Description	Size	U.S. $	Can. $	U.K. £
1	Tom	Blue; yellow/black eyes; pink ears	90 x 55	75.00	125.00	35.00
2	Jerry	Beige; pink ears; green base	50 x 30	75.00	125.00	35.00
—	Set (2)			225.00	275.00	80.00

HORSE SETS

1974-1981

Two sets of horses were produced intermittently between 1974 and 1981. Each set comprised a "Mare" and her two foals. Although the models were sold with black and gold "Wade England" labels stuck on the bases, most of them either peeled off or wore off. But even without labels, the distinctive Wade glaze and their ribbed bases make these models easily recognisable.

Set 1 1974-1981

Backstamp: **A.** Unmarked (1-3)
B. Black and gold label "Wade England" (1-3)

No.	Name	Description	Size	U.S.$	Can.$	U.K.£
1	Mare	Dark brown; light brown face	75 x 76	15.00	25.00	6.00
2	Foal, Lying	Dark brown; light brown face	32 x 55	15.00	25.00	6.00
3	Foal, Standing	Dark brown; light brown face	48 x 48	15.00	25.00	6.00
—	Set (3)			50.00	80.00	25.00

Set 2 1978-1981

Backstamp: **A.** Unmarked (1-3)
B. Black and gold label "Wade England" (1-3)
C. Embossed "Wade England" on rim (1-3)

No.	Name	Description	Size	U.S.$	Can.$	U.K.£
1	Mare	Honey; light brown mane	65 x 70	50.00	70.00	25.00
2	Foal, Lying	Honey; light brown mane	30 x 46	50.00	70.00	25.00
3	Foal, Sitting	Honey; light brown mane	38 x 38	50.00	70.00	25.00
—	Set (3)			150.00	250.00	80.00

LARRY AND LESTER, THE LEPRECHAUN TWINS

1974-1985

Size: 100 x 60 mm.
Backstamp: Black ink stamp "Made in Ireland"

No.	Name	Description	U.S.$	Can.$	U.K.£
1	Larry	Green hat; purple jacket; brown leggings	70.00	120.00	45.00
2	Lester	Yellow hat; green jacket; red leggings	70.00	120.00	45.00

LARRY AND LESTER DERIVATIVES

BOOKENDS

1974-1985

The leprechaun twins were added to a heavy porcelain, L-shaped base to form a pair of bookends.

Size: 115 x 75 mm.
Backstamp: Purple ink stamp "Made in Ireland"

No.	Description	U.S.$	Can.$	U.K.£
1	"Larry" on one base; "Lester" on the other; dark green bookends	250.00	325.00	125.00

LARGE LEPRECHAUNS

1974-1985

Although it appears that these models were in production for over ten years, they are rarely seen.

Size: 70 x 30 mm.
Backstamp: Unmarked

No.	Description	U.S.$	Can.$	U.K.£
1a	Grey-green	35.00	45.00	20.00
1b	Bright blue all over	45.00	55.00	25.00
1c	Brown all over	45.00	55.00	25.00
1d	Green hat; dark brown jacket; beige trousers	45.00	55.00	25.00
1e	Turquoise blue	45.00	55.00	25.00

LARGE LEPRECHAUN DERIVATIVES

LARGE LEPRECHAUN ON CONNEMARA MARBLE BASE

1974

This model is the original 1974 model mounted on a block of Connemara marble. It was intended for the tourist trade.

Backstamp: **A.** Gold label "Real Connemara Marble Made in Ireland"
B. Gold label "Lucky Irish Leprechaun Made in Ireland"

No.	Description	U.S.$	Can.$	U.K.£
1	Dark grey-green; gold label	75.00	100.00	50.00

LEPRECHAUN ON TOADSTOOL WITH CROCK OF GOLD

Circa 1975

This model is of a smiling leprechaun sitting on top of a toadstool with his hands resting on top of a crock of gold.

Backstamp: Black ink stamp "Made in Ireland"

No.	Description	Size	U.S.$	Can.$	U.K.£
1	Grey/brown	125	65.00	85.00	30.00
2	Grey/brown leprechaun; blue toadstool	145	75.00	100.00	50.00

WHOPPAS

1976-1981

Whoppas are the big brothers of *Whimsies* and were in production from 1976 to 1981. They were issued in three sets of five models. The original price was 65p each.

Set 1 Red Box 1976-1981

Backstamp: Embossed "Wade England"

No.	Name	Description	Size	U.S.$	Can.$	U.K.£
1a	Polar Bear	Beige brown; blue base	35 x 55	25.00	35.00	7.00
1b	Polar Bear	White; grey-blue base	35 x 55	25.00	35.00	7.00
2	Hippo	Grey; green base	35 x 50	25.00	35.00	7.00
3	Brown Bear	Red-brown; brown base	35 x 45	20.00	28.00	7.00
4	Tiger	Yellow/brown; green base	30 x 60	20.00	28.00	7.00
5	Elephant	Grey; green base	55 x 50	25.00	35.00	7.00

Set 2 Green Box 1977-1981

Backstamp: Embossed "Wade England"

No.	Name	Description	Size	U.S.$	Can.$	U.K.£
6	Bison	Brown; green base	40 x 50	25.00	35.00	7.00
7	Wolf	Grey; green base	60 x 45	30.00	40.00	10.00
8	Bobcat	Light brown; dark brown spots; green base	55 x 50	30.00	40.00	10.00
9	Chipmunk	Brown; brown base	55 x 40	30.00	40.00	10.00
10	Racoon	Brown; black stripes, eye patches; green base	40 x 50	30.00	40.00	10.00

Set 3 Brown Box 1978-1981

Backstamp: Embossed "Wade England"

No.	Name	Description	Size	U.S.$	Can.$	U.K.£
11	Fox	Red-brown; green base	30 x 60	35.00	45.00	20.00
12	Badger	Brown; cream stripe; green base	35 x 45	35.00	45.00	20.00
13	Otter	Brown; blue base	30 x 55	35.00	45.00	20.00
14	Stoat	Brown; green base	35 x 55	35.00	45.00	20.00
15	Hedgehog	Brown; green base	30 x 50	35.00	45.00	20.00

BABY PIXIE

Circa 1978-1980s

The *Baby Pixie* models can be found free standing, on a circular pin tray or on a shamrock leaf dish. Some pin trays have a 1950s mark on the base, which means they may have been old stock reissued with pixies on them to create new products.

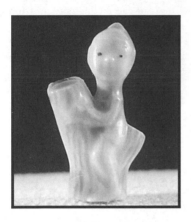 

Backstamp: **A.** Black ink stamp "Made in Ireland" (1)
B. Embossed "Made in Ireland, Porcelain Wade, Eire Tir-Adheanta" (2, 3)
C. Impressed "Irish Porcelain Made in Ireland Co. Armagh" (3)

No.	Name	Description	Size	U.S.$	Can.$	U.K.£
1	Baby Pixie	Blue suit, cap, boots	35 x 10	30.00	45.00	12.00
2	Baby Pixie Pin Tray	Blue suit; blue-green tray	40 x 75	25.00	35.00	10.00
3	Baby Pixie Shamrock Leaf Dish	Blue suit; blue-grey dish	40 x 75	25.00	35.00	10.00

NURSERIES (MINIATURES)

Circa 1979-1980

The *Nurseries* is a boxed set of five models from the Canadian Red Rose Tea *Miniature Nurseries*. For some reason these figures did not sell well to British collectors, so Wade discontinued the intended series with only five models issued. When these figures are out of their boxes, they are hard to distinguish from the Red Rose Tea models. As the *Nurseries* was advertised after the Corgies and Yorkshire terriers from the *Whimsies Dogs and Puppies* series (issued in 1979), the issue date for this series is set during late 1979.

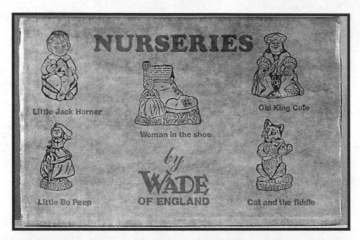

Backstamp: Embossed "Wade England"

No.	Name	Description	Size	U.S.$	Can.$	U.K.£
1	Old Woman in a Shoe	Honey; red-brown roof	40	6.00	4.00	6.00
2a	Old King Cole with Blue Hem	Beige; blue hat; pink sleeves; blue hem	40	6.00	4.00	4.00
2b	Old King Cole without Blue Hem	Beige; blue hat; pink sleeves	40	6.00	4.00	4.00
3	Little Jack Horner	Beige; blue plum; pink cushion	40	6.00	4.00	6.00
4	Little Bo-Peep	Light brown; blue apron; green base	45	4.00	3.00	3.00
5	The Cat and the Fiddle	Beige; yellow fiddle	45	30.00	15.00	9.00
—	Set (5)			50.00	35.00	30.00

WHIMSEY-ON-WHY

1980-1987

Whimsey-on-Why is a series of miniature porcelain houses based upon a mythical English village called Whimsey-on-Why. The highly accurate detail was achieved by the use of fired-on enamel transfers, which included the number of the model in an unobtrusive place. The original price for a set of eight models was £10, or the houses could be bought individually at prices ranging from 79p for a small model to £2.15 for a larger size.

Set 1 1980-Unknown

Set 1 was issued in spring 1980. The original price for "Pump Cottage" was 79p. "Morgans the Chemist," "Dr Healer's House" and the "Tobacconist's Shop" sold for 99p. The "Why Knott Inn" was 89p, "Bloodshott Hall" and "The Barley Mow" were £1.85 and "St. Sebastian's Church" was £2.15. All models are numbered.

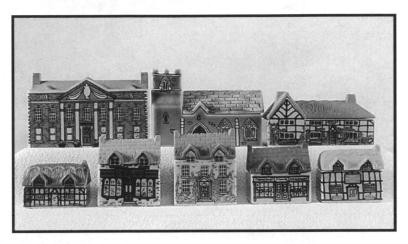

Backstamp: Embossed "Wade England"

No.	Name	Description	Size	U.S.$	Can.$	U.K.£
1	Pump Cottage	Brown thatch, beams	28 x 39	20.00	25.00	5.00
2	Morgan's the Chemist	Grey roof; yellow windows	40 x 39	20.00	25.00	9.00
3	Dr. Healer's House	Brown roof, door	40 x 39	20.00	25.00	9.00
4	Tobacconist's Shop	Brown roof; red doors	33 x 39	20.00	25.00	5.00
5	Why Knott Inn	Beige thatch; black beams	33 x 39	20.00	25.00	6.00
6	Bloodshott Hall	Red-brown; grey roof	50 x 80	20.00	30.00	8.00
7	St. Sebastian's Church	Grey; brown door	55 x 77	25.00	40.00	10.00
8	The Barley Mow	Beige roof; black wood	35 x 77	25.00	40.00	10.00

Set 2 1981-1982

This set was issued in spring 1981. "The Greengrocer's Shop" and "The Antique Shop" originally sold for 99p each. The price for the "Whimsey Service Station" and for "The Post Office" was £1.10. The "Whimsey School" cost £1.50, "The Watermill" and "The Stag Hotel" were £1.85 and "The Windmill" was £2.15.

Backstamp: A. Embossed "Wade England" (9-15)
B. Unmarked (16)

No.	Name	Description	Size	U.S.$	Can.$	U.K.£
9	The Greengrocer's Shop	Grey roof; green windows	35 x 35	20.00	30.00	8.00
10	The Antique Shop	Purple-brown roof	35 x 37	20.00	30.00	8.00
11	Whimsey Service Station	Beige roof; green pumps	40 x 38	20.00	30.00	10.00
12	The Post Office	Beige roof; yellow/blue windows	40 x 38	20.00	25.00	10.00
13	Whimsey School	Brown; grey roof; blue window	38 x 51	30.00	35.00	15.00
14	The Watermill	Red-brown; beige thatch	42 x 66	25.00	35.00	10.00
15	The Stag Hotel	Grey roof; black wood	45 x 66	25.00	35.00	10.00
16	The Windmill	White; copper pin	60 x 30	80.00	100.00	40.00

Set 3 1982-1983

Set 3 was issued in spring 1982. The "Tinker's Nook" originally sold for 89p, the "Whimsey Station" cost 99p, "Merryweather Farm" was £2.15, "The Vicarage" was £1.65, "The Manor" was £1.85, "Briar Row" was £1.95 and "Broomyshaw Cottage" and "The Sweet Shop" were each £1.10.

Backstamp: **A**. Embossed "Wade England" (18-24)
           B. "Wade Ireland" (17)

No.	Name	Description	Size	U.S.$	Can.$	U.K.£
17	Tinker's Nook	Red-brown roof; yellow/white windows	38 x 22	10.00	15.00	6.00
18	Whimsey Station	Red-brown; brown roof; yellow/blue windows	135 x 39	25.00	35.00	15.00
19	Merryweather Farm	Cream; brown roof; blue/yellow windows	48 x 55	50.00	60.00	25.00
20	The Vicarage	Pink; beige roof; blue/yellow windows	41 x 51	55.00	75.00	35.00
21	Broomyshaw Cottage	Beige; brown roof; blue/yellow windows	40 x 40	10.00	10.00	10.00
22	The Sweet Shop	Grey roof; black wood; blue windows	40 x 40	10.00	15.00	10.00
23	Briar Row	Beige thatch; yellow/blue windows	33 x 78	25.00	35.00	10.00
24	The Manor	Red-brown; brown roof; blue/yellow windows	42 x 66	20.00	30.00	10.00

Set 4 1984-1985

Only three new *Whimsey-on-Why* models were released during 1984—"The District Bank," "The Old Smithy" and "The Picture Palace"—the same year Wade Ireland introduced its *Bally-Whim Irish Village* (marketed by George Wade & Son Ltd.). The remaining five models of this set were produced in early 1985.

The original price for the "District Bank" was £1.75, "The Old Smithy" was £1.30 and "The Picture Palace" was £2.35. The original prices for the remaining models are not known.

Backstamp: **A.** Embossed "Wade England" (25-31)
B. Unmarked (32)

No.	Name	Description	Size	U.S.$	Can.$	U.K.£
25	The District Bank	Red-brown; brown roof	43 x 40	15.00	20.00	10.00
26	The Old Smithy	Yellow thatch; black wood	25 x 45	10.00	15.00	10.00
27	The Picture Palace	Black wood; red lettering	45 x 65	20.00	25.00	15.00
28	The Butcher Shop	Brown roof; green/grey front	33 x 25	20.00	25.00	15.00
29	The Barber Shop	Grey roof; green/yellow front	33 x 25	25.00	35.00	20.00
30	Miss Prune's House	Grey roof; black wood; yellow door	38 x 38	10.00	15.00	10.00
31	The Fire Station	Brown roof; red fire engine	33 x 30	15.00	20.00	12.00
32	The Market Hall	Brown roof	35 x 50	15.00	20.00	15.00

Set 5 1987-Unknown

The last *Whimsey-on-Why* set, issued in 1987, comprises four models. This brought the series to a close with a total of 36 models. The original prices of this set are unknown. For similar models see the section on *Whimsey-in-the-Vale*.

Backstamp: Embossed "Wade England"

No.	Name	Description	Size	U.S.$	Can.$	U.K.£
33	The School Teacher's House	Grey roof, walls	38 x 38	20.00	30.00	20.00
34	The Fishmonger's Shop	Brown roof	43 x 27	25.00	35.00	20.00
35	The Police Station	Blue; brown roof	43 x 27	25.00	35.00	20.00
36	The Library	Brown; grey roof	50 x 38	20.00	30.00	20.00

BALLY-WHIM IRISH VILLAGE

1984-1987

Due to the success of the English Whimsey-on-Why models, Wade Ireland introduced a set of eight Irish village houses. Because the Wade Ireland pottery ceased production of giftware in August 1987, only one *Bally-Whim Irish Village* set was made. Each model is marked in a hollow under the base. The model number is on the side.

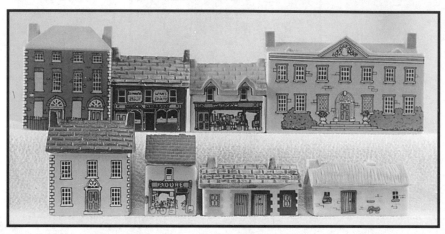

Backstamp: Embossed "Wade Ireland"

No.	Name	Description	Size	U.S.$	Can.$	U.K.£
1	Undertaker's House	Beige; brown roof, door	50 x 38	20.00	30.00	10.00
2	Moore's Post Office	Cream; brown roof	38 x 25	20.00	30.00	10.00
3	Barney Flynn's Cottage	Grey roof; red windows, door	28 x 45	20.00	30.00	10.00
4	Kate's Cottage	Yellow-brown roof	23 x 45	15.00	20.00	10.00
5	The Dentist's House	Dark brown; grey roof; red door	50 x 45	15.00	20.00	10.00
6	Mick Murphy's Bar	Green/grey	35 x 38	25.00	35.00	10.00
7	W. Ryans Hardware Store	Yellow/brown roof	35 x 38	25.00	35.00	10.00
8	Bally-Whim House	Grey; blue roof; honey door	40 x 82	25.00	35.00	10.00

WHIMSIE-LAND SERIES

1984-1988

Although the *English Whimsies* series was discontinued in 1984, George Wade and Son Ltd. continued to produce a range of inexpensive miniature animals, called the *Whimsie-land* series. Five sets of this series were issued between 1984 and 1988. There are five models per set, making a total of 25 figures.

All *Whimsie-land* models were issued in pastel coloured boxes with a complete numbered list of all the models in the series printed on the bottom. All these figures are marked on the back of the base. The original price was 49p each.

Note that the "Elephant" in this series is sometimes confused with the *English Whimsies* "Elephant," as the pose is similar; however, the *Whimsie-land* "Elephant" has open-cast legs.

PETS

Set 1 1984

Backstamp: Embossed "Wade England"

No.	Name	Description	Size	U.S.$	Can.$	U.K.£
1	Retriever	Beige; white face, underparts; green base	32 x 60	10.00	15.00	7.00
2	Puppy	Beige; white face, chest; pink tongue	35 x 36	10.00	15.00	7.00
3	Rabbit	Gold; brown front, base	50 x 25	15.00	20.00	7.00
4a	Kitten	Grey; blue wool	20 x 42	15.00	20.00	10.00
4b	Kitten	Grey; pink wool	20 x 42	15.00	20.00	7.00
5	Pony	Grey mane, tail; green base	37 x 47	15.00	20.00	7.00

145

WILDLIFE

Set 2 1984

Backstamp: Embossed "Wade England"

No.	Name	Description	Size	U.S.$	Can.$	U.K.£
6	Lion	Brown; gold mane; honey base	30 x 50	15.00	20.00	8.00
7	Tiger	Orange-brown; black stripes, base	22 x 50	10.00	15.00	8.00
8	Elephant	Grey; green base	35 x 40	20.00	30.00	8.00
9	Panda	Grey/white; green base	37 x 20	20.00	30.00	8.00
10	Giraffe	Brown; green base	50 x 35	20.00	30.00	8.00

FARMYARD

Set 3 1985

Backstamp: Embossed "Wade England"

No.	Name	Description	Size	U.S.$	Can.$	U.K.£
11	Cockerel	Grey wings, tail; pink comb; grey/green base	50 x 35	20.00	30.00	8.00
12	Duck	Grey back, tail; yellow beak; green base	45 x 35	20.00	30.00	8.00
13	Cow	Black patches; green base	30 x 45	25.00	35.00	10.00
14	Pig	Pink; green base	30 x 35	10.00	15.00	8.00
15	Goat	Grey patch; green base	35 x 35	10.00	15.00	8.00

HEDGEROW

Set 4 1986

Backstamp: Embossed "Wade England"

No.	Name	Description	Size	U.S.$	Can.$	U.K.£
16	Fox	Red-brown; honey face, chest, feet	35 x 35	30.00	40.00	20.00
17	Owl	White; yellow/black eyes	35 x 25	10.00	15.00	7.00
18	Hedgehog	Grey-brown; brown face, paws	25 x 35	10.00	15.00	8.00
19	Badger	Grey; black markings	25 x 35	10.00	15.00	7.00
20	Squirrel	Grey	35 x 25	10.00	15.00	7.00

BRITISH WILDLIFE

Set 5 1987

Backstamp: Embossed "Wade England"

No.	Name	Description	Size	U.S.$	Can.$	U.K.£
21	Pheasant	Honey; grey-blue markings	35 x 50	38.00	50.00	25.00
22	Field Mouse	Brown; yellow corn	35 x 30	38.00	50.00	25.00
23	Golden Eagle	Brown; dark brown rock	35 x 40	38.00	50.00	25.00
24	Otter	Brown; blue base	40 x 40	20.00	30.00	15.00
25	Partridge	White; black beak; green base	35 x 35	20.00	30.00	15.00

WHIMSIE-LAND SERIES DERIVATIVES

NEW WHIMTRAY

1987

During the summer of 1987, Wade produced a set of kidney-shaped trays it called *New Whimtrays*. Because the new *Whimsie-land* animals were used on them, they are often referred to as Whimsie-land trays.

Size: 90 x 110 mm.
Backstamp: Embossed "Wade England"

No.	Name	Description	U.S.$	Can.$	U.K.£
1a	Duck	Black tray	25.00	35.00	10.00
1b	Duck	Green tray	25.00	35.00	10.00
1c	Duck	Blue tray	25.00	35.00	10.00
2a	Owl	Black tray	25.00	35.00	10.00
2b	Owl	Green tray	25.00	35.00	10.00
2c	Owl	Blue tray	25.00	35.00	10.00
3a	Pony	Black tray	25.00	35.00	10.00
3b	Pony	Green tray	25.00	35.00	10.00
3c	Pony	Blue tray	25.00	35.00	10.00
4a	Puppy	Black tray	25.00	35.00	10.00
4b	Puppy	Green tray	25.00	35.00	10.00
4c	Puppy	Blue tray	25.00	35.00	10.00
5a	Squirrel	Black tray	25.00	35.00	10.00
5b	Squirrel	Green tray	25.00	35.00	10.00
5c	Squirrel	Blue tray	25.00	35.00	10.00

KEY RINGS, 1988

After the *Whimsie-land* series and the *New Whimtrays* were discontinued, surplus models were converted into key rings by adding a small chain and a ring. The *Whimsie-land* "Panda" was reglazed in black and white for this series.

Photograph not available
at press time

Backstamp: Embossed "Wade England"

No.	Name	Description	Size	U.S.$	Can.$	U.K.£
1	Badger	Grey; black markings	25 x 35		Unknown	
2	Duck	White/grey; yellow beak	45 x 35		Unknown	
3	Kitten	Grey/white; pink wool	20 x 42		Unknown	
4	Panda	Black/white	37 x 20		Unknown	
5	Puppy	Beige/white	35 x 36		Unknown	

IRISH WHIMTRAYS

Circa 1985

In the mid 1980s, Wade Ireland reissued *Whimtrays*, but as the original mould for the tray was worn, a new one was designed. The plinth on which the figure sits is not gently rounded, as was that of the original George Wade model. Instead it bends much farther out into the dish, making it easy to distinguish the two styles of trays. The figures attached to model numbers 1, 2, 3 and 4 are from the *First Whimsies* series; numbers 5, 6, and 7 were originally *English Whimsies*.

Backstamp: Embossed "Made in Ireland, Irish Porcelain, Wade 'Eire tir a dheanta'" in a circle around a crown and shamrock

No.	Name	Description	Size	U.S.$	Can.$	U.K.£
1	Polar Bear Cub	White; green tray	40 x 77	30.00	40.00	15.00
2	Husky	Fawn/white; green tray	50 x 77	30.00	40.00	15.00
3a	King Penguin	Black/white; black tray	50 x 77	15.00	20.00	8.00
3b	King Penguin	Black/white; green tray	45 x 77	30.00	40.00	15.00
4	Cockatoo	Yellow crest; black tray	50 x 77	30.00	40.00	15.00
5	Fawn	Brown; black tray	50 x 77	15.00	20.00	8.00
6	Duck	Blue/brown; blue tray	50 x 77	15.00	20.00	8.00
7	Trout	Brown; green tray	50 x 77	15.00	20.00	8.00

THOMAS THE TANK ENGINE

1986

Thomas the Tank Engine, based on the storybooks by Reverend Wilbert Awdry and on the British television cartoon, was a very short-lived series. Only two models were produced, "Thomas" and "Percy." They came in two forms, a money-box train and a miniature train. A prototype of "The Fat Controller" has been seen, but the model was not put into production. These four models are very rare.

Backstamp: **A.** Unmarked (1, 3)
              B. Black transfer "Wade Made in England" (1-4)

No.	Name	Description	Size	U.S.$	Can.$	U.K.£
1	Thomas the Tank Engine Money Box	Blue; red markings	110 x 165	275.00	350.00	140.00
2	Thomas the Tank Engine Miniature	Blue; red markings	28 x 40	130.00	175.00	65.00
3	Percy the Small Engine Money Box	Green; red markings	110 x 173	275.00	350.00	140.00
4	Percy the Small Engine Miniature	Green; red markings	28 x 38	130.00	175.00	65.00

MONEY BOXES

1987

In 1987 Wade issued three money boxes based on the earlier "Fawn" and "Noddy Toadstool Cottage" money boxes. Because the original moulds were worn, Wade made new moulds, which produced larger, heavier and less delicate-looking models than the originals. New colours were also used. The model in the "Kennel and Puppy" money box is the "Puppy" from the *Whimsie-land* series, and the "Large Leprechaun" was used on the "Toadstool Cottage." These models were sold in plain, unmarked boxes.

Backstamp: **A.** Black "Wade Made in England (1)
          B. Black "Wade England" on cap that covers hole in base (1)
          C. Unmarked (2, 3)

No.	Name	Description	Size	U.S.$	Can.$	U.K.£
1	Fawn	Light brown; brown markings	130 x 125	35.00	45.00	20.00
2	Kennel and Puppy	Brown roof; honey walls	95 x 125	35.00	45.00	20.00
3	Toadstool Cottage	Brown roof, door, gnome's shirt; green hat	140 x 155	60.00	80.00	40.00

THE DINOSAUR COLLECTION

1993

The *Dinosaur Collection* was issued in the wake of a series of documentary films about dinosaurs and the popular movie, *Jurassic Park*, released in early 1993. The imagination of the public was stirred by the subject, and it sparked the revival of dinosaur exhibits and a subsequent flood of dinosaur toys and models. This set of five models was issued in July 1993.

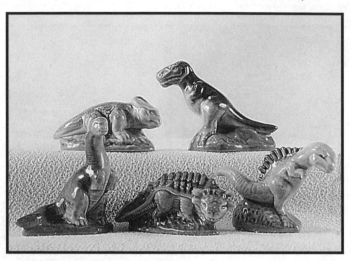

Backstamp: Embossed "Wade England"

No.	Name	Description	Size	U.S.$	Can.$	U.K.£
1	Camarasaurus	Brown/honey	50 x 45	6.00	8.00	4.00
2	Euoplocephalus	Red-brown/beige	28 x 50	6.00	8.00	4.00
3	Spinosaurus	Beige; grey spines	45 x 60	6.00	8.00	4.00
4	Protoceratops	Brown	30 x 50	6.00	8.00	4.00
5	Tyrannosaurus Rex	Brown/honey	50 x 60	6.00	8.00	4.00
5b	Tyrannosaurus Rex	Grey; greenish brown base	50 x 60	6.00	8.00	4.00
—	Set (5)			35.00	45.00	20.00

WHIMSEY-IN-THE-VALE

1993

In 1993 two new sets of houses were produced in the *Whimsey-in-the-Vale* series. Each set consists of five models, boxed individually and not numbered.

The moulds from the *Whimsey-on-Why* houses were used to make the following models in the *Whimsey-in-the-Vale* series:

Whimsey-on-Why Models

Why Knott Inn
Whimsey Service Station
Briar Row
The Fire Station
St. Sebastian's Church
The Barley Mow
The Antique Shop
The Post Office
The Market Hall
The Stag Hotel

Whimsey-in-the-Vale Models

Antique Shop
Florist Shop
Jubilee Terrace
St. John's School
St. Lawrence Church
Boar's Head Pub
Post Office
Rose Cottage
Town Garage
Vale Farm

Set 1

Backstamp: Embossed "Wade England"

No.	Name	Description	Size	U.S.$	Can.$	U.K.£
1	Antique Shop	White; beige roof; green/yellow trim	33 x 39	15.00	20.00	7.00
2	Florist Shop	White; light brown roof; green/yellow trim	40 x 38	15.00	20.00	7.00
3	Jubilee Terrace	White; beige roof; yellow stonework	33 x 78	15.00	20.00	7.00
4	St. John's School	White; dark brown roof; green windows, doors	33 x 30	15.00	20.00	7.00
5	St. Lawrence Church	Grey; green doors	55 x 77	15.00	20.00	7.00

Set 2

Backstamp: **A.** Embossed "Wade England" (1, 2, 3, 5)
         B. Unmarked (4)

No.	Name	Description	Size	U.S.$	Can.$	U.K.£
1	Boar's Head Pub	White; brown roof, windows; yellow doors	35 x 77	15.00	20.00	7.00
2	Post Office	White; dark brown roof; blue doors	35 x 37	15.00	20.00	7.00
3	Rose Cottage	White; beige roof; yellow windows, doors	40 x 38	15.00	20.00	7.00
4	Town Garage	White; beige roof; blue doors, windows	35 x 50	15.00	20.00	7.00
5	Vale Farm	Light brown; grey roof; dark brown beams	42 x 66	15.00	20.00	7.00

CHILDREN AND PETS

1993-1994

Children and Pets is a series comprising three figures modelled by Ken Holmes. Each is a limited edition of 2,500 and numbered on its base. The first model, "Welcome Home," was issued in June 1993, "Fireside Friend" was produced in the latter half of 1993 and "Togetherness" was issued in late autumn 1994. The models have polished wood bases with recessed tops shaped in the same outline as the figure above.

Children and Pets was sold direct from the Wade pottery as a mail order and was limited to two models per customer. The original price was £25.00 each.

Backstamp: Black transfer "Wade Limited Editions [name of model] Modelled by Ken Holmes"

No.	Name	Description	Size	U.S.$	Can.$	U.K.£
1	Welcome Home	Yellow jacket; brown trousers; white/black dog	100 x 125	100.00	135.00	50.00
2	Fireside Friend	Pink blanket; brown or black ears	90 x 110	100.00	135.00	50.00
3	Togetherness	Green skirt, ribbon; white/grey dog	130 x 95	100.00	135.00	50.00

BEAR AMBITIONS

1995

The Bear Ambitions set of six named Teddy Bears was re-issued in 1996 For Tom Smith and Company (the British Christmas Cracker manufacturers) in three different glaze colours for their 'Christmas Time Crackers' series (see page 258).

Backstamp: Embossed "Wade England"

No.	Name	Description	Size	U.S.$	Can.$	U.K.£
1	Admiral Sam	Honey	50	6.00	8.00	3.00
2	Alex the Aviator	Honey	45	6.00	8.00	3.00
3	Artistic Edward	Honey	40	6.00	8.00	3.00
4	Beatrice Ballerina	Honey	50	6.00	8.00	3.00
5	Locomotive Joe	Honey	50	6.00	8.00	3.00
6	Musical Marco	Honey	45	6.00	8.00	3.00

NENNIE SCOTTISH TERRIER

1996

Originally commissioned by Ms. F. Shoop (Ficol), "Nennie" was the first model in an intended series of Scottish dogs issued in a limited edition of 2,000 to raise funds for the STECS (Scottish Terrier Emergency Care Scheme). Unfortunately the series was cancelled and "Nennie," who was modelled on a rescued Scottish terrier, was sold by Wade Ceramics at the Wade Fair in Birmingham in April 1996 for £25.00.

Backstamp: White printed "Nennie produced exclusively for Ficol by Wade," print of 2 Scottie dogs and the edition No. in gold.

No.	Description	Size	U.S.$	Can.$	U.K.£
1	Black; grey streaks; pale blue collar; gold disc	25 x 65	70.00	80.00	40.00

WATER LIFE SET

1997

ALLIGATOR, GOLDIFSH AND WHALE

Backstamp: Black printed (on Whale) and red printed (on fish and alligator) "Wade Made in England"

No.	Name	Description	Size	U.S.$	Can.$	U.K.£
1	Alligator	Green	25 x 65	15.00	20.00	5.00
2	Goldfish	Orange fish; blue grey, orange streaked water	50 x 40	15.00	20.00	5.00
3	Whale	Light blue whale; blue waves	47 x 70	15.00	20.00	5.00

HERMIT CRAB, OCTOPUS AND SEAHORSE

Backstamp: Gold "Wade England" between two gold lines

No.	Name	Description	Size	U.S.$	Can.$	U.K.£
4	Hermit Crab	Orange crab; grey blue waves	30	15.00	20.00	5.00
5	Octopus	Grey octopus; seagreen-blue waves	50	15.00	20.00	5.00
6	Seahorse	Beige seahorse; dark blue waves	30	15.00	20.00	5.00

ANDY CAPP 40TH ANNIVERSARY

1997

To celebrate the 40th anniversary of the *Daily Mirror* cartoon series *Andy Capp*, ade Ceramics produced an Andy Capp and Flo cruet, an Andy Capp teapot and a toast rack with Flo and Andy Capp decal. The complete set could be purchased for £35.00 ($58.00 U.S).

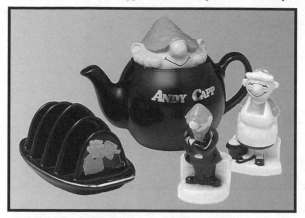

Backstamp: **A.** Printed "Andy Capp © 1997 Mirror Group Newspapers Ltd, Wade" (3, 4)
B. Printed "Andy Capp Andy © 1997 Mirror Group Newspapers Ltd, Wade" (1)
C. Printed "Andy Capp Flo © 1997 Mirror Group Newspapers Ltd, Wade" (2)

No.	Name	Description	Size	U.S.$	Can.$	U.K.£
1	Andy Capp Salt	Light green cap & scarf; black suit; white base	93	17.00	20.00	10.00
2	Flo Pepper	Yellow hair; light green hairband, blouse; black skirt, shoes; white base	103	17.00	20.00	10.00
3	Andy Capp Teapot	Green cap; flesh coloured face; black pot;	132	21.00	24.00	12.00
4	Toast Rack	Black; gold line; multi-coloured print of Flo & Andy Capp	70	14.00	16.00	8.00

MR. & MRS. SNOWMAN CRUET

1997

Backstamp: Unknown

No.	Name	Description	Size	U.S.$	Can.$	U.K.£
1	Mr. Snowman	Black hat, buttons; green white striped scarf	Unknown	12.00	17.00	9.00
2	Mrs. Snowman	Black hat; grey brown collar; brown muff	Unknown	12.00	17.00	9.00

WADE COLLECTOR'S FAIR
AND EVENT FIGURES

Westie, Madison Mouse and Rufus

1st U.S. WADE COLLECTOR'S FAIR —1996

WESTIE

This model of a West Highland terrier was produced for the 1st Wade Collectors Fair, which was held in conjunction with the International Jim Beam Bottles and Specialties Club. It was held at the Red Lion Hotel in Seattle, Washington, on July 6th and 7th, 1996. "Westie" was produced in a limited edition of 3,000 for the show and sold for $20.00 U.S. Unsold models were offered to club members through the Wade magazine.

Size: 75 x 78 mm.
Backstamp: Printed black and red "The Official International Wade Collectors Club," and black "Seattle 1996"

No.	Description	U.S.$	Can.$	U.K.£
1	White; black eyes, nose; pink tongue	55.00	75.00	45.00

2nd U.S. WADE COLLECTOR'S FAIR —1997

MADISON MOUSE

"Madison Mouse," named after Wisconson's capital, was produced for the 2nd Wade Collectors Fair held in conjunction with the International Jim Beam Bottles and Specialties Club in Oconomowoc, Wisconsin, U.S.A., July 12-13th 1997. "Madison Mouse" was produced in a limited edition for the show and sold for $30.00 U.S. Unsold models were offered to club members through the Wade Magazine.

Backstamp: Black and red printed circular "The Official International Wade Collectors Club Wisconson 1997"

No.	Description	Size	U.S.$	Can.$	U.K.£
1	Beige mouse; pink inside ears, tongue; blue eyes; yellow cheese	95 x 60	40.00	55.00	30.00

EVENT DRAW PRIZES

DADDY BEARS — 1997

Special one-of-a-kind Daddy Bears, in different colours from the original were presented in prize draws held at the Trentham Gardens Wade Show in April 1997 and in similar draws held at the July 1997 Wisconson, U.S.A. combined Wade / Jim Beam Fair and at the Arundel Swap Meet in August 1997 where they were also included in the 'Bran Tub' lucky dip. Each "One of a Kind Daddy Bear" came with a certificate of authenticity. Unfortunately records were not kept of the colours of the One of a Kind Daddy Bears, I would be grateful if the owners of these models would contact me at the address listed at the beginning of the book. See page 173 for Goldilocks and the Three Bears.

Backstamp: A. Unknown (1a, 1b)
B. Gold printed "Wade" between two lines (1c)

No.	Description	Colour	Size	U.S.$	Can.$	U.K.£
1a	Daddy Bear (Arundel)	Unknown	105		Rare	
1b	Daddy Bear (Trentham)	Unknown	105		Rare	
1c	Daddy Bear (Wisconsin)	Black hair, glasses, moustache & suit; red & black striped bow tie; red waistcoat; yellow buttons, spoon & plate	105		Rare	

WADE ON TOUR

RUFUS —1997

This model of a Dachshund was the Wade on Tour model for 1997 and was available at all the venues that the International Wade Collectors Club attended during that year. The cost of Rufus was £15.00

Backstamp: Printed "The Official International Wade Collectors Club Wade on Tour 1997"

No.	Description	Size	U.S.$	Can.$	U.K.£
1	Red brown dog; cobalt blue cushion	65 x 84	50.00	65.00	15.00

1st WADE SWAP MEET —1997

ARUNDEL DUCK

A model of a duck was produced by Wade for the first 'Wade Swap Meet' held at Arundel in August 1997 in conjunction with C&S Collectables. The duck was produced in a limited edition of 1,400 in dull yellow and 100 in white. The original cost of the yellow duck was £15.00 and the white duck was £20.00

Backstamp: Printed "O.I.W.C.C." (Logo) and "The Arundel Duck August 1997"

No.	Description	Size	U.S.$	Can.$	U.K.£
1a	Creamy white; light brown beak; blue-green base	95	300.00	400.00	200.00
1b	Dull yellow duck; brown beak; greenish base	95	75.00	100.00	50.00

ARUNDEL AUCTION MODELS —1997

Special 'One of a kind' coloured models were auctioned and given as prizes at the Wade Arundel Swap Meet in August 1997. Anyone having further information on these pieces should contact me at the address listed in the front of the book.

Please see listings under the regular issued pieces for
an illustration of the model.

Backstamps: Printed "Arundel Swap Meet" with O.I.W.C.C. Logo

No.	Name	Colour	Size	U.S.$	Can.$	U.K.£
1a	Arundel Duck	Blue duck; greenish base	95		Since these are	
1b	Arundel Duck	Green duck; greenish base	95	unique, or one-of-a-kind		
1c	Arundel Duck	Orange duck; greenish base	95	pieces, it is impossible		
2	Christmas Teddy Bear	Red hat; white trim; brown bear; blue sack	110	to arrive at a price for guide purposes.		
3	Dick Whittingtons Cat	Unknown	110			
4	Felicity Squirrel	Orange	105	Price must be		
5	Mother Goose	White; green bonnet, ribbon; pearl white bloomers; black shoes; dull yellow beak; red and white striped socks	110	determined between the buyer and seller.		
6a	Pantomime Dame	Blue dress	Unknown			
6b	Pantomime Dame	Green dress	Unknown			
7	Rufus	Red brown dog; green cushion; gold trim	65 x 84			
8	Water Life Goldfish & Whale	Goldfish: white face; orange body; black tipped fin & tail;	50 x 40			
		Whale: unknown	47 x 70			
9	Water Life Alligators	Unknown	25 x 65			

ARUNDEL TREASURE HUNT — 1997

The first prize in the Treasure Hunt was a Betty Boop Classic model in one of a kind colours. See page 184 for a photograph of the model in a different colourway.

Photograph not available
at press time

No.	Name	Colour	Size	U.S.$	Can.$	U.K.£
1	Betty Boop Classic	White moon; pearlised dress; yellow earrings & bracelet; brown "Bimbo" dog	95		Rare	

THE OFFICIAL INTERNATIONAL WADE COLLECTORS CLUB MEMBERSHIP FIGURES LIMITED EDITIONS

1995-1996 and 1994-1995 Membership Figures

1996-1997 and 1997-1998 Membership Figures

MEMBERSHIP FIGURES

THE WORKS CAT "BURSLEM" — 1994-1995

Produced in September 1994 for the Official International Wade Collectors Club, "The Works Cat 'Burslem'" was given free of charge to fully paid-up members during 1994 and 1995. It was modelled on a stray cat living at the pottery, whose favourite sleeping place was underneath the kilns. Burslem died in 1996. This is the first of the Collectors Club models. The cost was £15.00 UK or $32.00 overseas.

Backstamp: **A.** Large embossed "Wade"
            B. Unmarked

No.	Description	Size	U.S.$	Can.$	U.K.£
1	White; black patches	75 x 75	125.00	170.00	85.00

The 'Christmas Puppy' was produced for new and re-newing members of the "Official International Wade Collectors Club" (O.I.W.C.C.) The model was sent free of charge during 1995-1996. Membership cost was £15.00 for U.K. and $32 for overseas members.

Size: 57 mm. long
Backstamp: Embossed "Wade"

No.	Description	U.S.$	Can.$	U.K.£
1	Amber	70.00	95.00	35.00

The Scottie dog was produced for new and renewing members of the "Official International Wade Collectors Club" during 1996-1997. "Smudger" was named in a competition run by the Club. 1996-1997 was the first year that members received an enamel "Wade Official International Collectors Club" badge with their membership. The cost of joining the club for the 1996-1997 year was £18.00 U.K. and $36 U.S. for overseas membership.

Backstamp: Circular white printed "The Official International Collectors Club" red 'Wade' between two lines and white "Membership Special 1996-1997"

No.	Name	Description	Size	U.S.$	Can.$	U.K.£
1	Smudger	Black; grey hair detailing; brown eyes	70	45.00	60.00	30.00
2	Badge	Brass/enamel; black, gold, red design, lettering	29	8.00	10.00	5.00

THE WADE BABY — 1997-1998

The "Wade Baby" was sent free of charge to new and renewing members of the O.I.W.C.C. along with a badge which has a picture of the baby and the words "The Official Wade International Collectors Club." The cost to join the club was £23.00 or $36.00 U.S.

Backstamp: Unknown

No.	Description	Size	U.S.$	Can.$	U.K.£
1	Brown hair, teddy bear; white vest, pants; green shoes; dark blue base	83	36.00	50.00	23.00

LIMITED EDITION FIGURES

SNOWMAN AND SNOW WOMAN —1994-1995

The "Snowman" was produced in November 1994 in a limited edition of 1,000. The "Snow Woman" was produced for Christmas 1995 in a limited edition of 1,500.

Backstamp: **A.** Black transfer "Wade England" (1)
              B. Black transfer "Christmas 1995 Wade Made in England" with two lines (2)

No.	Name	Description	Size	U.S.$	Can.$	U.K.£
1	Snowman	Off white; black hat; dark blue scarf	125	130.00	175.00	65.00
2	Snow Woman	Off white; dark blue scarf; black purse, umbrella	127	70.00	90.00	40.00

Wade produced four models based on the fairy tale, "The Three Little Pigs." The first two figures produced, "The Straw House Pig" and "The Wood House Pig," were issued in a limited edition of 1,250 each. Due to high demand, the production of the next two models was increased to 1,500 each. The original price direct from Wade was £15.00 each.

Backstamp: A. Red print "Wade England" with two lines and black print "The Official Wade International Collectors Club The Big Bad Wolf 1995" (1)
B. Red print "Wade England" with two lines and black print "The Official Wade International Collectors Club House of Brick 1995" (2)
C. Red print "Wade England" with two lines and black print "The Official Wade International Collectors Club House of Straw 1995" (3)
D. Red print "Wade England" with two lines and black print "The Official Wade International Collectors Club House of Wood 1995" (4)

No.	Name	Description	Size	U.S.$	Can.$	U.K.£
1	Big Bad Wolf	Mottled grey; white patch on throat; red tongue; black nose, eyes, claws	101	65.00	90.00	45.00
2	Brick Pig	Pinky beige; red-brown trousers; grey brick wall	130	65.00	90.00	45.00
3	Straw Pig	Pinky beige; dark blue dungarees; yellow straw	123	90.00	120.00	60.00
4	Wood Pig	Pinky beige; brown cap; dark green dungarees; brown wood	117	90.00	120.00	60.00

SNOW CHILDREN — 1996

2,500 Snow Children were produced for Christmas 1996 and were available through the Wade Collectors Club until December 31st, 1996. The model was limited to one per member and cost £15.00 U.K..

Size: 120 mm.
Backstamp: Black Printed "Christmas 1996 Wade Made in England" with two black lines

No.	Description	U.S.$	Can.$	U.K.£
1	White; Boy dark blue hat, scarf; Girl pale blue hat/scarf; beige brown sleigh	60.00	85.00	25.00

GOLDILOCKS AND THE THREE BEARS — 1996

The first figurine in this series was Mummy Bear, and originally the production was intended to be 1,500 of each model but because of increasing club membership numbers the production was increased to 2,750. The cost of each figurine was £15. Two of the Daddy Bear models in a one of a kind decoration were given as door prizes at the Trentham Gardens Wade Fair and at the Wisconson, U.S.A. Wade/Jim Beam Fair held in July 1997. (See page 164).

Backstamp: Circular black & red printed "Official International Wade Collectors Club," Black printed "[name] 1996"

No.	Name	Description	Size	U.S.$	Can.$	U.K.£
1	Mummy Bear	Light brown; white cap,apron; dark blue dress; brown bowl	102	80.00	105.00	55.00
2	Daddy Bear	Light brown; dark blue suit; red bowtie; brown spoon, bowl	105	80.00	105.00	55.00
3	Goldilocks	Light brown chair; yellow hair; pink dress; white socks, porridge; brown spoon, bowl	85	80.00	105.00	55.00
4	Baby Bear	Light brown; dark blue dungarees; white shirt with yellow stripes; white hankie; brown spoon	80	45.00	60.00	30.00

This model of a seal pup on a rock was previously used in the English Whimsies 1980 and the Tom Smith 1992-1996 'Snowlife' series (see pages 126 and 253), the model was re-produced in a new colour for the 'Enrol a Friend' scheme, both the Wade Club member and the new member who enroled in the International collectors Club received a Seal Pup model.

Photograph not available
at press time

Size: 17 x 30
Backstamp: Embossed 'Wade England'

No.	Description	U.S.$	Can.$	U.K.£
1	White seal; blue rock base	5.00	8.00	4.00

OSCAR THE CHRISTMAS TEDDY BEAR — 1997

Backstamp: Printed circular "The Official International Wade Collectors Club Christmas Teddy 1997" with O.I.W.C.C. logo

No.	Description	Size	U.S.$	Can.$	U.K.£
1	Red hat; white trim; honey brown bear; brown ear and paw patches, sack; red, yellow, brown toys	110	38.00	45.00	20.00

A new series of four models was introduced in 1997 for the "Official International Wade Collectors Club" and were available to club members only and limited to one model. The production was limited to 4,000 of each model. The cost of each figurine was £15.

Backstamp: Circular black and red Printed "[Name] The Official International Wade Collectors Club 1997"

No.	Name	Description	Size	U.S.$	Can.$	U.K.£
1	Pantomime Horse	White; black mane, hooves, tail, spots; brown patch	90	40.00	55.00	25.00
2	Mother Goose	White; pale blue bonnet, ribbon, bloomers; black eyes, shoes; dull yellow beak; red and white striped socks	110	40.00	55.00	25.00
3	Dick Whittington's Cat	Grey cat; brown stick & lunch bag; light blue trousers; black boots; beige milestone	110	40.00	50.00	20.00
4	Pantomime Dame	Light blue hair; red cheeks; seagreen-blue dress; white bow; black shoes; red & white bloomers	Unknown	40.00	50.00	20.00

IF YOU OWN THIS BOOK YOU SHOULD BELONG TO THIS CLUB

THE OFFICIAL INTERNATIONAL WADE COLLECTORS CLUB

In 1998 The Official International Wade Collectors Club was founded to offer the Wade Collector information, support and an insight into the world of Wade, without which it would be impossible to build a meaningful collection.

ANNUAL MEMBERSHIP FIGURE

Now each year, these exclusive annual membership figures become collector items in their own right. "The Wade Baby" is the membership model for the 1997-1998 year.

MEMBERSHIP CERTIFICATE

Every new member receives a personalised membership certificate on joining.

This quarterly full-colour club magazine is packed with information on limited editions, club news, Wade fairs and events and "wanted" and "for sale" adverts.

Only club members can participate in purchasing the various club limited edition figures which are offered every year.

Each year a new collector's pin is included free with membership. The 1998 collector's pin features "The Wade Baby."

Royal Works, Westport Road, Burslem,
Stoke-on-Trent, ST6 4AP, England
In U.K. Tel 01782 255255   Fax 01782 575195
Overseas Tel 44 1782 255255   Fax 44 1782 575195

MEMBERSHIP OPTIONS

ANNUAL INDIVIDUAL MEMBERSHIP
(12 months from month of application)

UK Membership £18
Overseas Membership £23 or $36 US

ANNUAL FAMILY CLUB MEMBERSHIP
(12 months from month of application)

UK Membership £60
Overseas Membership £78 or $120 US

A family of 5 can enjoy full club membership
benefits. This is offered for the same payment,
any additional family members will be charged
at full rate. An enrollment fee based on at least four
four. All family memberships can be made in one
application. All additional memberships will
incorporate into the years period.

TWO YEAR MEMBERSHIP
(24 months from month of application)

UK Membership £32
Overseas Membership £42 or $66 US

Receive a series of newsletters that will keep members
informed of new and reintroduced models and wares.
Offer exclusive pieces for sale. Up to date information
regarding the availability of new and current models. You
will also have access to a members only special events.

ENROL A FRIEND

The "Enrol a Friend" scheme is available when
you introduce a new member for a 2 year
membership. Your friend will enjoy all the
benefits of club membership plus you will both
be sent a BONUS GIFT.

MEMBERSHIP APPLICATION FORM

Please enrol me/my family/my friend as a member(s):

Title . . . . . . First Name . . . . Last Name . . . .

Address . . . .

. . . .

Post/Zip Code . . . . Telephone Number . . . .

☐ My cheque for . . . . made to payable to Wade Ceramics Limited is enclosed
(cheques are accepted in Pounds Sterling and US Dollars)

☐ Debit my credit/charge card ☐ Visa ☐ Access ☐ American Express the sum of . . . .

Card No. ☐☐☐☐ ☐☐☐☐ ☐☐☐☐ ☐☐☐☐ ☐☐☐☐ Expiry ☐☐☐☐

Other 3 Family Names (for family membership): . . . .

Enrol a Friend and Both Receive a Bonus Gift

Title . . . . . . First Name . . . . Last Name . . . .

Address . . . .

. . . .

Post/Zip Code . . . . Telephone Number . . . .

My Membership Number . . . .

Friends Signature . . . . Date . . . .

I am/am not a member of the Jim Beam Bottle Club . . . . Number . . . .

Send to:

THE OFFICIAL INTERNATIONAL WADE COLLECTORS CLUB
Wade Ceramics Limited
Royal Works, Westport Road, Burslem, Stoke-on-Trent, ST6 4AP England
In UK: Tel 01782 255255 Fax 01782 575195
From Overseas: Tel 44 1782 255255 Fax 44 1782 575195

PRIVATELY COMMISSIONED MODELS

Robertson's Gollies on Bandstand

BALDING AND MANSELL

FLINTSTONES CHRISTMAS CRACKER PREMIUMS

1965

This set of four miniature comic, prehistoric animals was produced exclusively for Balding and Mansell Christmas cracker manufacturers (later Mansell, Hunt, Catty Ltd.). For other Christmas cracker models, see Great Universal Stores and Tom Smith and Company.

A box of Flintstones Christmas Crackers containing these models was auctioned in 1997 for £35.00.

Backstamp: Unmarked

No.	Name	Description	Size	U.S. $	Can. $	U.K. £
1	Rhino	Beige; blue eyes, ears	20 x 40	15.00	20.00	6.00
2	Dino	Beige; green eyes; black-brown base	35 x 35	15.00	20.00	6.00
3	Bronti	Brown; beige face, feet, base; blue ears	20 x 35	15.00	20.00	6.00
4	Tiger	Yellow-brown; black stripes, nose; brown feet	38 x 28	25.00	30.00	7.00

BRIGHTON CORPORATION

BRIGHTON PAVILION

1988

The *Brighton Pavilion* set consists of a circular pavilion and two oblong pavilions of the famous British landmark, a Turkish-style domed palace built by King George IV as a summer residence in the seaside town of Brighton. The building is now a museum, owned by the Brighton Corporation. The models, commissioned by the Brighton Corporation, were sold in the museum gift shop.

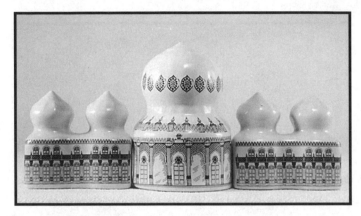

Backstamp: Unmarked

No.	Name	Description	Size	U.S. $	Can. $	U.K. £
1	Circular Pavilion	Blue/black/yellow doors, windows	75 x 53	15.00	20.00	8.00
2	Oblong Pavilion	Blue/black/yellow doors, windows	50 x 53	10.00	20.00	8.00

BROOKE BOND OXO LTD., ENGLAND

1969-1970

After the success of the *Miniature Animals* promotion by its sister company in Canada— Red Rose Tea—Brooke Bond Oxo Ltd. of London (England) offered nine figures from the same set in its 1969 promotion of Brooke Bond Teabags. One model was included in the 72-teabag box and two models in the 144-teabag box.

The first models were so popular that a further six models from Red Rose Tea were added to the series in late 1969 and early 1970, for a total of 15 models. All these figures are in the same colours as the original Red Rose Tea Canada issue. Some of them were later used by Wade in its *English Whimsies* series. They are listed in alphabetical order.

Backstamp: Embossed "Wade England"

No.	Name	Description	Size	U.S. $	Can. $	U.K. £
1	Bear Cub	Grey; beige face	30 x 40	7.00	5.00	2.00
2	Beaver	Grey-brown; honey brown face	35 x 45	6.00	6.00	2.00
3	Bison, Small	Honey brown body; dark brown head, mane	30 x 40	7.00	5.00	4.00
4	Bushbaby	Brown; blue ears; black eyes, nose	30 x 30	6.00	4.00	2.00
5	Butterfly	Green/brown; green tips; raised circles	10 x 45	10.00	8.00	5.00
6	Corgi	Honey brown; black nose	30 x 35	9.00	7.00	2.00
7	Duck	Blue/brown; yellow beak	30 x 40	9.00	7.00	2.00
8	Fantail Goldfish	Green/yellow; blue rock	30 x 35	10.00	8.00	5.00

No.	Name	Description	Size	U.S. $	Can. $	U.K. £
9	Fox	Dark brown; fawn face, chest	30 x 30	9.00	7.00	2.00
10	Frog	Green-yellow/green/yellow	15 x 30	8.00	5.00	3.00
11	Otter	Beige; blue base	30 x 35	7.00	5.00	2.00
12	Owl	Dark brown; light brown chest, face	35 x 20	8.00	6.00	2.00
13	Seal on Rock	Light brown; blue rock	35 x 35	10.00	8.00	5.00
14	Setter	Light brown; grey-green base	35 x 50	7.00	5.00	2.00
15	Trout	Brown; red tail; grey-green base	30 x 30	8.00	6.00	3.00

C&S COLLECTABLES

ARTHUR HARE SERIES

1993, 1996, 1997

C&S Collectables commissioned "Arthur Hare" and "Holly Hedgehog" in late 1993 and "Felicity Squirrel" in March 1996. A limited edition of 2,000 each of the blue-grey "Arthur Hare" and "Holly Hedgehog," modelled by Ken Holmes, were produced, along with 200 of the fawn "Arthur Hare." They are the first of a series of comic animals based on the characters from a British storybook, *The Adventures of Arthur Hare and the Silent Butterfly*.

Felicity Squirrel, modelled by Robert Feather and the third in the series, was produced in a limited edition of 1,250 in grey glaze and 250 in a dark red glaze. Collectors Corner of Colorado, U.S.A. had their name included in the backstamp of six of the dark red models and on 250 of the grey models. Edward Fox, introduced in 1997, is the fourth model in the series and was modelled by Robert Feather.

Backstamp: **A.** Black transfer "Arthur Hare © C&S Collectables Wade England" (1a, 1b)
B. Black transfer "Holly Hedgehog © C&S Collectables Wade England" (2)
C. Black transfer "Felicity Squirrel 1250 Limited Edition © C&S Collectables 1995 Arthur Hare Productions Wade England" between two lines (3b)
D. Printed 'Felicity Squirrel 250 Limited Edition Collectors Corner © 1995 Arthur Hare Productions Wade' with two lines
E. Printed in red "Genuine Wade" (3a)
F. Black printed"Edward Fox 1000 Limited Edition © C&S Collectables 1997 Arthur Hare productions Wade" (4)

No.	Name	Description	Size	U.S. $	Can. $	U.K. £
1a	Arthur Hare	Blue-grey/white; red tongue	130 x 100	75.00	100.00	35.00
1b	Arthur Hare	Fawn/white; red tongue	130 x 100	100.00	130.00	65.00
2	Holly Hedgehog	Beige; brown prickles; grey ball	95 x 70	50.00	75.00	30.00
3a	Felicity Squirrel	Dark red	105 x 68	55.00	80.00	40.00
3b	Felicity Squirrel	Grey; pink cheeks, inside ears; white tail tip	105 x 68	50.00	75.00	30.00
4	Edward Fox	Light orange; pink ears; black eyes, nose, mouth; white muzzle, tail tip, feet	115	45.00	60.00	30.00

ANDY CAPP AND FLO

1994-1995

Produced in early 1994 for C&S Collectables, "Andy Capp" depicts the cartoon character created by Reg Smythe in 1958 for the British *Daily Mirror* newspaper, and which now appears in papers throughout the world. The second model "Flo," Andy's long-suffering wife, was issued in 1995. In styles 1b and 2b, the models have a cigarette hand painted on the face. Only 100 each of these cigarette models were produced.

Size: 75 x 36 mm.
Backstamp: **A.** Black transfer "1994 © Mirror Group Newspapers Ltd C&S Collectables Wade England" (1a, 1b)
 B. Black transfer "1994 © Mirror Group Newspapers Ltd C&S Collectables Wade England Flo 1995" (2a, 2b)

No.	Name	Description	U.S. $	Can. $	U.K. £
1a	Andy Capp	Green cap, scarf; black suit; white hexagonal base	60.00	80.00	35.00
1b	Andy Capp, Cigarette	Green cap, scarf; black suit; white hexagonal base	110.00	150.00	55.00
2a	Flo	Yellow hair; green blouse, shoes; black skirt, bucket; white apron, base	50.00	70.00	30.00
2b	Flo, Cigarette	Yellow hair; green blouse, shoes; black skirt; white apron, bucket, base	110.00	150.00	55.00

WHIMBLES

"Whimbles" (a registered trade mark of C&S Collectables) were first produced for the U.K. Wade Show held at Birmingham on June 11th, 1995. The first Whimble was of Holly Hedgehog.

New Whimbles were introduced at the U.S.A. Wade Show held in Seattle, Washington, July 12-13th, 1996. The 'International Wade Collectors Club' logo Whimble (a World Globe with WADE across it) and the house shaped Whimble of 'Spooners' the collectors shop run by C&S Collectables in Arundel, West Sussex, England were produced in limited editions of 1,000.

The "Seattle Space Needle," "Three Bears" and "Puss in Boots" Whimbles were produced in association with Collectors Corner, (Wade Watch) of Arvada, U.S.A. in a limited edition of 500. 100 of the Seattle Space Needle Whimbles with only the "Needle" print and the Wade backstamp were produced for sale at the Seattle Space Needle complex. All additional Whimbles were produced in limited editions of 500.

Round Whimbles

1995-1997

Backstamp: Red transfer printed 'Whimbles by Wade' with two lines

No.	Name	Description	Size	U.S. $	Can. $	U.K. £
1a	"Holly Hedgehog"	White; gold band; black lettering, print	27	8.00	10.00	4.00
1b	"Felicity Squirrel"	White; gold band; black lettering, print	27	8.00	10.00	4.00
1c	"OIWCC" Logo	White; gold band; black/red lettering	27	8.00	10.00	4.00
1d	"Seattle Space Needle"	White; gold band; blue lettering, print	27	15.00	20.00	5.00
1e	"Betty Boop"	White; gold band; black lettering; black/red print	27	25.00	25.00	12.00
1f	"Arthur Hare"	White; gold band; red lettering; blue print	27	8.00	10.00	4.00
1g	"Whimbles by Wade"	White; gold band; red lettering	27	8.00	10.00	4.00
1h	"The Three Bears"	White; gold band; black lettering; brown print	27	8.00	10.00	4.00
1i	"Arundel Castle"	White; gold band; black lettering; multi-coloured print of castle	27	8.00	10.00	4.00
1j	"Puss in Boots"	White; gold band; ?? lettering; ?? print of cat	27	8.00	10.00	4.00
1k	"Edward Fox"	White; gold band; red lettering; brown print	27	8.00	10.00	4.00
1l	"Wisconsin Mouse"	White; gold band; black lettering; white mouse; fawn cheese	27	8.00	10.00	4.00

House Shaped Whimble

1996

Backstamp: Red transfer printed 'Whimbles by Wade' with two lines

No.	Name	Description	Size	U.S. $	Can. $	U.K. £
2	"Spooners"	White; black/red lettering; black hare; red door print	27	8.00	10.00	4.00

Boxed Sets of Whimbles

1996-1997

In September 1996 the first of specially boxed and numbered Whimbles were sold at the U.K. Wade Show held at Dunstable, Bedfordshire. The sets were issued in limited editions of 25 and sold for £15 for the boxed set of four and £25.00 for the boxed set of six. The sets consist of previously issued Whimbles with the current new design added.

Backstamp: Red transfer printed 'Whimbles by Wade' with two lines

No.	Name	Description	U.S. $	Can. $	U.K. £
1	Dunstable	Whimbles; Betty Boop; Arthur Hare; Spooners; Wade Club Logo; Seattle Space Needle	60.00	80.00	40.00
2	Trentham Gardens	Wade Club Logo; Arthur Hare; Spooners; Edward Fox; Puss in Boots; TheThree Bears	50.00	70.00	35.00
3	Wisconson	Wisconsin Mouse; Seattle Space Needle; Arthur Hare; Edward Fox	35.00	50.00	25.00

BETTY BOOP

1996-1997

Betty Boop was originally created by Max Fleisher in 1931 and was a popular North American Paramount films cartoon character of the 1930s. Betty was usually accompanied by her dog Bimbo. A comic strip cartoon of her was produced by King Features in the mid-late 1930s. Betty Boop cartoons appeared on North American television in the late 1950s and again in the early 1970s. Today she is as popular as ever with American and British collectors.

Betty Boop

1997

The first model in a series of Betty Boops commissioned by C&S Collectables is wearing a red dress. She was produced in a limited edition of 1,500 and sold for £35.00 including P&P direct from C&S Collectables. A limited edition of 500 Betty Boops in a blue dress were produced for the July 1997, Wisconson, U.S.A. Jim Beam/Wade Show. Those models not sold at the Wisconson show in July were sold at the August 1997, Arundel Swap Meet. 200 models were sold in Wisconson and 300 at Arundel.

Size: 95 mm.
Backstamps: A. Black printed circular "© 1996 King Features Syndicate, Inc. Fleisher Studios, Inc. 2000 Limited Edition (C&S) Betty Boop by Wade England" (1a)
B. Black printed circular "© 1996 King Features Syndicate, Inc. Fleisher Studios, Inc. 2000 Limited Edition (C&S) Betty Boop by Wade England" and black printed "Wisconson 1997" (1b)

No.	Description	U.S. $	Can. $	U.K. £
1a	Black hair, eyes, shoes; red dress; white collar, hem; green base	60.00	80.00	40.00
1b	Black hair, eyes, shoes; blue dress; pearlised collar, hem, base	100.00	130.00	65.00

Betty Boop Classic Wall Hanging Figurine

1997

The Betty Boop Classic wall hanging figurine is based on a famous photo of Marilyn Monroe standing on a subway grill with her dress blowing upward, in this version Betty Boop has her dog Bimbo with her and shows a red garter.

Size: Unknown
Backstamp: Black printed circular "© 1996 King Features Syndicate, Inc. Fleisher Studios, Inc. ™ Hearst Corporation. 1250 Limited Edition (C&S) With Certificate of Authenticity Betty Boop Classic by Wade England"

No.	Description	U.S. $	Can. $	U.K. £
2	Pearlised moon; white dress; gold earrings & bracelets; red garter; white & black dog	65.00	85.00	39.95

Betty Boop Christmas Surprise

1997

A special Christmas edition of Betty Boop sitting on a pile of Christmas parcels and with a sack of toys was issued in a limited edition of 2000. The original cost was £39.95 plus £5.00 P&P for overseas collectors.

Size: Unknown
Backstamp: Black printed circular "© 1996 King Features Syndicate, Inc. Fleisher Studios, Inc. ™ Hearst Corporation. 2000 Limited Edition (C&S) With Certificate of Authenticity Betty Boop Christmas Surprise by Wade England"

No.	Description	U.S. $	Can. $	U.K. £
3	Red hat & dress; white trim; black hair & shoes; blue & white parcels; brown sack	65.00	85.00	39.95

THE VILLAGE PEOPLE ARTHUR HARE SERIES

1997-1998

A new series of Arthur Hare models dressed in character clothes and modelled by freelance artist Andy Moss was introduced in December 1997. The first in the series was "Santhare Paws" he was first introduced on the day that C&S Collectables opened their new Collectables shop in Arundel, West Sussex and by telephone the next day. Other models to be produced in 1998 are "Shareriff" a cowboy hare, "Big Chief Bravehare" a North American Indian hare, and "P.C. Gotchare" a British policeman. Each model was issued in a limited edition of 500. The cost direct from C&S Collectables was £30.00.

Backstamp: Printed black and red circular "© 1997 C&S Collectables Limited Edition With Certificate of Authenticity Modelled by Andy Moss Special Limited Edition (C&S) Arthur Hare™ Santhare Paws by Wade England"

No.	Name	Description	Size	U.S. $	Can. $	U.K. £
1	Santhare Paws	Grey hare; red and white Santa coat; brown sack; black belt; pearlised base	124	55.00	70.00	35.00
2	Shareriff	Grey hare; brown hat; red shirt; yellow sheriff's badge; blue trousers	110	45.00	60.00	30.00
3	Big Chief Bravehare	Green feathered war bonnet; red shirt; yellow trousers	115	45.00	60.00	30.00
4	PC Gotchare	Dark blue helmet and jacket; yellow helmet badge brown truncheon	115	45.00	60.00	30.00

CAMTRAK

CHILDHOOD FAVOURITES SERIES

1995-1997

Dougal

1995

"Dougal," a cartoon dog from the British children's television series, "The Magic Roundabout," is the first model of this series, produced for Camtrak of Nottingham, England. It was issued in a limited edition of 2,000 figures. The first 220 models were fired twice, leaving the model with a dark mushroom-coloured face. This "Dougal" is known by collectors as "the brown-faced Dougal." The other 1,780 models were fired once only and have a lighter, pale ivory face.

The original price, direct from Camtrak, was £27.50, which included the cost of postage and handling. Serge Danot and AB Productions SA, indicated in the backstamp, are the owners of the copyright for "Magic Roundabout."

Backstamp: Transfer print "Camtraks Childhood Favourites No.1 Dougal by Wade © Serge Danot / AB Productions SA 1995 Licensed by Link Licensing Ltd."

No.	Name	Description	Size	U.S. $	Can. $	U.K. £
1a	Dougal	Dark straw-coloured body; mushroom face; black eyes, nose; red tongue	84 x 155	75.00	100.00	40.00
1b	Dougal	Dark straw-coloured body; pale ivory face;	84 x 155	60.00	80.00	30.00

Rupert Bear

1996

Rupert Bear was created by Mary Tourtel and was featured in a British Daily Newspaper as well as childrens books from the 1950s to the present. Rupert is the second in the Childhood Favourites series. He was produced in a limited edition of 1,900 green based models and 100 models with a gold base. The original price was £30.00.

Size: 130 mm.
Backstamp: Printed " Camtrak's Childhood Favourites by Wade No 2 Rupert © 1996 Express Newspapers plc Licensed by A.H.E/Nelvana"

No.	Description	U.S. $	Can. $	U.K. £
1a	White head; black eyes, nose; yellow/black checked scarf & trousers; red jacket; green base	90.00	120.00	60.00
1b	White head; black eyes, nose; yellow/black checked scarf & trousers; red jacket; gold base	275.00	370.00	185.00

Paddington Bear

1997

Paddington Bear, who was created by Michael Bond made his debut in 1958. He is the third model in the Childhood favourites series commissioned by Camtrak. The original price was £33.00.

Backstamp: Printed "Camtrak's Childhood Favourites No 3 Paddington © Paddington and Company LTD 1997 Licensed by Copyrights Wade Made in England"

No.	Description	Size	U.S. $	Can. $	U.K. £
1a	Red hat/boots; royal blue coat; white label; brown suitcase; grey base	90	70.00	95.00	48.00
1b	Red hat/boots; royal blue coat; white label; brown suitcase; gold base	90	225.00	300.00	150.00

DRACULA

1997

Wade produced Dracula in conjunction with "Nexus" a subsidiary name used by Camtrak, as Dracula was deemed too much of a contrast to Camtrak's cute "Childhood Favourites" series. Dracula was produced in the centenary year of the famous Bram Stoker character. The model which is standing on a wooden plinth was sold in a special 'window' shaped gift box. The production was limited to 2,500 models. Wade marketed 1,250 models in a matt glaze and Nexus (Camtrak) marketed 1,250 models in a high gloss glaze. The original cost was £85.00 for club members and £90.00 for non-members.

Size: 254 mm.
Backstamp: Unknown

No.	Description	U.S. $	Can. $	U.K. £
1a	Black hair, cloak; red lining (gloss)	150.00	180.00	90.00
1b	Black hair, cloak; red lining (matt)	150.00	180.00	90.00

RUPERT AND THE SNOWMAN

1998

This is the first in an intended series of "seasonal" models, the second model due for release in winter 1998 will be a Paddington Bear 40th anniversary special entitled "Paddingtons Snowy Day," the third in the series is to be a "Thomas The Tank Engine" model entitled "Thomas Gets Stuck in The Snow."

Photograph not available
at press time

Size: Unknown
Backstamp: Unknown

No.	Description	U.S. $	Can. $	U.K. £
1	Unknown		Unknown	

SOOTY AND SWEEP 50TH ANNIVERSARY

1998

Sooty and Sweep, who were glove puppets operated by Harry Corbett, were featured on a BBC children's program from 1950 to the 1980s. Camtrak has commissioned Sooty and Sweep figures to be produced in a limited edition of 2,000 and released in the spring of 1998.

Photograph not available
at press time

Backstamp: Unknown

No.	Description	U.S. $	Can. $	U.K. £
1a	Sooty (Teddy Bear)	Unknown		
1b	Sweep (Long-eared Dog)	Unknown		

PADDINGTON BEAR 40TH ANNIVERSARY

1998

1998 marks the 40th anniversary of Paddington Bear's arrival from Peru. Camtrak has commissioned a limited edition piece of 2,000 to be released for the occassion.

Photograph not available
at press time

Backstamp: Unknown

No.	Description	U.S. $	Can. $	U.K. £
1	Unknown	Unknown		

CARRYER CRAFT OF CALIFORNIA

PAINTED LADIES

1984-1986

The beautiful Victorian houses of San Francisco survived the 1906 earthquake, but by the 1960s they had deteriorated badly. A few owners then decided to repaint their homes in the flamboyant colours of the original era, and the Painted Ladies were reborn.

George Wade & Son Ltd. was commissioned by Carryer Craft of California (Iris Carryer was the elder daughter of Sir George Wade) to reproduce the Painted Ladies in porcelain. Because this short-lived series was made for export to the United States, only a very limited quantity were released onto the British market.

All models are marked with "Wade England" in black on their side walls. The boxed set comprises six models, but the "Pink Lady," "Brown Lady," "White Lady" and the "Cable Car" are the most difficult to find. The original price was £10 for a box of eight models.

Backstamp: Black transfer "Wade Porcelain England SF/[number of model]"

No.	Name	Description	Size	U.S. $	Can. $	U.K. £
SF/1	Pink Lady	Pink; black roof	55 x 25	65.00	85.00	40.00
SF/2	White Lady	White; grey roof	55 x 25	65.00	85.00	40.00
SF/3	Brown Lady	Brown; beige roof	65 x 30	65.00	85.00	40.00
SF/4a	Yellow Lady	Yellow; grey roof; black apex	63 x 30	60.00	80.00	35.00
SF/4b	Yellow Lady	Yellow; grey roof; blue apex	63 x 30	60.00	80.00	35.00
SF/5	Blue Lady	Blue; grey roof	70 x 38	60.00	80.00	35.00
SF/6a	Cable Car	Blue/green; red front; Fisherman's Wharf	20 x 38	90.00	120.00	55.00
SF/6b	Cable Car	Blue/green; yellow front; Dewars White Label	20 x 38	90.00	120.00	55.00

CIBA GEIGY

1969

In 1969 George Wade was commissioned by the British drug company Ciba Geigy to produce models of tortoises with the words *Slow Fe* and *Slow K* on their backs. These models were never issued as a retail line, but were presented to general practitioners by Ciba Geigy sales representatives as a promotional novelty to assist in marketing their iron and potassium preparations, Slow Fe (slow-release iron) and Slow K (slow-release potassium).

Approximately ten thousand of these models were produced. Wade retooled the "Medium (Mother)" tortoise from the *Tortoise Family* by embossing either the name Slow Fe or Slow K in the top shell.

Size: 35 x 75 mm.
Backstamp: Embossed "Wade Porcelain Made in England"

No.	Name	Description	U.S. $	Can. $	U.K. £
1	Slow Fe	Brown; blue markings	100.00	125.00	45.00
2	Slow K	Brown; blue markings	100.00	125.00	45.00

THE COLLECTOR

IN THE FOREST DEEP SERIES

1997

This new series commissioned by The Collector, of Church Street, London is of British animals Oswald Owl, Morris Mole and Santa Hedgehog. The models were first seen at the October 1997 Dunstable Wade show. Oswald and Morris were issued in limited editions of 1,000 and Santa was issuded in a limited edition of 2,000. The original cost per figure was £39.00 plus £2.00 for overseas airmail.

Backstamp: **A.** Printed "In The Forest Deep Series [name of model] for The Collector London Limited Edition of 1000 Wade"
B. Printed "In The Forest Deep Series Santa Hedgehog for The Collector London Limited Edition of 2000 Wade"

No.	Name	Description	Size	U.S. $	Can. $	U.K. £
1	Oswald Owl	Black mortar hat; dark brown back, brows, wings, log; light brown body; olive green base	113	60.00	80.00	39.00
2	Morris Mole	Grey body; buff chin, front, earthworms; brown mole hill; green base	105	60.00	80.00	39.00
3	Santa Hedgehog	Red & white Santa suit; black eyes, nose, belt, boots; light brown spines, face, paws; brown tree stump; buff toy sack; white snow base	132	60.00	80.00	39.00

E. AND A. CRUMPTON

THE LONG ARM OF THE LAW

1993-1995

The Long Arm Of The Law set was commissioned and designed by Elaine and Adrian Crumpton and modelled by Ken Holmes, for a limited edition of 2,000 each. "The Burglar" was issued in June 1993, the "Policeman" the following October, the "Barrister" in August 1994 and the "Prisoner" in June 1995. The prisoner was produced with black hair and brown hair. The first 400 "Policeman" models have impressed faces, due to production problems; the next 1,600 have hand-painted faces.

A mislaid "Policeman" mould resulted in the unauthorized production of a black-suited earthenware version which has an embossed Wade backstamp but was not produced by Wade Ceramics.

Painted Face (left)   Impressed Face (right)

Backstamp: **A.** Large embossed "Wade" (1)
B. Embossed "Wade" (2a, 2b, 4a, 4b)
C. Red transfer "Wade Made in England" (3)

No.	Name	Description	Size	U.S. $	Can. $	U.K. £
1	The Burglar	Black/white top; black cap, mask, shoes	85	50.00	70.00	40.00
2a	Policeman	Impressed face; dark blue uniform	90	80.00	105.00	55.00
2b	Policeman	Painted face; dark blue uniform	90	55.00	75.00	35.00
3	Barrister	Black gown, shoes; grey trousers	80	60.00	80.00	30.00
4a	Prisoner	Black hair, ball, chain; white suit with black arrows; grey shoes	70	60.00	80.00	30.00
4b	Prisoner	Brown hair; black ball, chain; white suit with black arrows; grey shoes	70	90.00	120.00	50.00

PETER ELSON

GINGERBREAD CHILDREN

1996

A hollow model of the "Gingerbread Children" (a waving girl & boy) was commissioned by Peter Elson, U.K. following the success of the 1995 "Giant Gingerbread Man." Produced in a limited edition of 2,000 they were sold at the Dunstable Wade show in September 1996 at an original cost of £15.00 each.

Size: 884 x 884 mm.
Backstamp: Embossed "Wade"

No.	Description	U.S. $	Can. $	U.K. £
1	Brown; dark green base	65.00	85.00	45.00

G&G COLLECTABLES

SCOOBY-DOO

1994

"Scooby-Doo" was commissioned by G&G Collectables for a limited edition of 2,000 numbered models.

Size: 115 x 85 mm.
Backstamp: Black transfer "© H/B Inc Scooby-Doo Limited Edition of 2,000 Wade England G & G Collectables"

No.	Description	U.S. $	Can. $	U.K. £
1	Brown; black spots; blue collar; gold medallion	85.00	110.00	45.00

SCRAPPY DOO

1995

This model was issued in a limited edition of 2,000. The original price was £29.95.

Size: Unknown
Backstamp: Transfer print "© H/B Inc Scrappy Doo Limited Edition of 2,000 Wade England G&G Collectables"

No.	Description	U.S. $	Can. $	U.K. £
1	Brown; black nose, eyes; blue collar; yellow medallion; green base	75.00	110.00	45.00

YOGI BEAR AND BOO BOO

1997

Hanna Barbera's cartoon 'Yogi Bear' was produced in a limited edition of 1,500 in early 1997 for G & G Collectables. Boo Boo, the second model in the series, was available in late 1997. The original cost of both models was £34.00 plus £3.00 postage for overseas collectors.

Backstamp: **A.** Printed Black printed "Wade England Yogi Bear" "©1997 H.B.Prod Inc Worldwide Edition of 1500 G&G Collectables"

B. Printed Black printed "Wade England Boo Boo" "©1997 H.B.Prod Inc Worldwide Edition of 1500 G&G Collectables"

No.	Name	Description	Size	U.S. $	Can. $	U.K. £
1	Yogi Bear	Dark brown bear; green hat, tie; white collar; dark blue waistcoat; brown picnic basket, tree stump; green and white base	130	55.00	70.00	35.00
2	Boo Boo	Brown bear; black eyes, nose, bow tie & waistcoat; white honey pot; light brown tree stump	114	55.00	70.00	35.00

MR. JINKS

1997

Mr Jinks a Hanna-Barbera cartoon character of the late 1950s-1960s was commissioned by G&G Collectables and first seen at the October 1997 Dunstable Wade Show. Mr Jinks, who was modelled by Ken Holmes, will be joined sometime in 1998 by Pixie and Dixie to make a set of three.

Backstamp: Unknown

No.	Name	Description	Size	U.S. $	Can. $	U.K. £
1	Mr Jinks	Orange cat; black eyes & nose; blue bow tie; yellow cheese; white base	Unknown	75.00	100.00	50.00

SANTA CLAUS

1997

This model of Santa Claus in a chimney was commissioned by G&G Collectables in a limited edition of 1,000 and was modelled by Nigel Weaver. The cost direct from G&G Collectables was £36.00 + £1.50 P&P.

Backstamp: Unknown

No.	Name	Description	Size	U.S. $	Can. $	U.K. £
1	Santa Claus	Red and white hat and jacket; black belt and gloves; grey chimney; white snow	133	55.00	75.00	36.00

GAMBLE AND STYLES

MR. PUNCH AND JUDY

1996, 1997

A model of Mr. Punch sitting on a white drum was commissioned by Peggy Gamble and Sue Styles in a limited edition of 2,000; 1,800 are dressed in burgundy and 200 are in green. The model was sold at the 3rd Wade Collectors Fair, held in Birmingham, England, in 1996, for a cost of £45.00. Each figure is numbered and issued with a matching, numbered card signed by Gamble and Styles. A corgi is on the card and backstamp because the two women breed these dogs.

This beautifully modelled figure of Judy is the second in a limited edition series commissioned by Peggy Gamble and Sue Styles, Judy is seated and holding a baby on her lap. Judy was issued in a limited edition of 1,800 models. The original issue price was £42.00. The signature of modeller Ken Holmes is included in the backstamp.

Backstamp: **A.** Black transfer outline of a corgi, "P&S" stamped on the body, "Wade" between two black lines and the issue number (1)

B. Black transfer outline of a Corgi, "P&S" stamped on the body, "Modelled by K Holmes Wade" and the issue number (2)

No.	Name	Description	Size	U.S. $	Can. $	U.K. £
1a	Mr. Punch	Burgundy hat, suit; white ruff; yellow hat tassel, socks; black stick, shoes; white drum	165	95.00	125.00	45.00
1b	Mr. Punch	Green hat, suit; white ruff, yellow hat tassel, socks; black stick, shoes; white drum	165	95.00	125.00	45.00
2	Judy	White mop cap, collar & cuffs; black string bow; pale blue dress; baby in white cap & gown	150	95.00	125.00	45.00

GENERAL FOODS

A planned promotion for General Foods of England that included miscellaneous animals of two or three colours and *Miniature Nursery Rhymes* characters in one-colour glazes was cancelled before it began. A number of models that had been intended for the promotion were released onto the market for a short time in late 1990.

MISCELLANEOUS ANIMALS

1990

TS: Tom Smith   EW: *English Whimsies*   WL: *Whimsie-land* series

Photograph not available
at press time

Backstamp: Embossed "Wade England"

No.	Name	Description	Size	U.S. $	Can. $	U.K. £
1	Badger (TS British Wildlife)	Light grey/white; green base	25 x 40	10.00	12.00	4.00
2	Chimpanzee (EW)	Olive/green-brown	35 x 35	12.00	15.00	6.00
3	Owl (WL)	White; orange beak; green base	35 x 25	10.00	15.00	7.00
4	Panda (WL)	Black/white	37 x 20	20.00	30.00	8.00
5	Penguin (TS 1987)	Black/white; orange beak	45 x 17	10.00	12.00	4.00
6	Rabbit (EW)	White; pinky beige; pink nose	30 x 30	8.00	6.00	2.00
7	Zebra (EW)	Black; green grass	40 x 35	9.00	11.00	4.00

MINIATURE NURSERY RHYMES

1990

These models are all in one colour.

Photograph not available
at press time

Backstamp: Embossed "Wade England"

No.	Name	Description	Size	U.S. $	Can. $	U.K. £
1	Jack	Beige	35 x 35	6.00	8.00	4.00
2	Jill	Beige	35 x 35	6.00	8.00	4.00
3	Little Bo-Peep	Green	45 x 25	10.00	12.00	6.00
4	Little Jack Horner	Beige	40 x 20	6.00	8.00	4.00
5	Mother Goose	Beige	40 x 32	6.00	8.00	4.00
6	Old King Cole	Light blue	40 x 35	15.00	20.00	10.00
7	Old Woman Who Lived in a Shoe	Beige	40 x 40	6.00	8.00	4.00
8	Pied Piper	Green	50 x 30	10.00	12.00	6.00
9	Red Riding Hood	Pink	45 x 20	10.00	12.00	6.00
10	Tom the Piper's Son	Blue	40 x 35	15.00	20.00	10.00
11	Wee Willie Winkie	Blue	45 x 25	15.00	20.00	10.00

GOLD STAR GIFTHOUSE

NURSERY FAVOURITES

1990-1991

Only five of the original 20 *Nursery Favourites* models were reissued for the Gold Star Gifthouse, a California Wade dealer. The last two models are the hardest to find of the original *Nursery Favourites*.

Backstamp: A. Embossed "Wade England 1990" (1, 2, 3)
B. Embossed "Wade England 1991" and ink stamp "GSG" (4)
C. Embossed "Wade England 1991" (5)

No.	Name	Description	Size	U.S. $	Can. $	U.K. £
1	Mary Mary	Brighter than original; blue dress; yellow hair; pink shoes; green base	75 x 45	35.00	45.00	15.00
2	Polly Put the Kettle On	Same colours as original; brown; pink cap, kettle	75 x 35	35.00	45.00	15.00
3	Tom Tom the Piper's Son	Brighter than original; blue-grey kilt; yellow/honey jacket	65 x 55	35.00	45.00	15.00
4	Old Woman in a Shoe	Blue bonnet, dress; beige dog, door	60 x 55	50.00	60.00	35.00
5	Goosey Goosey Gander	Same as original; beige; pink beak	66 x 55	35.00	45.00	40.00

GRANADA TELEVISION

CORONATION STREET HOUSES

1988-1989

The *Coronation Street Houses* set was commissioned by Granada Television as a promotional item for its long-running television series, "Coronation Street," and sold at the studio gift shop and by mail order. Only three models of the set were produced, although others were planned. The figures are very similar to the *Whimsey-on-Why* houses. They were sold on cards with details of the series printed on the back.

Backstamp: Embossed "Wade England"

No.	Name	Description	Size	U.S. $	Can. $	U.K. £
1	Alfs Corner Shop	Brown; grey roof	45 x 33	20.00	25.00	10.00
2	No:9 The Duckworths	Yellow/grey windows, door	45 x 33	20.00	25.00	10.00
3	The Rovers Return	Brown; grey roof	45 x 48	20.00	25.00	10.00

GREAT UNIVERSAL STORES

For a number of years, Tom Smith and Company marketed a line of Christmas crackers through Great Universal Stores (G.U.S.).

SNOW LIFE

Set 1 1993-1994

The Tom Smith *Snow Animals* series was reissued for G.U.S., with the addition of the Tom Smith *Survival Animals* "Whale" in grey and the Red Rose *Miniature Nurseries* "Goosey Goosey Gander," coloured white and renamed the "Snow Goose." The reindeer model can be found with or without a gap between the legs.

Although there are ten models in this set, the box only contains eight crackers. This can cause problems for collectors wishing to complete a set and will cause a future rise in price for some figures. The following initials indicate the origin of the models:

TS: Tom Smith
WL: *Whimsie-land* series

EW: *English Whimsies*
RR: Red Rose *Miniature Nurseries*

Backstamp: Embossed "Wade England"

No.	Name	Description	Size	U.S.$	Can.$	U.K.£
1	Hare (TS)	White	45 x 33	15.00	20.00	3.00
2	Fox (WL)	Red-brown	35 x 36	15.00	20.00	3.00
3	Polar Bear (EW)	White	27 x 45	10.00	12.00	4.00
4	Owl (WL)	White	35 x 25	15.00	20.00	3.00
5	Walrus (EW)	Beige	34 x 36	12.00	15.00	3.00
6	Penguin (EW)	Blue-grey	49 x 21	15.00	20.00	3.00
7	Seal Pup (EW)	Blue-grey	26 x 39	15.00	20.00	3.00
8	Reindeer (TS)	Beige	34 x 35	15.00	20.00	3.00
9	Whale (TS)	Grey	22 x 52	15.00	20.00	3.00
10	Snow Goose (RR)	White	33 x 37	12.00	15.00	3.00

ENDANGERED SPECIES

Set 2 1994

The following initials indicate the origin of the models:

EW: *English Whimsies*　　　　　　TS: Tom Smith
WL: *Whimsie-land* series

Backstamp: Embossed "Wade England"

No.	Name	Description	Size	U.S.$	Can.$	U.K.£
1	Tiger (EW)	Honey brown	37 x 30	15.00	20.00	5.00
2	Cockatoo (TS)	Green	41 x 47	8.00	10.00	3.00
3	Rhino (EW)	Grey	25 x 43	8.00	6.00	4.00
4	Leopard (EW)	Honey brown	20 x 47	6.00	8.00	4.00
5	Gorilla (EW)	Brown	37 x 28	4.00	6.00	3.00
6	Orang-Utan (EW)	Brown	30 x 34	5.00	7.00	4.00
7	Koala Bear (EW)	Beige	35 x 29	6.00	9.00	4.00
8	Polar Bear (EW)	White	27 x 45	10.00	12.00	4.00
9	Whale (TS)	Grey	22 x 52	8.00	10.00	4.00
10	Fox (WL)	Light brown	35 x 36	8.00	10.00	10.00

TALES FROM THE NURSERY

Set 3 1994-1995

Also reissued for G.U.S. was the Tom Smith *Tales from the Nurseries* set. There are slight colour variations from the previous set in "Hickory Dickory Dock," "Little Bo-Peep," "Humpty Dumpty," "Queen of Hearts," "Little Jack Horner" and "Ride a Cock Horse." The remaining models are the same colour as before. The following initials indicate the origin of the models:

RR: Red Rose Tea   TS: Tom Smith

Backstamp: Embossed "Wade England"

No.	Name	Description	Size	U.S.$	Can.$	U.K.£
1	Hickory Dickory Dock (RR)	Beige	45 x 20	8.00	10.00	3.00
2	Little Bo Peep (RR)	Purple	45 x 25	8.00	10.00	3.00
3	Humpty Dumpty (RR)	Blue-grey	35 x 23	8.00	10.00	3.00
4	The Cat and the Fiddle (RR)	Beige front; grey back; yellow fiddle	47 x 31	8.00	10.00	3.00
5	Dr. Foster (RR)	Dark brown	45 x 30	8.00	10.00	3.00
6	Queen of Hearts (RR)	Apricot	43 x 25	8.00	10.00	4.00
7	Little Jack Horner (RR)	Honey	38 x 20	8.00	10.00	3.00
8	Little Boy Blue (TS)	Blue	41 x 25	10.00	12.00	4.00
9	Tom Tom the Piper's Son (RR)	Honey; blue-grey tam, kilt	40 x 34	8.00	10.00	3.00
10	Ride a Cock Horse (TS)	Green	36 x 41	10.00	12.00	4.00

MISCELLANEOUS MODELS

Set 4

EW: *English Whimsies*   TS: Tom Smith

Backstamp: Unknown

No.	Name	Description	Size	U.S.$	Can.$	U.K.£
1	Beaver (EW)	Dark brown	35 x 45	8.00	6.00	2.00
2	Camel (EW)	Beige	35 x 55	9.00	11.00	4.00
3	Circus lion (TS)	Honey	40 x 22	5.00	12.00	4.00
4	Giraffe (EW)	Beige	35 x 35	7.00	5.00	2.00
5	Langur (EW)	Dark brown	35 x 30	5.00	7.00	4.00
6	Pine marten (EW)	Honey	34 x 34	6.00	5.00	2.00
7	Pony (TS)	Beige	25 x 30	10.00	12.00	4.00
8	Puppy (TS)	Honey	25 x 30	10.00	12.00	4.00
9	Racoon (EW)	Light brown	25 x 35	15.00	12.00	4.00
10	Zebra (EW)	Grey	40 x 35	9.00	11.00	4.00

HARRODS OF KNIGHTSBRIDGE

DOORMAN EGG CUP, MONEY BOX, CRUET AND COOKIE JAR

1991-1996

These models were produced for Harrods of Knightsbridge. The egg cups, produced in 1991, are in the shape of a Harrods doorman and were sold in the store at Easter, packaged with miniature chocolate eggs, and at Christmas, filled with sweets or sugared almonds. The money box, issued in 1993, is the same shape as the egg cups, only larger. Its original selling price at Harrods was £16.95. The cookie jar was released in 1996 and features a younger looking doorman.

Backstamp: Black transfer "Harrods Knightsbridge"

No.	Name	Description	Size	U.S. $	Can. $	U.K. £
1	Egg Cup	Green cap, coat; gold buttons, trim	103 x 48	35.00	45.00	30.00
2	Money Box	Green cap, coat; gold buttons, trim	175 x 125	45.00	60.00	50.00
3	Pepper Cruet Saluting	Green cap, coat; gold buttons, trim	105	30.00	45.00	25.00
4	Salt Cruet Holding Package	Green cap, coat; gold buttons, trim	105	30.00	45.00	25.00
5	Cookie Jar	Green cap, coat; gold buttons, trim	185	60.00	80.00	35.00

K.P. FOODS LTD.

K.P. FRIARS

1983

The *K.P. Friars* set was commissioned by K.P. Foods Ltd. to promote the sales of its potato crisps (chips). The first model, the "Father Abbot," was free with a given number of tokens from the packets. The remaining five models could be obtained with tokens, plus a small charge.

The "Father Abbot" came either in a cardboard box with a friar's design on it or in a small box with a cellophane front. The rest of the figures were issued together as a set of five, in a box with a folding cardboard lid or one with a cellophane sleeve. Although *K.P. Friars* was issued as a set of five (and in late 1983, as a set of six, with the inclusion of the "Father Abbot"), for some reason the last three models —"Brother Crispin," "Brother Angelo" and "Brother Francis"— are the hardest to find, so have higher collectors' prices. Each model stands on a square base, with the name of the friar embossed on the front.

Backstamp: Embossed "Wade"

No.	Name	Description	Size	U.S. $	Can. $	U.K. £
1	Father Abbot	Beige head, base; brown robes	45 x 18	15.00	20.00	5.00
2a	Brother Peter	Beige head, base; brown robes	40 x 18	12.00	17.00	7.00
2b	Brother Peter	Honey head, base; grey robes	40 x 18	12.00	17.00	7.00
3	Brother Benjamin	Beige head, base; brown robes	40 x 18	12.00	17.00	7.00
4	Brother Crispin	Beige head, base; brown robes	40 x 20	45.00	60.00	20.00
5	Brother Angelo	Beige head, base; brown robes	48 x 20	45.00	60.00	20.00
6a	Brother Francis	Beige head, base; brown robes	42 x 20	45.00	60.00	20.00
6b	Brother Francis	Honey head, base; grey robes	42 x 20	45.00	60.00	20.00

KING AQUARIUMS LTD.

1976-1980

The *Aquarium Set* was produced for King Aquariums Ltd., a British company that supplied aquarium products to pet stores. Intended as ornaments for fish tanks, these models were not on sale in gift stores.

The "Bridge" is marked with "Wade England" embossed at the base of each span, whereas the other figures are marked on the back rims. The "Mermaid," "Diver" and "Lighthouse" are easily found, but the "Seahorse," "Water Snail/Whelk" and "Bridge" are much scarcer.

Backstamp: Embossed "Wade England"

No.	Name	Description	Size	U.S. $	Can. $	U.K. £
1	Mermaid	Beige; yellow hair; grey-green base	60 x 58	45.00	60.00	30.00
2	Diver	Honey brown; brown base	70 x 28	25.00	35.00	15.00
3a	Lighthouse	Beige, honey brown; grey-green base	75 x 45	50.00	70.00	30.00
3b	Lighthouse	Honey brown; grey-green base	75 x 45	50.00	70.00	30.00
4	Bridge	Beige; light brown bases	45 x 80	120.00	160.00	60.00
5	Seahorse	Blue/beige pattern	70 x 30	225.00	300.00	100.00
6	Water Snail/Whelk	Honey brown; green-grey shell	30 x 35	100.00	125.00	45.00

LEVER REXONA

NURSERY RHYME MODELS

1970-1971

Lever Rexona, makers of Signal 2 toothpaste, offered 24 miniature *Nursery Rhyme* models as a promotion, one model per box. The same models were used in the 1972-1979 Canadian Red Rose Tea promotion.

Photograph not available
at press time

Backstamp: Unknown

No.	Name	Description	Size	U.S. $	Can. $	U.K. £
1	Humpty Dumpty	Honey; pink cheeks; blue bowtie; brown wall	45 x 35	7.00	5.00	5.00
2	Little Boy Blue	Blue hat, coat; honey trousers	43 x 25	15.00	12.00	6.00
3	Puss in Boots	Brown; blue boots; green base	45 x 20	10.00	8.00	12.00
4	The Three Bears	Dark brown; honey base	35 x 38	35.00	20.00	20.00
5	The Pied Piper	Light brown coat; green bush	50 x 30	10.00	8.00	6.00
6	Baa Baa Black Sheep	Black	25 x 30	15.00	12.00	15.00
7	The Queen of Hearts	Pink hat; beige dress; two red hearts	45 x 25	15.00	8.00	10.00
8	Red Riding Hood	Beige dress; red/pink hood, cape; green base	45 x 20	6.00	5.00	6.00
9	Gingerbread Man	Red-brown; grey-green base	40 x 28	45.00	35.00	25.00
10	Mother Goose	Blue hat, bodice; honey dress, goose	40 x 32	10.00	8.00	15.00
11	Little Miss Muffet	Honey/grey dress; red-brown spider	45 x 20	10.00	6.00	10.00
12	Wee Willie Winkie	Yellow hair, candle; beige nightshirt	45 x 25	10.00	7.00	6.00
13	Hickory Dickory Dock	Red-brown/honey clock; brown mouse	45 x 20	6.00	4.00	6.00
14	Goosey Gander	Honey head, neck; dark brown wings; pink beak	30 x 35	8.00	6.00	4.00
15	Jack	Light brown; blue shirt, bucket	35 x 35	10.00	6.00	9.00
16	Jill	Yellow hair; beige dress; blue bucket	35 x 35	10.00	6.00	9.00
17	Dr. Foster	Light brown; yellow tie; blue puddle	45 x 25	10.00	6.00	10.00
18	TomTom the Piper's Son	Honey; blue hat, kilt; brown jacket	40 x 35	15.00	8.00	8.00
19	Little Bo Peep	Light brown; blue apron; green base	45 x 25	5.00	4.00	6.00
20	Old Woman Who Lived in a Shoe	Red-brown roof; honey woman	40 x 40	8.00	4.00	6.00
21	The House that Jack Built	Honey; red-brown roof	35 x 35	12.00	8.00	15.00
22	The Cat and the Fiddle	Beige cat; yellow fiddle	45 x 25	35.00	15.00	10.00
23	Little Jack Horner	Beige; blue plum; pink cushion	40 x 20	6.00	4.00	6.00
24	Old King Cole (Gap)	Beige; blue hat, hem; pink sleeves	40 x 35	7.00	4.00	6.00

PEX NYLONS

FAIRY AND CANDLE HOLDER

Circa 1952

One of the first promotional models produced by Wade was made at the Wade (Ulster) Pottery in the early 1950s for Pex Nylons. It was a model of a fairy sitting in a pink water lily, and was also produced as a candle holder, although only a very limited number of the candle holders exists. The models were issued with Wade labels; however, they are often seen unmarked because the labels have fallen off.

In the late 1950s, the surplus fairy models were sent to the George Wade Pottery, with the intention of using them in a water babies series. Because of high production costs, however, the series was never issued.

Backstamp: **A.** Unmarked (1-2)
B. Black and gold label "Made in Ireland by Wade Co. Armagh" (1-2)

No.	Name	Description	Size	U.S.$	Can.$	U.K.£
1a	Fairy	Blue wings; blue/pink/yellow flowers	55 x 35	450.00	600.00	225.00
1b	Fairy	Pink wings; blue/pink/yellow flowers	55 x 35	450.00	600.00	225.00
1c	Fairy	Yellow wings; blue/pink/yellow flowers	55 x 35	450.00	600.00	225.00
2	Fairy Candle Holder	Pink; green	25 x 75	300.00	400.00	130.00

POS-NER ASSOCIATES

SHERWOOD FOREST

1989-1995

Each model in the *Sherwood Forest* set was limited to a production run of 5,000.

Backstamp: Embossed "Mianco [year of issue] Wade England"

No.	Name	Description	Size	U.S. $	Can. $	U.K. £
1	Robin Hood	Green/honey brown	70 x 30	35.00	45.00	18.00
2	Maid Marian	Grey-blue/brown	65 x 25	35.00	45.00	20.00
3	Friar Tuck	Red-brown/honey brown	45 x 30	35.00	35.00	18.00

WHIMBLE FRIAR TUCK

1997

This Whimble was commissioned by Pos-ner Associates through C&S Collectables and has a print of "Friar Tuck" on the front.

Photograph not available
at press time

Backstamp: Red printed "Whimbles by Wade" with two lines

No.	Name	Description	Size	U.S. $	Can. $	U.K. £
1	Friar Tuck	White; gold band; black lettering; beige print	27	4.00	6.00	3.00

R.H.M. FOODS OF ENGLAND

BISTO KIDS

1977

The *Bisto Kids* salt and pepper cruets were marked "Wade Staffordshire" on their bases, because even though they were made in the Wade Ireland Pottery, they were intended for the British market. They were produced in November and December 1977 for Rank, Hovis & McDougall Foods Co. (R.H.M.) of England and were based on a pair of well-known characters in advertisements for Bisto Gravy Powder on British television. To receive the *Bisto Kids*, one had to mail in two tokens from the packet tops, plus a cheque for £1.95.

Backstamp: Brown transfer "Copyright RHM Foods Ltd. & Applied Creativity, Wade Staffordshire"

No.	Name	Description	Size	U.S. $	Can. $	U.K. £
1	Bisto Girl	Yellow hair, blouse; brown hat	115 x 48	100.00	125.00	50.00
2	Bisto Boy	Red hat; blue braces, trousers; grey jacket	110 x 58	100.00	125.00	50.00
—	Set (2)			180.00	200.00	100.00

RED ROSE TEA (CANADA) LTD.

MINIATURE ANIMALS

First Issue 1967-1973

In early 1967, when the sales of Red Rose Tea were in decline and the company was falling behind its competitors, it decided to start a promotional campaign to win back customers. In its campaign Wade miniature animals were used as free premiums in packages of Red Rose Tea Bags.

The first 12 promotional models were released in early 1967 and used in a trial run in Quebec, Canada, to test the public's reaction. The idea proved so successful that the series was quickly increased to 32 models in autumn 1967. The models were then offered nationally, region by region across Canada. Their popularity was so great that the promotional area and period (originally intended for two to three years) was extended to cover all of Canada for six years (from 1967 to 1973).

The models marked with "Wade England" in a recessed base were the first of this series to be produced. When the dies on six of these—the "Bear Cub," "Beaver," "Bushbaby," "Kitten," "Owl" and "Squirrel"—were retooled in 1967, the marks were placed on the back rim of the models.

The "Bison" and "Hippo" are found in two sizes because, when the original dies broke, the new dies produced smaller models. In fact, there can be slight size variations in all the models listed below.

A second "Rabbit" was made with open ears because the closed ears on the first version were too difficult to fettle. The first issue "Trout" was unmarked, and the back of the base differs slightly from the second issue, which is marked "Wade England" on the back rim.

This first issue was later produced as *English Whimsies,* except for the "Fantail Goldfish," "Butterfly," "Frog," "Poodle," "Crocodile," "Terrapin," "Seal on Rock" and "Rabbit" with closed ears.

Two variations have been found in the "Hedgehog" model. Type A has a deep recess base with three pads around the rim, and Type B has a shallow recess base with two pads, one at either end of the rim.

The following list is in alphabetical order.

Backstamp: **A.** Embossed "Wade England" on rim (1, 2a, 3a, 4a, 4b, 6a, 8, 9, 11, 12, 13, 14, 16, 18a, 18b,19a, 19b, 20, 21, 22, 23a, 24, 25a, 25b, 26, 27, 28, 29a, 31a, 32)
   B. Embossed "Wade England" in recessed base (2b, 3b, 5, 6b, 7, 10b, 15a, 15b, 17, 23b, 29b, 30a, 30b, 30c)
   C. Embossed "Wade England" on disk (10a)
   D. Unmarked (31b)

No.	Name	Description	Size	U.S. $	Can. $	U.K. £
1	Alsatian	Grey; tan face	30 x 40	9.00	7.00	2.00
2a	Bear Cub	Grey; beige face	30 x 40	7.00	5.00	2.00
2b	Bear Cub	Grey; beige face	30 x 40	20.00	15.00	5.00
3a	Beaver	Grey-brown; honey brown face	35 x 45	8.00	6.00	2.00
3b	Beaver	Grey-brown; honey brown face	35 x 45	20.00	15.00	5.00
3bb	Beaver	Honey brown	35 x 45	8.00	6.00	2.00
4a	Bison, Large	Honey brown body; dark brown head, mane	32 x 45	14.00	10.00	4.00
4aa	Bison, Large	Honey brown	30 x 45	8.00	12.00	15.00
4b	Bison, Small	Honey brown body; dark brown head, mane	28 x 40	7.00	5.00	4.00
5	Bluebird	Beige body, tail; blue wings, head	15 x 35	10.00	8.00	4.00
6a	Bushbaby	Brown; blue ears; black eyes, nose	30 x 30	6.00	4.00	2.00
6b	Bushbaby	Brown; blue ears; black eyes, nose	30 x 30	7.00	5.00	3.00
7a	Butterfly	Olive/brown; green tips; raised circles	10 x 45	10.00	8.00	5.00
7b	Butterfly	Honey brown	10 x 45	10.00	8.00	5.00
8	Chimpanzee	Dark brown; light brown face, patches	35 x 35	7.00	5.00	2.00

No.	Name	Description	Size	U.S. $	Can. $	U.K. £
9	Corgi	Honey brown; black nose	30 x 35	9.00	7.00	2.00
10a	Crocodile	Brownish green	14 x 40	10.00	8.00	5.00
10b	Crocodile	Brownish green	14 x 40	10.00	8.00	5.00
11	Duck	Blue/brown; yellow beak	30 x 40	9.00	7.00	2.00
12	Fantail Goldfish	Green/yellow; blue rock	30 x 35	10.00	8.00	5.00
13	Fawn	Brown; blue ears; black nose	30 x 30	7.00	5.00	2.00
14	Fox	Dark brown; fawn face, chest	30 x 30	9.00	7.00	2.00
15a	Frog	Green	15 x 30	7.00	5.00	3.00
15b	Frog	Yellow	15 x 30	7.00	5.00	3.00
16	Giraffe	Beige	35 x 35	7.00	5.00	2.00

No.	Name	Description	Size	U.S. $	Can. $	U.K. £
17a	Hedgehog	Light brown; honey face; black nose	23 x 40	9.00	7.00	2.00
17b	Hedgehog	Dark red brown; honey face; black nose	23 x 40	9.00	7.00	2.00
18a	Hippo, Large	Honey brown	25 x 45	16.00	12.00	4.00
18b	Hippo, Small	Honey brown	20 x 40	6.00	4.00	2.00
19a	Kitten	Dark/light brown; pink wool	30 x 30	8.00	6.00	2.00
19b	Kitten	Dark/light brown; red wool	30 x 30	10.00	8.00	4.00
20	Lion	Light brown; dark brown head, mane	35 x 45	8.00	6.00	2.00
21	Mongrel	Dark brown back; light brown front	35 x 35	7.00	5.00	2.00
22	Otter	Beige; blue base	30 x 35	7.00	5.00	2.00
23a	Owl	Dark/light brown	35 x 20	8.00	6.00	2.00
23b	Owl	Dark/light brown	35 x 20	20.00	12.00	6.00
24	Poodle	White	40 x 45	10.00	7.00	4.00

Closed-eared rabbit (left), Open-eared rabbit (right)

No.	Name	Description	Size	U.S. $	Can. $	U.K. £
25a	Rabbit	Beige; closed ears	30 x 30	22.00	12.00	7.00
25b	Rabbit	Beige; ears open	30 x 30	8.00	6.00	2.00
26	Seal on Rock	Brown; blue rock	35 x 35	8.00	4.00	5.00
27	Setter	Brown; grey-green base	35 x 50	7.00	5.00	2.00
28	Spaniel	Honey brown; green nose	35 x 35	8.00	5.00	2.00
29a	Squirrel	Grey; brown head, legs; yellow acorn	35 x 30	7.00	5.00	2.00
29b	Squirrel	Grey; brown head, legs; yellow acorn	35 x 30	12.00	9.00	5.00
30a	Terrapin	Beige; brown markings	10 x 40	8.00	6.00	4.00
30b	Terrapin	Beige; grey markings	10 x 40	8.00	6.00	4.00
30c	Terrapin	Beige; purple-blue markings	10 x 40	8.00	6.00	4.00
31a	Trout	Brown; red tail; grey-green base	30 x 30	8.00	6.00	3.00
31b	Trout	Brown; red tail; grey-green base	30 x 30	8.00	6.00	3.00
32	Wild Boar	Brown; green on base	30 x 40	15.00	12.00	4.00

MINIATURE NURSERIES

Second Issue 1972-1979

A series of 24 miniature nursery rhyme characters was given away free in the second Red Rose Tea promotion. For the first two years these models were only distributed in selected areas; it was not until 1973 that they were distributed throughout Canada.

When a new die replaces a worn one, variations in models sometimes occur, as in "The Queen of Hearts" and "Old King Cole." Models with colour variations may indicate a painter's whim or that a particular glaze was temporarily out of stock. All the models are marked "Wade England" around the rim of the base.

Because over 20 million of these models are reported to have been made, only the undamaged models are worth keeping. Thin, more breakable models in mint condition are worth more than the solid, heavier models, which stand up to rough handling better. Only five of the models listed were released in England and none in the United States.

The Queen of Hearts
Two large hearts   Two small hearts

No.	Name	Description	Size	U.S. $	Can. $	U.K. £
1a	Humpty Dumpty	Honey brown; blue tie; brown wall	45 x 35	7.00	5.00	5.00
1b	Humpty Dumpty	Honey brown; brown wall	45 x 35	7.00	5.00	5.00
2	Little Boy Blue	Blue hat, coat; brown trousers	43 x 25	15.00	12.00	6.00
3	Puss in Boots	Brown; blue boots; green base	45 x 20	10.00	8.00	12.00
4a	The Three Bears	Dark brown, honey brown base	35 x 38	35.00	20.00	20.00
4b	The Three Bears	Light brown, honey brown base	35 x 38	35.00	20.00	20.00
5a	The Pied Piper	Light brown coat; green bush	50 x 30	10.00	8.00	6.00
5b	The Pied Piper	Pink/brown coat; green bush	50 x 30	10.00	8.00	6.00
6	Baa Baa Black Sheep	Black all over	25 x 30	15.00	12.00	15.00
7a	The Queen of Hearts	2 small hearts; beige dress; pink hat	45 x 25	15.00	8.00	10.00
7b	The Queen of Hearts	2 large hearts; beige dress; pink hat	45 x 25	15.00	8.00	10.00
7c	The Queen of Hearts	8 small hearts; beige dress; pink hat	45 x 25	40.00	55.00	20.00
8	Little Red Riding Hood	Beige dress; red cape; green base	45 x 20	6.00	5.00	6.00

No.	Name	Description	Size	U.S. $	Can. $	U.K. £
9	Gingerbread Man	Red-brown; grey-green base	40 x 28	45.00	35.00	25.00
10a	Mother Goose	Brown hat; honey brown dress	40 x 32	10.00	8.00	15.00
10b	Mother Goose	Blue hat; honey brown dress	40 x 32	10.00	8.00	15.00
11	Little Miss Muffet	Honey/grey dress; red-brown spider	45 x 20	10.00	6.00	10.00
12	Wee Willie Winkie	Yellow hair; beige nightshirt	45 x 25	10.00	7.00	6.00
13	Hickory Dickory Dock	Red-brown/honey brown	45 x 20	6.00	4.00	6.00
14	Goosey Goosey Gander	Honey brown head; pink beak	30 x 35	8.00	6.00	4.00
15a	Jack	Brown; blue shirt; brown bucket	35 x 35	10.00	6.00	9.00
15b	Jack	Brown; blue shirt; blue bucket	35 x 35	10.00	6.00	9.00
16	Jill	Yellow hair; beige dress; blue bucket	35 x 35	10.00	6.00	9.00

Note: The above pricing table is listed in photograph order from bottom left to upper right.

Old King Cole
Gap between feet   No gap between feet

Backstamp: Embossed "Wade England"

No.	Name	Description	Size	U.S. $	Can. $	U.K. £
17a	Dr. Foster	Light brown all over	45 x 25	10.00	6.00	10.00
17b	Dr. Foster	Light brown; blue puddle	45 x 25	10.00	6.00	10.00
17c	Dr. Foster	Light brown; yellow tie; blue puddle	45 x 25	10.00	6.00	10.00
17d	Dr. Foster	Brown; grey puddle	45 x 25	10.00	6.00	10.00
18a	Tom Tom the Piper's Son	Honey brown; blue tam, kilt	40 x 35	15.00	8.00	8.00
18b	Tom Tom the Piper's Son	Honey brown; brown tam, kilt	40 x 35	15.00	8.00	8.00
18c	Tom Tom the Piper's Son	Honey brown; grey tam, kilt	40 x 35	15.00	8.00	8.00
19	Little Bo-Peep	Brown; blue apron; green base	45 x 25	5.00	4.00	6.00
20a	Old Woman Who Lived in a Shoe	Honey brown; red-brown roof	40 x 40	8.00	4.00	6.00
20b	Old Woman Who Lived in a Shoe	Honey brown	35 x 40	7.00	4.00	5.00
21	The House that Jack Built	Honey brown; red-brown roof	35 x 35	12.00	8.00	15.00
22	The Cat and the Fiddle	Beige front; grey back; yellow fiddle	45 x 25	35.00	15.00	10.00
23	Little Jack Horner	Beige; pink cushion; blue plum	40 x 20	6.00	4.00	6.00
24a	Old King Cole	Gap; brown body, shoes, pot; blue hat, cloak	40 x 35	7.00	4.00	6.00
24b	Old King Cole	Gap; brown body, pot blue hat, cloak, shoes	40 x 35	7.00	4.00	6.00
24c	Old King Cole	No gap; brown body shoes, pot blue hat	40 x 35	7.00	4.00	6.00
24d	Old King Cole	No gap; brown body; blue hat, cloak, shoes, pot	40 x 35	7.00	4.00	6.00

Note: The above pricing table is listed in photograph order from bottom left to upper right.

WHOPPAS

Third Issue 1981

In 1981 the English series of *Whoppas* came to an end, and the surplus stock was used for Red Rose Tea Canada premiums. To obtain a model, Canadian collectors had to mail in the tab from a box of Red Rose Tea, plus $1.00 for postage. All are marked "Wade England" around the rim of the base. Numbers 1 through 5 are from Wade's *Whoppas*, set 1; 6 to 10 are from *Whoppas*, set 2; 11 to 15 are from *Whoppas*, set 3.

Backstamp: Embossed "Wade England"

No.	Name	Description	Size	U.S. $	Can. $	U.K. £
1	Polar Bear	White; grey-blue base	35 x 55	25.00	35.00	7.00
2	Hippo	Grey; green base	35 x 50	25.00	35.00	7.00
3	Brown Bear	Red-brown; brown base	35 x 45	20.00	28.00	7.00
4	Tiger	Yellow/brown; green base	30 x 60	20.00	28.00	7.00
5	Elephant	Grey	55 x 50	25.00	35.00	7.00
6	Bison	Brown; green base	40 x 50	25.00	35.00	7.00
7	Wolf	Grey; green base	60 x 45	30.00	40.00	10.00
8	Bobcat	Light brown; dark brown spots; green base	55 x 50	30.00	40.00	10.00
9	Chipmunk	Brown; dark brown base	55 x 40	30.00	40.00	10.00
10	Racoon	Brown; black stripes, eye patches; green base	40 x 50	30.00	40.00	10.00
11	Fox	Red-brown; green base	30 x 60	35.00	45.00	20.00
12	Badger	Brown; cream stripe; green base	35 x 45	35.00	45.00	20.00
13	Otter	Brown; blue base	30 x 55	35.00	45.00	20.00
14	Stoat	Brown; green base	35 x 55	35.00	45.00	20.00
15	Hedgehog	Brown; green base	30 x 50	35.00	45.00	20.00

MINIATURE ANIMALS

Fourth Issue 1982-1984

Six animal models from the first Red Rose Tea Canada Promotion were re-issued some with slight colour variations and seventeen models from the 1971-1984 English Whimsies series were added to make this fourth promotion of twenty three animals. New dies resulted in 3 sizes of pig.

Backstamp: Embossed "Wade England"

No.	Name	Description	Size	U.S. $	Can. $	U.K. £
1	Angel Fish	Grey; dark grey stripes; blue base	35 x 30	15.00	12.00	5.00
2	Beaver	Brown; honey brown face	35 x 45	8.00	6.00	2.00
3	Bushbaby	Beige	30 x 30	5.00	7.00	5.00
4	Camel	Dark grey	35 x 35	9.00	11.00	4.00
5	Collie	Honey brown/green	35 x 35	10.00	8.00	4.00
6	Corgi	Honey brown; black nose	30 x 35	9.00	7.00	2.00
7	Cow	Light orange	35 x 35	12.00	12.00	4.00
8	Fox	Dark brown	30 x 30	9.00	7.00	2.00

Backstamp: Embossed "Wade England"

No.	Name	Description	Size	U.S. $	Can. $	U.K. £
9	Giraffe	Beige	35 x 35	7.00	5.00	2.00
10	Gorilla	Dark grey; green	35 x 25	8.00	8.00	4.00
11	Horse	Black	35 x 35	15.00	12.00	4.00
12	Lamb	White	30 x 25	8.00	10.00	4.00
13	Langur	Beige; brown stump	35 x 30	5.00	7.00	4.00
14	Leopard	Yellow-brown	17 x 45	6.00	8.00	4.00
15	Orang-Utan	Dark brown	30 x 30	5.00	7.00	5.00

Backstamp: Embossed "Wade England"

No.	Name	Description	Size	U.S. $	Can. $	U.K. £
16	Pelican	Brown/yellow; green base	45 x 40	20.00	25.00	6.00
17a	Pig, large	Beige	27 x 44	25.00	20.00	10.00
17b	Pig, medium	Beige	25 x 40	25.00	20.00	10.00
17c	Pig, small	Beige	25 x 35	25.00	20.00	10.00
18	Pine Martin	Yellow/brown	30 x 30	6.00	5.00	2.00
19a	Rabbit ears open	Beige	30 x 30	8.00	6.00	2.00
19b	Rabbit ears closed	Beige	30 x 30	22.00	12.00	7.00
20	Rhino	Dark grey	17 x 45	8.00	6.00	4.00
21	Seahorse	Yellow/brown; blue base	50 x 17	20.00	25.00	7.00
22	Turtle	Dark grey	15 x 50	10.00	8.00	4.00
23	Zebra	Beige	40 x 35	9.00	11.00	4.00

Note: The above pricing tables are listed in photograph order from bottom left to upper right.

RED ROSE TEA U.S.A. LTD. (REDCO FOODS LTD.)

The Canadian Red Rose Tea promotion was so successful that it was extended to the United States in 1983. Red Rose estimates that over 200 million Wade models have been distributed in packets of Red Rose Tea in the U.S.A. and in Canada during its promotions.

In many states figurine promotions overlap, with some model series still being offered in one area whilst a new series is offered in another.

MINIATURE ANIMALS

First Issue 1983-1985

In this first American series, two of the models, the "Hare" and "Squirrel," were not original *English Whimsies*, but models from the 1980-1981 Tom Smith *British Wildlife* set. All figures are in all-over, one-colour glazes, and they may vary slightly from the measurements indicated below. They are listed in alphabetical order. The following initials indicate the origin of the models:

EW: *English Whimsies*   TS: Tom Smith *British Wildlife* set
RR: Red Rose Tea

Backstamp: Embossed "Wade England"

No.	Name	Description	Size	U.S. $	Can. $	U.K. £
1	Bear Cub (RR/EW)	Beige	30 x 40	5.00	7.00	5.00
2	Bison (RR/EW)	Dark brown	30 x 40	6.00	8.00	4.00
3	Bluebird (RR/EW)	Beige	15 x 35	6.00	8.00	6.00
4	Bushbaby (RR/EW)	Beige	30 x 30	5.00	7.00	5.00
5	Chimpanzee (RR/EW)	Honey brown	35 x 35	5.00	7.00	5.00
6	Elephant (EW)	Blue; no eyes	35 x 45	12.00	15.00	10.00
7	Hare (TS)	Blue	50 x 30	6.00	12.00	6.00
8	Hippo (RR/EW)	Honey brown	23 x 35	12.00	12.00	4.00
9	Lion (RR/EW)	Honey brown	35 x 45	5.00	8.00	4.00
10	Otter (RR/EW)	Beige	30 x 35	6.00	5.00	2.00
11	Owl (RR/EW)	Dark brown	35 x 20	6.00	5.00	10.00
12	Seal (RR/TS)	Blue	35 x 35	8.00	12.00	6.00
13a	Squirrel (TS)	Dark blue	40 x 40	6.00	12.00	12.00
13b	Squirrel (TS)	Grey-blue	40 x 40	6.00	12.00	12.00
14	Turtle (EW)	Light grey	15 x 50	10.00	8.00	4.00
15	Wild Boar (RR/EW)	Beige	30 x 40	8.00	10.00	4.00

All the models in this series are in all-over, one-colour glazes. Some of these figures are in the same colours used in the 1982-1984 Canada Red Rose Tea promotion. The following initials indicate the origin of the models:

EW: *English Whimsies*   TS: Tom Smith
RRC: Red Rose Tea Canada

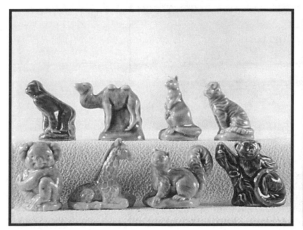

Backstamp: Embossed "Wade England"

No.	Name	Description	Size	U.S. $	Can. $	U.K.£
1	Koala Bear (EW)	Beige	35 x 25	6.00	9.00	4.00
2	Giraffe (EW/RRC)	Beige	35 x 35	7.00	5.00	2.00
3	Pine Martin (EW/RRC)	Honey brown	30 x 30	6.00	5.00	2.00
4	Langur (EW/RRC)	Dark brown	35 x 30	6.00	8.00	5.00
5	Orang-Utan (EW/RRC)	Dark brown	30 x 30	5.00	7.00	5.00
6	Camel (EW/RRC)	Beige	35 x 35	9.00	11.00	4.00
7	Kangaroo (EW)	Honey brown	45 x 25	10.00	15.00	5.00
8	Leopard (EW/RRC)	Yellow brown	17 x 45	6.00	8.00	4.00
9	Zebra (EW/RRC)	Grey	40 x 35	5.00	8.00	8.00
10	Polar Bear (EW/TS)	White	30 x 30	10.00	12.00	4.00
11	Gorilla (EW/RRC)	Dark brown	35 x 25	4.00	6.00	3.00
12	Racoon (EW)	Dark brown	25 x 35	4.00	6.00	5.00
13	Rhino (EW/RRC)	Blue-grey	17 x 45	8.00	6.00	4.00
14	Beaver (EW/RRC)	Light brown	35 x 45	6.00	10.00	6.00
15	Tiger (EW)	Honey brown	35 x 25	15.00	20.00	5.00

Note: The above pricing table is listed in photograph order from bottom left to upper right.

The 15 models offered in the 1985-1990 Red Rose Tea promotion were increased to 20 in late 1990, with the addition of five Tom Smith 1988-1989 models (indicated below by TS). By late 1993 in New York State, Philadelphia, Florida and in Portland, Maine, the models were no longer included free in boxes of teabags, but could be obtained by sending in the UPC code and a small shipping and handling charge. In other areas of the U.S., the 20 animal figurines were available until mid 1995.

Backstamp: Embossed "Wade England"

No.	Name	Description	Size	U.S. $	Can. $	U.K. £
16	Spaniel Puppy (TS)	Honey brown	25 x 30	10.00	12.00	4.00
17	Kitten (TS)	Grey	25 x 33	6.00	8.00	5.00
18	Rabbit (TS)	Dark brown	30 x 25	8.00	10.00	4.00
19	Pony (TS)	Beige	25 x 30	10.00	12.00	4.00
20	Cock-a-teel (TS)	Green	35 x 30	8.00	10.00	3.00

Note: The above pricing table is listed in photograph order from bottom left to upper right.

Fourth Issue 1992

Due to increasing demand, Red Rose U.S.A offered these models as a mail-in offer with their packages of decaffeinated tea in early 1992. This series includes the same models as offered in the second issue in different colourways with the addition of the third issue models in the same colourways.

This series was limited to mail order because packaging methods for decaffeinated tea did not allow for the inclusion of the model in the tea packet. For each model a special card was required from the tea packet, plus a postage charge of $1.00 for one to three models, $2.00 for four to nine models and $3.00 for ten to 15 models.

All these figures are in all-over, one-colour glazes, unless otherwise stated. The following initials indicate the origin of the models:

| EW: *English Whimsies* | TS: Tom Smith |
| RRC: Red Rose Tea Canada | RRU: Red Rose Tea U.S.A. |

Backstamp: Embossed "Wade England"

No.	Name	Description	Size	U.S. $	Can. $	U.K. £
1	Koala Bear (EW/RRU)	Dark grey; beige stump	35 x 25	15.00	25.00	6.00
2	Giraffe (EW/RRC)	Beige	35 x 35	7.00	5.00	2.00
3	Pine Marten (EW/RRC)	Yellow-brown	30 x 30	6.00	5.00	2.00
4	Langur (EW/RRC)	Light brown; brown stump	35 x 30	5.00	7.00	4.00
5	Orang-Utan (EW/RRC)	Brown	30 x 30	5.00	7.00	5.00
6	Camel (EW/RRC)	Dark grey	35 x 35	9.00	11.00	4.00
7	Kangaroo (EW/RRU)	Honey brown	45 x 25	10.00	15.00	5.00
8	Leopard (EW/RRC/RRU)	Mottled olive brown	17 x 45	6.00	8.00	5.00
9	Zebra (EW/RRC/RRU)	Light grey	40 x 35	5.00	8.00	8.00
10	Polar Bear (EW/TS/RRU)	White	30 x 30	10.00	12.00	4.00
11	Gorilla (EW/RRC)	Black	35 x 25	20.00	26.00	14.00
12	Racoon (EW/RRU)	Brown	25 x 35	4.00	6.00	5.00
13	Rhino (EW/RRC/RRU)	Blue-grey/light grey	17 x 45	8.00	6.00	4.00
14	Beaver (EW/RRC/RRU)	Dark brown	35 x 45	3.00	3.00	3.00
15	Tiger (EW/RRU)	Mottled olive brown	35 x 25	15.00	20.00	6.00
16	Cock-a-teel (TS)	Green	35 x 30	8.00	10.00	3.00
17	Kitten (TS)	Grey	25 x 33	6.00	8.00	5.00
18	Pony (TS)	Beige	25 x 30	10.00	12.00	4.00
19	Rabbit (TS)	Dark brown	30 x 25	10.00	12.00	6.00
20	Spaniel Puppy (TS)	Honey	25 x 30	10.00	12.00	4.00

Note: For an illustration of model numbers 16-20 please see previous page.

CIRCUS ANIMALS

In late 1993 Red Rose offered a reissue of the most popular of the Tom Smith cracker models , *The Circus* set, originally issued in England from 1978 to 1979 (indicated below by the initials TS). The original moulds were used, and there is only a slight variation in colour from the older models.

Left: Tom Smith *Circus* Elephant (blue)
Right: Red Rose (U.S.A.) Elephant (pale blue)

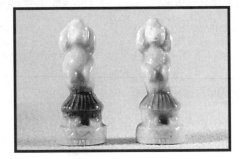

Left: Tom Smith *Circus* Poodle (dark blue)
Right: Red Rose (U.S.A.) Poodle (light blue)

Backstamp: Embossed "Wade England"

No.	Name	Description	Size	U.S. $	Can. $	U.K. £
1	Brown Bear (TS)	Dark brown	35 x 30	5.00	12.00	4.00
2	Chimpanzee Boy (TS)	Brown	40 x 20	5.00	12.00	8.00
3	Chimpanzee Girl (TS)	Brown	40 x 20	5.00	12.00	8.00
4	Elephant, Sitting (TS)	Pale blue	30 x 30	5.00	12.00	6.00
5	Elephant, Standing (TS)	Pale blue	30 x 25	5.00	12.00	6.00
6	Pony (TS)	Beige	45 x 22	5.00	12.00	4.00
7	Lion (TS)	Honey brown	40 x 22	5.00	12.00	4.00
8	Poodle (TS)	White; blue skirt	35 x 30	5.00	12.00	6.00
9	Sea Lion (TS)	Light grey	40 x 30	5.00	12.00	8.00
10	Tiger (TS)	Honey brown	43 x 20	5.00	12.00	4.00

Sixth Issue 1996-Present

Five new Circus models were produced for Redco Foods (Red Rose Tea U.S.A.) and were available in all U.S.A. states where Red Rose Tea is sold from July of 1996. The five new models were added to the Circus set which was first introduced in 1993 making a total of fifteen models for this series. The models were available in boxes of 100 and 48 count Orange Pekoe and Cut Black tea bags and also in 48 count Decaffeinated Tea bags. Red Rose advertising proclaims that over 200 million Wade Whimsicals have been distributed between 1983-1996.

Backstamp: Embossed 'Wade England'

No.	Name	Description	Size	U.S. $	Can. $	U.K. £
11	Clown Water Bucket	Light green	44	5.00	12.00	5.00
12	Clown Custard Pie	Pale blue	40	5.00	12.00	5.00
13	Human Cannonball	Light grey	30	5.00	12.00	5.00
14	Ringmaster	Light grey	44	5.00	12.00	5.00
15	Strongman	Honey brown	40	5.00	12.00	5.00

RICHLEIGH PROMOTIONS

THE CHILDREN OF THE WORLD

1997

The first model in this new series commissioned by Richard and Leigh Leford of Richleigh Promotions, "The Japanese Girl," was produced in two colour ways in winter 1997. Each colour version was issued in a limited edition of 1,000 together with a certificate of authenticity. The original cost per figure was £33.00 plus £5.00 for overseas mail.

Size: 114
Backstamp: Unknown

No.	Name	Description	U.S. $	Can. $	U.K. £
1a	Japanese Girl	Black hair; blue kimono; pink fan; light brown base	48.00	65.00	33.00
1b	Japanese Girl	Black hair; green kimono; blue fan; light brown base	48.00	65.00	33.00

ROBELL MEDIA PROMOTIONS LTD.

MR. HAPPY

1997

Mr. Happy, a character from the Mr, Men childrens story books by Roger Hargreaves, was produced for child members of the 'Mr. Men & Little Miss Club' and was marketed by Robell Media Promotions. The cost of Mr. Happy direct from the club was £15.99.

Backstamp: Black printed 'Genuine Wade Porcelain Robell Produced exclusively for the Mr. Men & Little Miss Club Mr. Men and Little Miss TM & © 1997 Mrs Roger Hargreaves', 'Mr. Happy and Little Miss' logo

No.	Name	Description	Size	U.S. $	Can. $	U.K. £
1	Mr. Happy	Yellow; black eyes, mouth; black lettering on green base	100	50.00	70.00	35.00

JAMES ROBERTSON & SONS

ROBERTSON'S JAM GOLLIES AND BANDSTAND
1963-1965

Golliwogs became the trademark of James Robertson & Sons after one of Mr. Robertson's sons visited the United States in the early 1900s. He purchased a golliwog doll for his children, and it was so loved by the family that they decided to use it as their trademark. In 1910 a golliwog first appeared on items from James Robertson Preserve Manufacturers Limited, such as labels and price lists.

Beginning in 1963 a Robertson's promotional campaign offered a series of eight golliwog musicians in exchange for ten paper golliwog labels per model and 6d in postage stamps. George Wade and Son Ltd. produced five models for a trial period only, to see how production costs compared to a version made in Portugal. At some time in 1965, Robertson's changed from using the Wade model to the cheaper Portuguese one.

None of the golliwogs is marked with a Wade stamp or label, but it is relatively easy to spot a Wade model amongst the hundreds of golliwogs seen at antique and collector shows. Only the Wade figures are standing on white bases. All the models have a raised "Robertson" mark on the front rim of the base, and all the *Gollies* are black, with blue coats and red trousers.

Wade records confirm that, out of the eight promotional models, it only produced five golliwog musicians—"Accordian Golliwog," "Clarinet Golliwog," "Bass Golliwog," "Saxophone Golliwog" and "Trumpet Golliwog." The three additional models, not confirmed by Wade and most likely produced by another manufacturer, are "Drum Golliwog," "Guitar Golliwog" and "Vocalist Golliwog."

Due to changing race relations laws in Great Britain during the late 1970s and early 1980s, the original name, *Golliwog*, was changed to *Golly Doll* or *Gollies*. The models below are listed by their original names.

Backstamp: **A.** Embossed "Robertson" (1-5)
               B. Red transfer print "Wade England" (6)

No.	Name	Description	Size	U.S. $	Can. $	U.K. £
1	Accordion Golliwog	Blue jacket; red pants; white/yellow accordion	65 x 25	250.00	325.00	125.00
2	Clarinet Golliwog	Blue jacket; red pants; black clarinet	65 x 25	250.00	325.00	125.00
3	Bass Golliwog	Blue jacket; red pants; white/yellow/brown bass	65 x 25	250.00	325.00	125.00
4	Saxophone Golliwog	Blue jacket; red pants; yellow saxophone	65 x 25	250.00	325.00	125.00
5	Trumpet Golliwog	Blue jacket; red pants; yellow trumpet	65 x 25	250.00	325.00	125.00
6	Bandstand	White	50 x 230	200.00	300.00	100.00

ST. JOHN AMBULANCE BRIGADE (U.K.)

BERTIE BADGER

1989-1994

"Bertie Badger" was produced in a limited edition of 5,000 as a promotional item for the British St. John Ambulance Brigade in late 1989. It was given as a reward to child members of the brigade after they completed three years of service and training. Those models that are unmarked were produced from 1989 to 1994; those embossed with the Wade mark were made only in 1994.

Size: 100 x 50 mm.
Backstamp: **A.** Unmarked
B. Embossed "Wade"

No.	Description	U.S. $	Can. $	U.K. £
1	Black/white; white coveralls, shoes,	300.00	385.00	145.00

SALADA TEA CANADA

WHIMSEY-ON-WHY

1984

Six models from the *Whimsey-on-Why* sets 1, 2 and 3 were introduced as a short promotional offer by Salada Tea Canada between September and December 1984.

Backstamp: Embossed "Wade England"

No.	Name	Description	Size	U.S. $	Can. $	U.K. £
1	Pump Cottage	Brown thatch; white walls; yellow doors	28 x 39	20.00	25.00	5.00
2	Tobacconist's Shop	Brown roof; red doors	33 x 39	20.00	25.00	5.00
3	The Greengrocer's Shop	Grey roof; green windows, doors	35 x 35	20.00	30.00	8.00
4	The Antique Shop	Purple-brown roof; blue/yellow windows	35 x 37	20.00	30.00	8.00
5	The Post Office	Beige roof; yellow/blue windows	40 x 38	20.00	25.00	10.00
6	Whimsey Station	Red-brown; brown roof	35 x 39	25.00	35.00	15.00

SHARPS CHOCOLATE

HONEY BROWN SMILING RABBIT

1970

The "Honey Brown Smiling Rabbit" was produced in 1970 as a premium with Sharps Chocolate Easter eggs. The box was shaped like a hollow log, and the rabbit was fixed beside an egg containing milk chocolate buttons. The original price was 7/9d.

Size: 65 x 43 mm.
Backstamp: Unmarked

No.	Description	U.S. $	Can. $	U.K. £
1a	Honey brown; large dark brown eyes	40.00	50.00	25.00
1b	Honey brown; small brown eyes	40.00	50.00	25.00

BO-PEEP

1971

The following year Wade produced the "Honey Brown Bo-Peep," also as a premium with Sharps Chocolate Easter eggs. The model was fixed beside an egg containing milk chocolate buttons, and was packaged in a box decorated with a design of sheep and trees. The original price was 8/-.

Size: 70 x 28 mm.
Backstamp: Embossed "Wade England"

No.	Description	U.S. $	Can. $	U.K. £
1a	Honey brown	40.00	50.00	25.00
1b	Honey brown; dark blue hair, apron and flowers	40.00	50.00	25.00

SIMONS ASSOCIATES, INC.

Circa 1975

Some time in the mid 1970s, Wade exported a set of 24 *English Whimsies* to Simons Associates, Inc., of Los Angeles, California. The models were packaged in a plastic bubble on a blue card. The front of the card has a colourful design of a tree, smiling sun, baby birds in a nest, butterfly, snail and toadstools. Also printed there is "Whimsies Miniatures Collection Solid English Porcelain," and each package is numbered in the top left corner. On the back is printed: "Collect all these Whimsies miniatures / little creatures from the farm, forest and jungle of solid porcelain," and on the top right hand corner, "Whimsies Wade of England Est. 1810," along with the Union Jack and the American flag.

The values are given for models intact on their cards as they are indistinguishable from Red Rose Tea or English Whimsies models outside the packet. Note that these models were not given the same issue numbers as *English Whimsies*, although they are identical to the originals.

Backstamp: A. Embossed "Wade England" (1-3, 5-8)
B. Embossed "Wade England" in a recessed base (4)

No.	Name	Description	Size	U.S. $	Can. $	U.K. £
1	Rabbit	Beige	30 x 30	9.00	7.00	3.00
2	Fawn	Brown; blue ears	30 x 30	8.00	6.00	3.00
3	Mongrel	Dark brown back; light brown front	35 x 35	8.00	6.00	3.00
4	Squirrel	Grey; brown head, legs; yellow acorn	35 x 30	13.00	10.00	6.00
5	Elephant	Grey; black eyes	55 x 50	21.00	16.00	7.00
6	Setter	Brown; black nose	35 x 50	8.00	6.00	3.00
7	Cat	Beige	40 x 17	21.00	26.00	8.00
8	Collie	Golden brown	35 x 35	11.00	9.00	5.00

Backstamp: **A.** Embossed "Wade England" (9-11, 14-16)
B. Embossed "Wade England" in a recessed base (12, 13)

No.	Name	Description	Size	U.S. $	Can. $	U.K. £
9	Zebra	Light brown; green base	40 x 35	10.00	12.00	5.00
10	Bear Cub	Grey; beige face	30 x 40	8.00	6.00	3.00
11	Field Mouse	Yellow brown	35 x 25	13.00	12.00	4.00
12	Owl	Dark brown; light brown chest, face	35 x 20	21.00	12.00	7.00
13	Kitten	Dark/light brown; pink or red wool	30 x 30	11.00	9.00	5.00
14	Chimpanzee	Dark brown; light brown face, patches	35 x 35	8.00	6.00	3.00
15	Horse	Grey; green base	35 x 35	16.00	13.00	5.00
16	Duck	Blue/brown; yellow beak	30 x 40	10.00	8.00	3.00

Backstamp: **A.** Embossed "Wade England" (17-23)
B. Embossed "Wade England" in a recessed base (24)

No.	Name	Description	Size	U.S. $	Can. $	U.K. £
17	Spaniel	Honey brown; black nose	35 x 35	9.00	6.00	3.00
18	Giraffe	Beige	35 x 35	8.00	6.00	3.00
19	Lion	Light brown; dark brown head, mane	35 x 45	9.00	7.00	3.00
20	German Shepherd	Grey; tan face (formerly Alsatian)	30 x 40	10.00	8.00	3.00
21	Lamb	Fawn; green base	30 x 25	9.00	11.00	5.00
22	Pine Marten	Honey brown	30 x 30	7.00	6.00	3.00
23	Corgi	Honey brown	30 x 35	10.00	8.00	3.00
24	Hedgehog	Dark brown; light brown face	23 x 40	10.00	8.00	3.00

TOM SMITH AND COMPANY

The world famous Christmas cracker manufacturer, Tom Smith and Company Ltd., collaborated with George Wade and Son Ltd. over a number of years to produce a series of miniature animals exclusively for the Christmas and party cracker market. Each series of animals was used exclusively by Tom Smith for two years, after which time the design rights reverted back to Wade, then they could be reused for other premiums or included in the *English Whimsies* series.

The first models issued for Tom Smith and Company were eight figures previously used in the 1967-1973 Red Rose Tea Canada series. Next came a set of ten *Safari Park* models. All but two of the models
uote Symbol"¾the "Lion" and the "Musk Ox"
uote Symbol"¾were from either Red Rose Tea Canada or the *English Whimsies* series. The "Polar Bear" and "Koala Bear" differ in colour from the *English Whimsies* models. Each is marked with "Wade England" embossed on the rim of the base.

Only the first five figures in the *Safari Park* series can be distinguished from those in the *English Whimsies* series; therefore, they have a higher collector's value.

ANIMATE CRACKERS

1973-1975

Backstamp: Embossed "Wade England" on the rim or in a recessed base

No.	Name	Description	Size	U.S. $	Can. $	U.K. £
1	Fantail Goldfish	Light green; blue base	30 x 35	10.00	8.00	5.00
2	Pine Marten	Honey	30 x 30	6.00	5.00	2.00
3	Terrapin (recessed)	Dark green	10 x 40	8.00	6.00	4.00
4	Wild Boar	Beige; green base	30 x 40	15.00	12.00	4.00
5	Alsatian	Dark brown/honey	30 x 40	9.00	7.00	2.00
6	Bluebird (recessed)	Light brown; blue wings	15 x 35	10.00	8.00	4.00
7	Bullfrog (recessed)	Light green	15 x 30	25.00	32.00	10.00
8	Butterfly (recessed)	Honey; blue wing tips	10 x 45	10.00	8.00	5.00

ELEPHANT AND PIG

Circa 1975

Wade produced for Tom Smith a very small number of biscuit-glazed miniature elephants and gloss-glazed pigs. The elephant has a hole in the end of the trunk and the pig has a hole in the rump and were intended as indoor firework holders for sparklers.

Backstamp: Unmarked

No.	Name	Description	Size	U.S. $	Can. $	U.K. £
1	Elephant	Charcoal grey	27 x 35	50.00	75.00	25.00
2	Pig	White	25 x 50	50.00	75.00	25.00

SAFARI PARK

1976-1977

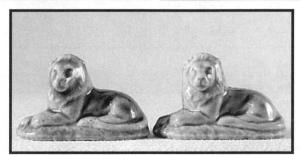

Honey brown, green base (left), Honey brown (right)

Backstamp: Embossed "Wade England"

No.	Name	Description	Size	U.S. $	Can. $	U.K. £
1a	Lion	Honey brown	30 x 45	12.00	15.00	5.00
1b	Lion	Honey brown; green base	30 x 45	12.00	15.00	5.00
2	Musk Ox	Grey; brown horns	27 x 30	12.00	15.00	7.00
3	Koala Bear	Black; brown stump	35 x 25	15.00	25.00	6.00
4	Polar Bear	Brown; black nose; grey/blue base	30 x 30	12.00	15.00	5.00
5	Tiger	Golden yellow	35 x 25	15.00	20.00	5.00
6	Langur	Light brown; dark brown stump	35 x 30	5.00	7.00	4.00
7	Walrus	Brown; grey base	30 x 30	12.00	15.00	3.00
8	Racoon	Brown; grey-green base	25 x 35	15.00	12.00	4.00
9	Kangaroo	Dark brown; light brown base	45 x 25	18.00	24.00	5.00
10	Orang-Utan	Ginger	30 x 30	5.00	7.00	5.00

CIRCUS

1978-1979

These ten models were set on drum bases, which are marked on their rims. These figures were reissued for Red Rose Tea U.S.A., with only a very slight variation in colour.

Backstamp: Embossed "Wade England"

No.	Name	Description	Size	U.S. $	Can. $	U.K. £
1	Brown Bear	Dark brown	35 x 30	5.00	12.00	4.00
2	Chimpanzee Boy	Beige; blue teapot	40 x 20	10.00	12.00	4.00
3	Chimpanzee Girl	Beige; blue skirt	40 x 20	10.00	12.00	4.00
4	Elephant, Sitting	Blue	30 x 30	8.00	12.00	4.00
5	Elephant, Standing	Blue	30 x 25	8.00	12.00	4.00

Backstamp: Embossed "Wade England"

No.	Name	Description	Size	U.S. $	Can. $	U.K. £
6	Pony	Beige	45 x 22	5.00	12.00	4.00
7	Lion	Honey brown	40 x 22	5.00	12.00	4.00
8	Poodle	White; blue skirt	35 x 30	8.00	12.00	4.00
9	Sea Lion	Dark grey	40 x 30	8.00	12.00	4.00
10	Tiger	Honey brown	43 x 20	5.00	12.00	4.00

Backstamp: Embossed "Wade England"

No.	Name	Description	Size	U.S. $	Can. $	U.K. £
1	Mole	Dark grey	25 x 40	10.00	15.00	4.00
2	Partridge	Beige; green base	30 x 20	10.00	15.00	5.00
3	Weasel	Beige; green base	35 x 40	10.00	15.00	5.00
4	Dormouse	Honey; green base	30 x 35	10.00	15.00	5.00
5	Fox	Brown	35 x 40	10.00	15.00	4.00
6	Badger	Dark grey	25 x 40	10.00	15.00	4.00
7	Squirrel	Red-brown	40 x 40	10.00	15.00	4.00
8	Hare	Yellow-brown	50 x 30	10.00	15.00	4.00

FARMYARD ANIMALS

1982-1983

The "Goose" was previously used in the 1971-1979 Red Rose *Miniature Nurseries* series; the earlier model has a pink beak.

Backstamp: Embossed "Wade England"

No.	Name	Description	Size	U.S. $	Can. $	U.K. £
1	Goose	Honey/brown; brown beak	35 x 40	8.00	6.00	4.00
2	Pig	Pale pink	25 x 40	12.00	18.00	4.00
3a	Goat	White; green base	40 x 40	12.00	18.00	6.00
3b	Goat	Beige; green base	40 x 40	12.00	18.00	6.00
4	Duck	White; blue base	25 x 30	18.00	24.00	6.00
5	Horse	Brown; green base	40 x 30	12.00	18.00	4.00
6	Cow	Orange-brown	30 x 40	12.00	18.00	4.00
7	Collie	Honey brown; brown base	25 x 50	12.00	18.00	4.00
8	Bull	Dark brown	30 x 50	12.00	18.00	4.00

SURVIVAL ANIMALS

1984-1985

From 1984 onwards, all Tom Smith crackers models were produced in a one-colour glaze. The "Sea Lion" was previously used as the "Seal" in the 1967-1973 Red Rose *Miniature Animals* series; the earlier model is brown on a blue base. The "Bison" had been number 51 of the *English Whimsies* series, where it is honey brown and dark brown.

Backstamp: Embossed "Wade England"

No.	Name	Description	Size	U.S. $	Can. $	U.K. £
1	Sea Turtle	Green-grey	25 x 45	15.00	20.00	6.00
2	Whale	Blue	25 x 50	20.00	25.00	7.00
3	Gorilla	Brown	40 x 40	15.00	20.00	6.00
4	Bison	Dark brown	28 x 40	6.00	8.00	4.00
5	Sea Lion	Blue	38 x 30	8.00	12.00	6.00
6	Eagle	Honey	35 x 23	15.00	20.00	5.00
7	Polar Bear	White	27 x 45	15.00	20.00	5.00
8	Armadillo	Dark grey	25 x 45	15.00	20.00	5.00

WILDLIFE

1986-1987

These models are reissued *English Whimsies* in all-over, one-colour glazes. Listed below are all the models that have been found in this series, although a number of British collectors have reported finding different figures in their crackers than were illustrated on the outer box (models 9 through 15). It is believed that surplus models from previous Red Rose Tea and Tom Smith promotions were used to fill the orders in time for Christmas sales.

The following initials indicate the origin of the models:

RR: Red Rose Canada
TSB: Tom Smith *British Wildlife* set

EW: *English Whimsies*
TSF: Tom Smith *Farmyard* set

Backstamp: Embossed "Wade England"

No.	Name	Description	Size	U.S. $	Can. $	U.K. £
1	Penguin (EW)	White	45 x 17	10.00	12.00	5.00
2	Rhino (EW)	Grey/brown	25 x 35	8.00	6.00	4.00
3	Leopard (EW)	Honey	17 x 45	6.00	6.00	4.00
4	Kangaroo (EW)	Beige	45 x 25	10.00	15.00	5.00
5	Koala Bear (EW)	Honey	35 x 25	6.00	8.00	4.00
6	Dolphin (EW)	Dark blue	30 x 40	12.00	15.00	5.00
7	Wild Boar (RR/EW)	Beige	30 x 40	8.00	10.00	4.00
8	Orang-Utan (EW)	Dark brown	30 x 30	5.00	7.00	5.00

No.	Name	Description	Size	U.S. $	Can. $	U.K. £
9	Collie (TSF)	Dark brown	25 x 50	15.00	18.00	4.00
10	Goat (TSF)	White	40 x 40	12.00	18.00	6.00
11	Duck (TSF)	Light blue	25 x 30	18.00	20.00	6.00
12	Squirrel (TSB)	Dark brown	40 x 40	12.00	15.00	4.00
13	Zebra (EW)	Blue-grey	40 x 35	5.00	8.00	8.00
14	Bison (RR/EW)	Brown	30 x 40	5.00	7.00	3.00
15	Hare (TSB)	Dark brown	50 x 30	10.00	12.00	6.00

MISCELLANEOUS MODELS

1987-1996

Wade re-coloured surplus models from the English Whimsies, Red Rose Tea Whimsies, Whimsielands and former Tom Smith Crackers for the Tom Smith Group who included them with other small gifts in their Bric-a-Brac, Catering, De Luxe, Luxury, Gallerie Noel, Table Decoration and Victorian Crackers. Only one or two models were used in each box of crackers and there is no reference to Wade on the outer box. Tom Smith do not keep records of these odd Wade models, the only way to find them is to look closely at Tom Smith advertising leaflets and packaging where they can be seen amongst plastic toys and paper hats.

The following initials indicate the origin of the figures:

EW: *English Whimsies*   RR: Red Rose
TSB: Tom Smith *British Wildlife* set   TSS: Tom Smith *Survival* set
TSD: Tom Smith *Dogs* set

1987 Issue

Backstamp: Embossed "Wade England"

No.	Name	Description	Size	U.S. $	Can. $	U.K. £
1	Little Bo-Peep	Brown	45 x 25	5.00	6.00	3.00
2	Hickory Dickory Dock	Beige	45 x 20	8.00	10.00	3.00
3	Humpty Dumpty	Brown	45 x 35	8.00	10.00	3.00
4	Old King Cole	Blue	40 x 35	15.00	20.00	10.00
5	Old Woman in a Shoe	Blue	40 x 40	15.00	20.00	10.00
6	Wee Willie Winkie	Blue	45 x 25	15.00	20.00	10.00
7	Hare (TSB)	Yellow-brown	50 x 30	10.00	12.00	4.00
8	Gorilla (TSS)	Dark brown	40 x 40	4.00	6.00	3.00

1989 Issue

Backstamp: Embossed "Wade England"

No.	Name	Description	Size	U.S. $	Can. $	U.K. £
1	Little Bo-Peep (RR)	Brown; blue apron	45 x 25	5.00	4.00	6.00
2	Hickory Dickory Dock (RR)	Honey/dark brown	45 x 20	6.00	4.00	6.00
3	Wee Willie Winkie (RR)	Beige; yellow hair	45 x 25	10.00	7.00	6.00
4	Kangaroo (EW)	Honey brown	45 x 25	10.00	15.00	5.00
5	Koala Bear (EW)	Beige	35 x 25	6.00	8.00	4.00

1990 Issue

Backstamp: Embossed "Wade England"

No.	Name	Description	Size	U.S. $	Can. $	U.K. £
1	Old King Cole (RR)	Brown; blue hat	40 x 35	7.00	4.00	6.00
2	Hare (TSB)	Dark brown	50 x 30	10.00	12.00	6.00
3	Squirrel (TSB)	Blue	40 x 40	6.00	12.00	12.00

1991 Issue

Backstamp: Embossed "Wade England"

No.	Name	Description	Size	U.S. $	Can. $	U.K. £
1	Koala Bear (EW)	Honey brown	35 x 25	6.00	8.00	4.00
2	Poodle (RR/TSD)	Dark orange	40 x 45	12.00	15.00	3.00

1992 Issue

Backstamp: Embossed "Wade England"

No.	Name	Description	Size	U.S. $	Can. $	U.K. £
1	Bluebird (RR/EW)	Blue	15 x 35	40.00	50.00	12.00
2	Bulldog (TSD)	Beige	35 x 35	10.00	15.00	3.00
3	Mongrel (RR/EW)	Blue	35 x 35	10.00	15.00	3.00

1996 Issue

Three *English Whimsies* models were used in assorted Tom Smith crackers. The "Duck" can be found in Tom Smith Catering, De Luxe and Luxury crackers, the "Camel" was used in the Gallerie Noel crackers, and the "Fieldmouse" is in Catering, De Luxe, Luxury and Table Decoration crackers.

Photograph not available
at press time

Backstamp: Unknown

No.	Name	Description	Size	U.S. $	Can. $	U.K. £
1	Camel (EW)	Light brown	35 x 35	9.00	11.00	4.00
2	Duck (EW)	Green	30 x 40	15.00	20.00	6.00
3	Fieldmouse	Honey	35 x 25	12.00	11.00	3.00
4	Swimming Duck	Beige	25 x 30	18.00	20.00	6.00

VILLAGE OF BROADLANDS

1988

Due to high production costs, only five of these models were produced for Tom Smith and Company. A further set of five figures was planned, but never issued.

They come from the same moulds as the following *Whimsey-on-Why* models, but are in different colours:

Whimsey-on-Why	Village of Broadlands
Whimsy School	The Chapel
Whimsey Station	The Coach House Garage
Pump Cottage	The Thatched Cottage
The Sweet Shop	The Pink House
The Greengrocer's Shop	The Village Store

Photograph not
available at press time

Backstamp: Embossed "Wade England"

No.	Name	Description	Size	U.S. $	Can. $	U.K. £
1	The Chapel	Grey; brown door	38 x 51	30.00	40.00	15.00
2	The Coach House Garage	White; black beams	35 x 39	30.00	40.00	15.00
3	The Thatched Cottage	White; brown roof	28 x 39	30.00	40.00	15.00
4	The Pink House	Pink; grey roof	40 x 40	30.00	40.00	15.00
5	The Village Store	Brown	35 x 35	30.00	40.00	15.00

FAMILY PETS

1988-1989

Backstamp: Embossed "Wade England"

No.	Name	Description	Size	U.S. $	Can. $	U.K. £
1	Cockatoo	Green	35 x 30	8.00	10.00	3.00
2	Spaniel Puppy	Honey brown	25 x 30	10.00	12.00	4.00
3	Guinea Pig	Honey brown	20 x 30	10.00	15.00	4.00
4	Rabbit	Brown	30 x 25	8.00	10.00	4.00
5	Mouse	White	15 x 25	12.00	15.00	4.00
6	Persian Kitten	Blue	25 x 33	8.00	10.00	4.00
7	Shetland Pony	Beige	25 x 30	8.00	12.00	5.00
8	Tropical Fish	Green	20 x 30	10.00	15.00	3.00

WORLD OF DOGS

1990-1991

Only two of these figures were new issues; the others were reissued *English Whimsies* and the first issue of Red Rose Tea Canada models in a new all-over, one-colour glaze.

Backstamp: Embossed "Wade England"

No.	Name	Description	Size	U.S. $	Can. $	U.K. £
1	Alsatian (RR/EW)	Dark brown	30 x 40	10.00	15.00	3.00
2	Poodle (RR)	Apricot	40 x 45	12.00	15.00	3.00
3	Husky (EW)	White	35 x 30	12.00	15.00	3.00
4	Corgi (RR/EW)	Honey brown; no eyes, nose	30 x 35	10.00	15.00	3.00
5	West Highland Terrier (new)	White	30 x 30	10.00	15.00	3.00
6	Mongrel (RR/EW)	Blue-grey	35 x 35	10.00	15.00	3.00
7	Bulldog (new)	Beige	35 x 35	10.00	15.00	3.00
8	Spaniel (RR/EW)	Black	35 x 35	10.00	15.00	3.00

BIRDLIFE SERIES

1992-1993

All the models in the *Birdlife* series, except for the "Wren," had been previously issued, either as *English Whimsies,* as other Tom Smith cracker models or as *Whimsie-land* figures. The "Eagle" and the "Goose" were former Tom Smith models, but this time were produced in different coloured glazes than the originals. The following initials indicate the origin of the models:

EW: *English Whimsies*   TS: Tom Smith
WL: *Whimsie-land*   RRT: Red Rose Tea Canada *Miniature Nurseries*

Backstamp: Embossed "Wade England"

No.	Name	Description	Size	U.S. $	Can. $	U.K. £
1	Wren	Beige	33 x 24	15.00	20.00	5.00
2	Duck (WL)	White	45 x 35	12.00	15.00	5.00
3	Cockerel (WL)	Green	50 x 35	12.00	15.00	5.00
4	Partridge (WL)	Beige	35 x 35	12.00	15.00	5.00
5	Barn Owl (WL)	Grey-blue	35 x 25	12.00	15.00	5.00
6	Eagle (TS *Survival*)	Beige	35 x 23	12.00	15.00	5.00
7	Pelican (EW)	Brown	45 x 40	20.00	20.00	5.00
8	Goose (RRT /TS)	White	35 x 40	12.00	15.00	5.00

SNOWLIFE ANIMALS

1992-1996

All the models in this set, except the "Reindeer," had been previously issued as *English Whimsies,* Tom Smith cracker figures or in the *Whimsie-land* series. The models are produced in a different all-over, one-colour glaze from the originals. The following initials indicate the origin of the models:

EW: *English Whimsies*   TS: *Tom Smith*   WL: *Whimsie-land*

Backstamp: **A.** Embossed "Wade Eng" (1a, 1b)
B. Embossed Wade England" (2-10)

No.	Name	Description	Size	U.S. $	Can. $	U.K. £
1a	Reindeer	Gap between legs; beige	30 x 35	12.00	15.00	5.00
1b	Reindeer	No gap; beige	30 x 35	10.00	12.00	4.00
2	Walrus (EW)	Beige	30 x 30	12.00	15.00	3.00
3	Penguin (EW)	Grey-blue	45 x 17	10.00	12.00	4.00
4	Polar Bear (EW)	White	27 x 45	10.00	12.00	4.00
5	Seal Pup (EW)	Grey	17 x 30	15.00	20.00	3.00
6	Snowy Owl (WL "Owl")	White	35 x 25	15.00	20.00	3.00
7	Fox (WL)	Brown	35 x 35	8.00	10.00	10.00
8	Snowshoe Hare (TS "Hare")	White	50 x 30	15.00	20.00	3.00
9	Whale (TS)	Grey	22 x 52	8.00	10.00	4.00
10	Snow Goose (RR)	White	33 x 37	12.00	15.00	5.00

TALES FROM THE NURSERIES

1994-1996

Some of the models from the Red Rose Tea *Miniature Nurseries* were reissued for this set. Two new figures were added in 1994, "Ride a Cock Horse" and a newly modelled "Boy Blue." All the models are in an all-over, one-colour glaze. Although there are ten models in this set, the box contains only eight crackers, making some models more difficult to find than others.

Backstamp: Embossed "Wade England"

No.	Name	Description	Size	U.S.$	Can.$	U.K.£
1	Little Bo-Peep	Wine	45 x 25	8.00	10.00	3.00
2	Little Boy Blue	Pale blue	45 x 25	10.00	12.00	4.00
3	The Cat and the Fiddle	Light grey	45 x 25	8.00	10.00	3.00
4	Dr. Foster	Dark brown	45 x 25	0.00	0.00	.00
5	Hickory Dickory Dock	Light brown	45 x 20	8.00	10.00	3.00
6	Humpty Dumpty	Pale blue	45 x 35	8.00	10.00	3.00
7	Little Jack Horner	Honey	40 x 20	6.00	8.00	4.00
8	Queen of Hearts	Apricot	45 x 25	8.00	10.00	4.00
9	Ride a Cock Horse	Green	45 x 35	10.00	12.00	4.00
10	Tom Tom the Piper's Son	Honey	65 x 55	8.00	10.00	3.00

CAT COLLECTION

1996

Eight of these cats are reissued from *English Whimsies*, the *Whimsie-land Series* and from Red Rose Tea's *Miniature Nurseries*. Some are in new colours, but others are similar to the Red Rose Tea U.S.A. issues. Two new cat models—one stalking and the other standing—were produced for this series. Although there are only eight crackers in a box, there are ten models in the set. The initials after the model indicates its origin.

EW: *English Whimsies*   WL: *Whimsie-land Series*   RR: Red Rose *Miniature Nurseries*

Backstamp: Embossed "Wade England"

No.	Name	Description	Size	U.S.$	Can.$	U.K.£
1	Cat (EW)	Light brown	40 x 17	8.00	10.00	4.00
2	The Cat and the Fiddle (RR)	Dark brown	45 x 25	8.00	10.00	4.00
3	Cat Stalking (new)	Apricot	23 x 43	12.00	15.00	5.00
4	Cat Standing (new)	Light brown	35 x 34	12.00	15.00	5.00
5	Kitten, sitting (EW)	Apricot	30 x 30	8.00	10.00	4.00
6a	Kitten, lying (WL)	Dark blue	20 x 42	8.00	10.00	4.00
6b	Kitten, lying (WL)	Pale blue	20 x 42	8.00	10.00	4.00
7	Leopard (EW)	Honey	17 x 45	8.00	10.00	5.00
8	Lion (EW)	Honey	35 x 45	8.00	10.00	5.00
9	Puss in Boots (RR)	Light grey	45 x 20	8.00	10.00	5.00
10	Tiger (EW)	Honey	35 x 25	15.00	20.00	6.00

CHRISTMAS TIME CRACKERS

1996

Tom Smith used the *Bear Ambitions* set, which was originally produced as a Wade giftware line, in its Christmas crackers. Four of the models are glazed in different colours from the originals, which were all honey brown.

Backstamp: Embossed "Wade England"

No.	Name	Description	Size	U.S. $	Can. $	U.K. £
1	Admiral Sam	Dark brown	50	10.00	12.00	4.00
2	Alex the Aviator	Light brown	45	10.00	12.00	4.00
3	Artistic Edward	Light brown	40	10.00	12.00	4.00
4	Beatrice Ballerina	Honey	50	6.00	8.00	3.00
5	Locomotive Joe	Dark brown	50	10.00	12.00	4.00
6	Musical Marco	Honey	45	6.00	8.00	3.00

SPILLERS DOG FOODS LTD.

RETRIEVER

1991

Commissioned by Spillers Dog Foods, this model could be obtained by sending in a certain number of tokens from packets of the dog food.

Size: 26 x 53 mm.
Backstamp: Embossed "Wade England"

No.	Description	U.S. $	Can. $	U.K. £
1	Honey brown; green base	15.00	20.00	15.00

MARGARET STRICKLAND

POLACANTHUS MONEY BOX, THE ISLE OF WIGHT DINOSAUR

1994

Margaret Strickland, a resident of the Isle of Wight, England, commissioned the "Polacanthus Money Box." This model is an artist's impression taken from the skeleton of a Polacanthus dinosaur, whose remains have only been found on the Isle of Wight. It was produced in May 1994, in a limited, numbered edition of 2,000.

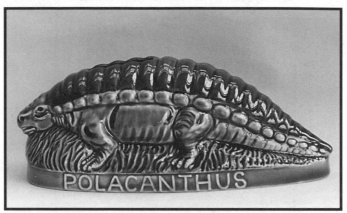

Size: 79 x 205 mm.
Backstamp: Black transfer "Wade" in Isle of Wight outline, numbered

No.	Description	U.S. $	Can. $	U.K. £
1	Honey/dark brown; green base; coin slot in top	85.00	110.00	50.00

TRAUFLER

A slip-cast "Sheep" in two colours and sizes and the "Cockerel Salt Pot" and the "Hen Pepper Pot" were produced by Wade for Traufler, a tableware manufacturer, to compliment its imported tablewares, which featured sheep, shepherds and farmyard scenes. These models were also produced by another manufacturer (also unmarked). Those figures not made by Wade have darker faces, more eyelashes and ears that are closer to their faces.

SHEEP

1992

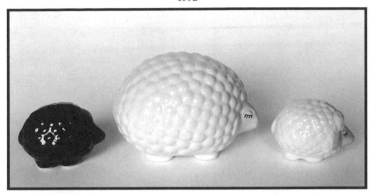

Backstamp: Unmarked

No.	Name	Description	Size	U.S. $	Can. $	U.K. £
1a	Sheep, Large	Cream; pink face	85 x 145	25.00	35.00	16.00
1b	Sheep, Large	Black	85 x 145	25.00	35.00	16.00
2a	Sheep, Small	Cream; pink face	65 x 45	20.00	30.00	15.00
2b	Sheep, Small	Black	65 x 45	20.00	30.00	15.00

COCKEREL AND HEN

1992

Backstamp: Unmarked

No.	Name	Description	Size	U.S.$	Can.$	U.K.£
1a	Cockerel Salt Pot	White; red/black markings	110 x 55	30.00	40.00	15.00
1b	Cockerel Salt Pot	Yellow; pink comb; black markings	115 x 80	30.00	40.00	15.00
2a	Hen Pepper Pot	White; red/blackmarkings	90 x 55	30.00	40.00	15.00
2b	Hen Pepper Pot	Yellow; pink comb; black markings	90 x 70	30.00	40.00	15.00

DAVID TROWER ENTERPRISES

Popeye Collection

1997

Popeye, a much loved cartoon character who made his cartoon debut in 1933, was the first model issued in an intended series of four to be modeled by Ken Holmes and produced by Wade Ceramics for DavidTrower Enterprises. The three other models are Brutus, Olive Oyl and Swee'pea and Wimpy. The models were sold in colourful presentation boxes with certificates of authenticity. Popeye's original price was £35.00 and was issued in a limited edition of 2,000. Brutus, who was issued in a limited edition of 1,500, and Olive Oyl, issued in a limited edition of 2,000, cost £36.00.

Backstamp: **A.** Printed 'Wade Popeye ™ & © 1997 King Features Synd Inc. Limited Edition of 2000 © David Trower Enterprises"
B. Printed 'Wade Brutus ™ & © 1997 King Features Synd Inc. Limited Edition of 1500 © David Trower Enterprises"
C. Printed 'Wade Olive Oyl and Swee'Pea ™ & © 1998 King Features Synd Inc. Limited Edition of 2000 © David Trower Enterprises"

No.	Name	Description	Size	U.S.$	Can.$	U.K.£
1	Popeye	White hat with black band; brown pipe in mouth; red collar with black band; black shirt with yellow buttons & navy blue cuffs; yellow belt with white buckle; navy blue trousers; black shoes; brown circular base	120	55.00	70.00	35.00
2	Brutus	Blue hat & trousers; black hair, eyes, beard & t-shirt; orange shirt; brown belt; white buckle	129	*55.00	75.00	36.00
3	Olive Oyl & Swee'pea	Olive: black hair, skirt & shoes; red blouse; blue belt; Swee'pea: white hat; red suit	Unknown	55.00	75.00	36.00

U.K. WADE COLLECTORS FAIRS

1994 BIRMINGHAM — SPANIEL

The "Spaniel" was produced for the first Official U.K. Wade Collectors Fair, held in Birmingham, England, on September 25, 1994, at the National Motorcycle Museum. It was a limited edition of 1,000 models, and the issue price was £12.50. The model came with a numbered certificate of authenticity and was signed by the managing director of Wade Ceramics Ltd.

Backstamp: Large embossed "Wade"

No.	Description	Size	U.S. $	Can. $	U.K. £
1	Honey brown	75 x 60	140.00	185.00	85.00

1995 BIRMINGHAM — GREY-HAIRED RABBIT

This model was produced in a limited edition of 1,250. It was available exclusively at the 1995 Official U. K. Wade Collectors Fair, held at the National Motorcycle Museum in Birmingham on June 11. It sold for £12.50 and came with a numbered certificate of authenticity, signed by the managing director of Wade Ceramics Ltd.

Backstamp: Embossed "Wade"

No.	Description	Size	U.S. $	Can. $	U.K. £
1	Grey-brown	87 x 60	110.00	150.00	55.00

1996 BIRMINGHAM — SMILING FROG

This model was produced for the 3rd Wade Collectors Fair, held at the Birmingham Motorcycle Museum on April 14, 1996. It was issued in a limited edition of 1,250 and was available for £12.50 only on the day of the fair. Each model has a numbered certificate.

Size: 60 x 80
Backstamp: Embossed "Wade"

No.	Description	U.S. $	Can. $	U.K. £
1	Green	80.00	105.00	45.00

1996 DUNSTABLE — TIMID MOUSE

Produced in a limited edition of 1,750, this model was issued for the 4th Wade Collectors Fair, held in Dunstable, Bedfordshire, in September 1996. Because of numerous requests to the Official International Wade Club from overseas members who were unable to attend the Dunstable Wade Show, 250 of the "Timid Mouse" models were made available to club members who sent their name and address plus their club membership number to U.K. Fairs Ltd, the show organisers.

The cost of the Timid Mouse on the day of the fair was £18.00.

Size: 60 x 100
Backstamp: Embossed "Wade" with black printed "Limited Edition of 1,750 Exclusively For Dunstable Wade Fair 1996"

No.	Description	U.S. $	Can. $	U.K. £
1	Light brown; black eyes, nose; green/brown base	70.00	95.00	40.00

1997 TRENTHAM GARDENS — THE AUSTRALIAN KANGAROO

The Kangaroo, the first in a series of Australian animals, was produced for the 5th Wade Collectors Fair held at Trentham Gardens, Staffordshire on the 20th of April 1997. The Kangaroo was produced in a limited edition of 1,500 with a special issue of 150 models for International Wade Club members living overseas. The cost of the Kangaroo on the day of the fair was £18.00.

Backstamp: Black printed "The Kangaroo 1 of 1,500 Exclusive Limited Edition For The Trentham Gardens Wade Fair 1997 ©UK Fairs LTD & Wade Ceramics LTD"

No.	Description	Size	U.S. $	Can. $	U.K. £
1	Orange brown; greenish base	127	55.00	75.00	35.00

1997 DUNSTABLE —THE AUSTRALIAN KOALA

The Koala, the second in the Australian animals series, was produced for the 6th Wade Collectors Fair held at Dunstable, Bedfordshire on the 5th of October 1997. It was produced in a limited edition of 1,500, with a special issue of 150 models for overseas Wade Club members. The cost of the Koala on the day of the fair was £20.00.

Backstamp: **A.** Black printed "The Koala Bear 1 of 1,500 Exclusive Edition for Dunstable Wade Fair 1997 ©UK Fairs Ltd & Wade Ceramics Ltd"
B. Black printed "The Koala Bear 1 of 150 Exclusive Edition of Dunstable Wade Fair Special Produced Solely For Overseas Wade Collectors ©UK Fairs Ltd & Wade Ceramics Ltd"

No.	Description	Size	U.S. $	Can. $	U.K. £
1	Beige brown; black eyes, nose; green gum leaves; brown tree stump	127	55.00	75.00	35.00

UK INTERNATIONAL CERAMICS LTD.

THE FLINTSTONES COLLECTION

1996-1998

Fred and Wilma Flintstone, from a popular television series of the 1970s, were the first two models offered as a pair, in a limited edition of 1,500. Betty and Barney Rubble (the Flintstones neighbours) followed a few months later. Pebbles, the Flintstone's daughter, and Bamm-Bamm, the Rubble's son, are the last two models in the series and will be available in 1998. The original issue price was £68.00 for the pair. The UK postage was free, overseas postage cost £5.

Backstamp: **A.** Printed "Fred™, The Flintstones™ Limited Edition of 1500 © 1996 H-B Prod., Inc © UKI Ceramics Ltd Licensed by CPL"

B: Printed "Wilma™, The Flintstones™ Limited Edition of 1500 © 1996 H-B Prod., Inc © UKI Ceramics Ltd Licensed by CPL"

C: Printed "Barney ™, The Flintstones ™ Limited Edition of 1500 © 1996 H-B Prod., Inc © UKI Ceramics Ltd Licensed by CPL"

D: Printed "Betty ™, The Flintstones ™ Limited Edition of 1500 © 1996 H-B Prod., Inc © UKI Ceramics Ltd Licensed by CPL"

No.	Name	Description	Size	U.S.$	Can.$	U.K.£
1	"Fred"	Black hair, eyes, spots on coat; blue neck scarf; orange coat; stone base	120	65.00	85.00	40.00
2	"Wilma"	Brown hair; black eyes; red mouth; white necklace, dress; stone base	125	65.00	85.00	40.00
3	"Barney"	Yellow hair; black eyes; brown coat; stone base	105	65.00	85.00	35.00
4	"Betty"	Black hair, eyes, dress strap; red mouth; white button; pale blue dress; stone base	115	65.00	85.00	35.00

FELIX THE CAT

1997

Felix The Cat was created shortly after World War I by Otto Messmer and Pat Sullivan. His first cartoon appeared in 1919. This Felix The Cat model was modelled by Andy Moss, and was produced in a limited edition of 1500. Each figure came with a numbered certificate and was in a special presentation box. The original cost was £38.00 plus £5.00 for postage to overseas collectors.

Backstamp: Black printed "WADE TM™ 1997 FTC PROD. INC. Limited edition of 1500 ™ UKI CERAMICS LTD Licensed by El Euro lizenzen, Munchen"

No.	Description	Size	U.S. $	Can. $	U.K. £
1	Black cat & lettering; white face & base; red tongue	135	55.00	75.00	38.00

NODDY AND BIG EARS
Style Two
1997

Noddy and Big Ears, created by Enid Blyton in her famous "Noddy" books, are the first two models in an intended set of four. They should prove to be just as popular today as they were in 1958 when they were originally produced by Wade. (See page 86) Unlike their 1950s predecessors, these models are slip cast (hollow) and much larger. They were sold as a pair at £68.00 plus £5.00 P&P for overseas collectors.

Backstamp: A. Black printed "Wade © UKI Cer. Ltd 1997 © D.W. 1949/90 Licenced by B.B.C. WL Ltd Noddy™ Limited Edition 1500"
      B. Black printed "Wade © UKI Cer. Ltd 1997 © D.W. 1949/90 Licenced by B.B.C. WL Ltd Big Ears™ Limited Edition 1500"

No.	Name	Description	Size	U.S. $	Can. $	U.K. £
1	Big Ears	Red hat; dark blue coat; yellow bow tie with red stripes; yellow trousers with green strips; brown shoes; white base	138	80.00	105.00	45.00
2	Noddy	Dark blue hat, bows; red shirt, shoes, light blue shorts; yellow scarf with red spots; white base	110	80.00	105.00	45.00

WADE CERAMICS LTD.

THE CAMELOT COLLECTION

1997

The Camelot Collection, a new series of models based on the legend of King Arthur, was introduced at the Wade / Jim Beam Fair held in Wisconson in July 1997. There are five slipcast (hollow) models in the collection: King Arthur, Queen Guinivere, Sir Lancelot, the Wizard Merlin and the Lady of the Lake. 200 each of the Camelot Collection models had a "C&S" backstamp added to the regular backstamp. These models are available to North American collectors from Village Antiques and Gifts, Lake Orion, Michigan, U.S.A at $39.00 each. British collectors could purchase the models from the Wade shop at £20.00.

Backstamp:
A. Black printed "Camelot Collection logo and "Arthur" The Camelot Collection Wade"
B. Black printed "Camelot Collection logo and "Guinivere The Camelot Collection Wade"
C. Black printed "Camelot Collection logo and "Lancelot" The Camelot Collection Wade"
D. Black printed "Camelot Collection logo and "Merlin" The Camelot Collection Wade"
E. Black printed "Camelot Collection logo and "Lady of the Lake" The Camelot Collection Wade"
F. Black printed "C&S" logo, "Camelot Collection" logo and (name of model) "The Camelot Collection Wade"

No.	Name	Description	Size	U.S. $	Can. $	U.K. £
1	King Arthur	Light brown; brown cloak; dull yellow crown, cloak chain, cross belt; dull yellow sword with black pummel & hilt	108	45.00	60.00	20.00
2	Queen Guinivere	Light brown; brown dress; dark green collar, cuffs; dull yellow belt	108	45.00	60.00	20.00
3	Sir Lancelot	Light brown; brown cloak	108	45.00	60.00	20.00
4	The Wizard Merlin	Light brown; blue grey hooded cloak; brown staff	108	45.00	60.00	20.00
5	The Lady of the Lake	Light brown; brown cloak; dull yellow sword; dark blue / green base	83	45.00	60.00	20.00

ROBERT WILLIAMSON

GINGERBREAD MAN

1995

A hollow model of a giant gingerbread man was commissioned by Robert Williamson. It was available for sale at the 2nd U.K. Fairs Wade Show in Birmingham at a cost of £15.00.

Size: 105 x 80 mm.
Backstamp: Embossed "Wade"

No.	Description	U.S. $	Can. $	U.K. £
1	Ginger brown	70.00	90.00	35.00

UNKNOWN COMPANY

3 FOR 49C WHIMSIES

Circa 1972

A small number of red carded Whimsies which state "Look Wow Genuine Porcelain by Wade of England Your Choice 3 for 49c Build an Entire Set" on the front have been found in Canada and the U.S.A. There has been no further information found as to who for and when these models were produced. It is probable that they were for a chain of North American Dime Stores. A fieldmouse on one of the red card models has a recess base as did some of the early 1967-1973 Canadian Red Rose Tea models, others are from the 1971-1984 English Whimsies series, which would suggest that surplus stock was distributed to this company. A date of early 1970s is estimated for these models. The values given are for models intact on their cards as they are indistinguishable from Red Rose Tea or English Whimsie models outside the packet.

Backstamp: **A.** Embossed 'Wade England' in recessed base (1, 3)
B. Embossed 'Wade England' on rim (2, 4)

No.	Name	Description	Size	U.S. $	Can. $	U.K. £
1	Bear Cub	Honey brown	34 x 20	12.00	15.00	10.00
2	Bison, large	Honey brown	34 x 46	12.00	15.00	10.00
3	Fieldmouse	Honey brown	35 x 25	12.00	15.00	10.00
4	Setter	Brown; grey green base	35 x 50	7.00	5.00	2.00

UNKNOWN COMPANY

Sometimes models are found in North America, the United Kingdom or even as far away as Australia which cannot be categorised in any Company Promotion, due to the fact that they were not found in original packaging or seen listed in Company Promotional Advertising. Models found in North America could have been transported by collectors from the U.K. and models found in the U.K. could have been transported from North America.

These models, in all over one colour glazes, are promotional models and most likely Redco Foods (Red Rose Tea U.S.A.) or Tom Smith (Miscellaneous) Cracker Models, any information is welcome. The following initials indicate the origin of the model.

EW: *English Whimsies*   TS: Tom Smiths

Backstamp: Embossed "Wade England" on rim

No.	Name	Description	Size	U.S. $	Can. $	U.K. £
1	Elephant (EW)	Dark grey	55 x 50	12.00	15.00	10.00
2a	Persian Kitten (TS)	Dark brown	25 x 33	8.00	10.00	4.00
2b	Persian Kitten (TS)	Honey brown	25 x 33	8.00	10.00	4.00
2c	Persian Kitten (TS)	Black	25 x 33	8.00	10.00	4.00

Note: The black kitten is suspect as Wade rarely use black models.

INDEX

WADE Whimsies

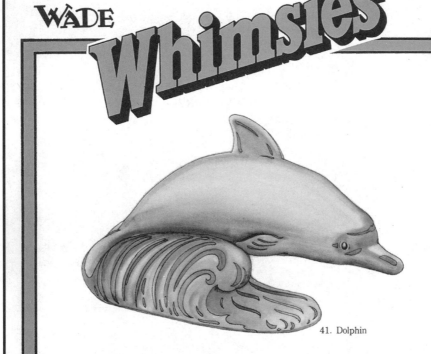

41. Dolphin

they're great to collect

42. Pelican   43. Angel Fish   44. Turtle   45. Sea-Horse

284

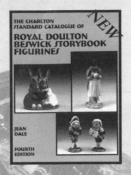

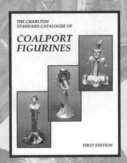

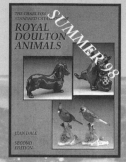